CW00591381

Understanding the New European Community

Understanding the New European Community

William Nicoll

Honorary Director General
Council of the European Community

Trevor C. Salmon

Jean Monnet Professor of European Integration Studies
University of St Andrews

HARVESTER
WHEATSHEAF

New York   London   Toronto   Sydney   Tokyo   Singapore

First published 1990 as
Understanding the European Communities
This edition published 1994 by
Harvester Wheatsheaf
Campus 400, Maylands Avenue
Hemel Hempstead
Hertfordshire, HP2 7EZ
A division of
Simon & Schuster International Group

Typeset in 10/12pt Garamond
by Hands Fotoset, Leicester

Printed and bound in Great Britain by
Biddles Ltd, Guildford and King's Lynn

British Library Cataloguing in Publication Data

A catalogue record for this book is available from
the British Library

ISBN 0-7450-1162-4

---

1   2   3   4   5   98   97   96   95   94

Contents

Tables, figures and exhibits

FIGURES

EXHIBITS

Preface

In this second edition we have caught up with developments in the European Community since the first edition in 1989, and have taken the story as far as the meeting of the European Council in Edinburgh in December 1992, and its aftermath which is also a convenient break-point as it coincided with the completion of the Single Market. The business of integration is unfinished, but it is timely to provide a basis for understanding the significance of recent events.

Again we have combined the resources of an academic and an experienced practitioner, but on this occasion we have also profited from comments of students and others on the first edition.

We have changed the title, using the language adopted in the Treaty on European Union of 1992, although it seems premature to use the title 'the European Union'.

Abbreviations

ACP	African Caribbean and Pacific states
CAP	Common Agricultural Policy
CCP	Common Commercial Policy
CET	Common External Tariff
CFP	Common Fisheries Policy
CFSP	Common Foreign and Security Policy
COREPER	Committee of Permanent Representatives
COPA	Committee of Professional Agricultural Organizations
CSA	Special Agricultural Committee
CSCE	Conference on Security and Co-operation in Europe
DB	Draft Budget
DG	Directorate-General
EAGGF	European Agricultural Guidance and Guarantee Fund
EBRD	European Bank for Reconstruction and Development
EC	European Communities
ECB	European Central Bank
ECJ	European Court of Justice
ECOFIN	Economic and Finance Council
ECSC	European Coal and Steel Community
ecu	European currency unit
EDC	European Defence Community
EDF	European Development Fund
EEA	European Economic Area
EEC	European Economic Community
EES	European Economic Space

EFTA	European Free Trade Association
EIB	European Investment Bank
EMS	European Monetary System
EMU	European Monetary Union
EP	European Parliament
EPC	European Political Co-operation
EPU	European Political Union
ERDF	European Regional Development Fund
ERM	Exchange Rate Mechanism
ESCB	European System of Central Banks
ESPRIT	European Strategic Programme for Research and Development in Information Technology
EU	European Union
EURATOM	European Atomic Energy Community
EUREKA	European Programme for High Technology Research and Development
GATT	General Agreement on Tariffs and Trade
GDP	Gross Domestic Product
GNP	Gross National Product
IGC	Inter-governmental Conference
JET	Joint European Torus
JRC	Joint Research Centre
MEP	Member of the European Parliament
MCAs	Monetary Compensation Amounts
mfn	most favoured nation
NACC	North Atlantic Co-operation Council
NATO	North Atlantic Treaty Organization
OEEC	Organization for European Economic Co-operation
OECD	Organization for Economic Co-operation and Development
OJ	Official Journal
PHARE	Poland and Hungary: Aid for the Reconstruction of Economies
SEA	Single European Act
SEM	Single European Market
STABEX	Stabilized Export Earnings
UN	United Nations
UNCTAD	United Nations Conference on Trade and Development
WEU	Western European Union

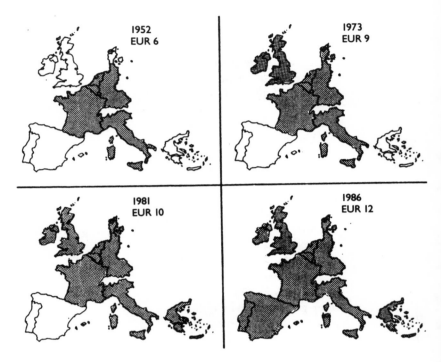

1952
EUR 6

1973
EUR 9

1981
EUR 10

1986
EUR 12

The Europe of the European Communities

The Historical Background

1 The Construction of Europe to the Treaties of Rome

This chapter traces some of the intellectual grand designs about the possible forms of association between European states and nations over the centuries, and then looks more specifically at the steps leading to the Treaties of Rome of 1957.

PRE-1945 IDEAS

Throughout its history, the European continent has been restless, fragile and contradictory,[1] competitive and pluralist.[2] Responding, unlike the subjects of the Chinese, Japanese and Ottoman empires, to no central rule-making authority, and divided from each other by language and religion, and by princely, and later national, aspirations, the Europeans vied with and stimulated each other to create a civilization, proprietarily described simply as 'civilization', which it became their manifest destiny to spread across the planet. But if there were common strands in their expansionism – Christianity, the Graeco-Roman heritage of philosophy and law, the humanism of the Renaissance and (much later) the principles of representative democracy – the Western Europeans were in more or less constant strife with each other in the four centuries up to the middle of the twentieth.[3] With exponential growth of efficiency in the technology of killing and maiming, there was a massive rise in the numbers of combatants involved in any fighting, and the effective disappearance of the distinction between combatant and non-combatant.[4] War-making also served to promote industrial development. War was even ideologically glorified as the means of cultivating the noblest instincts of man,[5] and the chivalry which had formed part of a martial code was diluted in the assertion of a principle of hegemony, whether because the belligerent maintained that he had the monopoly of respectable peace aims, or because his was rightfully the master race.

A European born in 1900 and still alive in 1955 would have spent one-fifth of his or her life in war years, would have known of the killing fields of Flanders, witnessed the blighting of the Brave New World of the League of Nations, seen in the newsreels the horror of Belsen, the firestorm of Dresden and the vaporization of Hiroshima, lived through the breakdown of the Great Alliance which was supposed to underpin and enforce the peacekeeping objectives of the United Nations, and listened to the debate about whether a third atom bomb might be used to stem the advance of Chinese–North Korean forces.[6] He or she would also have known that at the end of the Second World War, the seat of power moved east and west, from the chanceries of the European capitals to Moscow and to Washington. The Europeans' home continent was no longer a world power.

Over the years, many prepared for or waged war, irrespective of whether they wished for peace, but others devoted themselves to the cause of ending war and making peace last. It seemed to most of them that the guarantee of peace would be the acceptance of laws and the setting-up of international institutions. Just as law prescribes the relations between citizens, so law could do the same between states and, if directly applied, between citizens of these separate states. Various thinkers applied themselves to suggesting how this could be put into practice.

The 'Grand Design', attributed to Henry IV of France (1553–1610) and notably to his minister Sully, is almost certainly apocryphal. It was, in its legendary form, for a 'Great Republic' of Europe, bringing together the divided kingdoms and principalities (and religions within Christendom) to coexist in peace.[7] William Penn (1644–1718), the great English and later American Quaker, having been obliged by his unpopularity within his family and with the law in England to travel extensively in Europe, had been an eyewitness of the devastation of the longlasting seventeenth-century wars. In 1693 he published an essay on the present and future peace of Europe. He advocated the institution of a European estates general or parliament, which would mediate on disputes among the sovereigns and, in an anticipation of what the United Nations would call 'uniting for peace', would enforce the result of its deliberations against any dissidents.[8]

The German philosopher Immanuel Kant (1724–1804) published in 1795 his treatise *Zum Ewigen Frieden* ('Towards Perpetual Peace'). For Kant the existence of the state implied aggression: the state of nature was the state of war. Man's power over nature, the power to make law, could change this state. Disputes could be resolved, not by victory in war but by judicial means.[9] These means were not, however, what would today be called international law, because the latter existed then only because of war, actual or imminent. Kant's version of pacific law was for a federation of free states, freely consented to. Kant, as he himself acknowledged, had no greater success than any other thinker in resolving the paradox of structural imbalance: how can the federation be strong enough to coexist with its members without being dominated by them, but not so strong as to destroy them and subject them to an imperial sway?

Saint-Simon (1760–1825) had lived through the War of American Independence and its constitution-building aftermath. He published in 1814, with Augustin Thierry, 'On the Reorganization of European Society'. Unlike Penn and Kant he moved from the notion of the participating state to the participating people, to be represented by a European parliament, independent of the national states and empowered to settle disagreements among them. Saint-Simon did not take up the Kantian paradox.

The Italian Carlo Cattaneo (1801–69) did so, and based his solution on what in the 1980s came to be known as 'subsidiarity'. This principle teaches that government can be organized in layers – from the local community up to world level – each layer possessing the competence which it can discharge better than those above or below it. Seen from the viewpoint of a unitary state, this is decentralization. Seen from the smallest unit it is federation, and one in which there need be no contradiction between the loyalties paid to each layer – a Yorkshireman can comfortably be a Northerner, an Englishman, a Briton, a European and a citizen of the world (see below pp. 289–93).

These and other appeals and treatises were not greatly heeded. Nation-states consolidated themselves by conquest, satellitization of their neighbours, and rebellion against a foreign ruler, in the name of freedom and national unity. This was an alternative path to

European unity – the one followed by Napoleon. But it was predestined to evoke the opposition and armed response of the nations, which did not want to be subservient or which feared to share the continent with too powerful a partner.

The outbreak of European war in 1914 affirmed the reality of the existence and consolidation over four centuries of the nation-state, unified within its frontiers, governed by a single decision centre which engaged all its subjects, and devoted to increasing the relative power of the state by all available means: war if not diplomacy or commerce. The brotherhood of man, an airy vision,[10] was dissipated when, notably, the socialists in the Reichstag voted through the war credits in 1914. The Treaty of Versailles, signed on 28 June 1919, five years to the day from the assassination of the Archduke Ferdinand, demonstrated again that war and victory do not make lasting law. A fundamentally insecure and self-igniting system had been put together and the League of Nations, the peace-seeking and peace-making organ, stood no chance of success.

To some it was clear from the beginning that another structure was needed to provide stability in Europe, correctly seen as the key to stability in the world. This was the advocacy of Richard Coudenhove Kalergi, a Hungarian nobleman, who founded in 1923 the Pan-European movement and won the support of several leading and active politicians, especially in France.[11] Aristide Briand, Prime Minister of France, having obtained in advance the support of his German colleague Gustav Stresemann, delivered on 7 September 1929, at the 10th General Assembly of the League of Nations, a speech in which he outlined a plan for European union. At the request of the League's members, the French government elaborated the plan into a memorandum, 'The Organization of a Regime of European Federal Union', presented in May 1930 to a world in the grips of economic depression. The British reaction was crucial and negative. While warmly disposed towards inter-governmental European economic co-operation, and perhaps later extending it to political co-operation, His Majesty's Government gave weight to 'the peculiar and indissoluble connection of the British Isles with the worldwide territories of the British Empire and . . . the prestige and efficiency of the League of Nations which is the sheet anchor of British policy'.[12] The French memorandum, remitted to the attentions of the Committee for the Study of European Unity, was rejected by the General Assembly of the League.

British names are conspicuously missing from the roll-call of Europeanists. This is not to say that there was no awareness of the problem of European fractiousness and of the insecurity of the classic British pursuit of European balance. In 1897, diamond jubilee year, in the heyday of British imperialism, the Prime Minister, Lord Salisbury wrote:

> The federated action of Europe, if we can maintain it, is our sole hope of escaping from the constant terror and calamity of war, the constant pressure of the burdens of an armed peace, which weigh down the spirits and darken the prospect of every Nation in this part of the world. The Federation of Europe is the only hope we have.[13]

As war clouds gathered in Europe, Lord Beveridge (later known as the architect of the post-war welfare state) founded the Federal Union, drawing together the efforts of such as P. H. Kerr (Lord Lothian), author in 1935 of 'Pacifism is not enough, nor patriotism either'.[14] To this movement, which enjoyed little support, a federal community of nations, which need not initially be world-wide, was the only way of abolishing the institution of war: patriotism was not enough and non-violent resistance, which also had powerful and sincere advocates,[15] would not succeed either. Neither would international socialism, unless it also created the federal community. Kerr observed that the search for national advantage through trade protectionism and the drive for markets was being supported by capitalists and socialists alike. Miss Barbara Wootton, socialist and co-founder of the Federal Union, reached a similar conclusion in her pamphlet 'Socialism and federation' in 1940. As long as there was 'international anarchy', international no law, a socialist had to choose between taking up arms against his comrades or giving in to aggression. He had usually chosen the former. Hence international socialism lay in ruins.

The 1930s saw the world economic and trade war, the closing in of markets, the search for self-sufficiency, the command economy of the Third Reich[16] and the collapse of world trade.[17]

This was the economic expression of the nation-state, pursuing national advantage in a zero-sum game. The nation-states went to the political and shooting war of the 1940s, appeasement having failed to curtail the territorial demands of Hitler's Germany. Britain and France drew the line after the occupation, in the spring of 1939, of Bohemia and Moravia, parts of Czechoslovakia, which had not already been ceded by the Munich Pact of 1938. The German offensive against Poland in September 1939, followed by the occupation of Luxembourg, Belgium, the Netherlands, Denmark and Norway, the Italian invasion of Greece and the attack on France in June 1940, ushered in five years which were to prove the final demonstration of international anarchy. The execution in December 1941 of the long-prepared plan for the Strike South by Japanese imperialism made warring anarchy global, from Murmansk to Midway.

On either side, the first war aim was the defeat and probably the territorial occupation of at least part of the opposition. The Reich envisaged a new order under German hegemony in Europe and in Russia, as well as in the African colonies of the defeated nations.[18] Japan wanted to create the Greater Asia Co-Prosperity Sphere in the service of its empire. But neither was able, under the stresses of waging war, or willing to give much attention to the economic restructuring of the lands they had conquered. Occupied Europe did not become a single market.

British war aims were simple: to win. Harold Nicolson has described[19] how, as a junior minister at the Ministry of Information in 1940, he was charged with preparing a statement of war aims (in essence 'socialism' at home – that is, the welfare state – and pooled resources in Europe), which the War Cabinet decided against adopting. But the problem of a future Europe at peace did not go away. On 21 October 1942, when there was still a long dark way to go towards victory, Winston Churchill, the Prime Minister, sent Anthony Eden, the Foreign Secretary, the following minute:

> I must admit that my thoughts rest primarily in Europe – the revival of the glory of Europe, the parent continent of the modern nations and of civilization. It would be a measureless disaster if Russian barbarianism overlaid the culture and independence of the ancient States of Europe. Hard as it is to say now, I trust that the European family may act unitedly as one under a Council of Europe. I look forward to a United States of Europe in which the barriers between the nations will be greatly minimized and unrestricted travel will be possible. I hope to see the economy of Europe studied as a whole. . . . Of course we shall have to work with the Americans in many ways and in the greatest ways, but Europe is our prime care. . . . It would be easy to debate upon these themes. Unhappily the War has prior claims on our attention.[20]

The winning of the war and Anglo-American planning for post-war world organization[21] were the leading preoccupations of allied statesmen, but some Europeans, including those who were suffering grievously, were searching for answers to the questions of economic and political organization in Western Europe. In London, the governments in exile of the Netherlands, Luxembourg and Belgium were discussing co-operative and integrational plans, which laid the basis for the Benelux organization (Belgium and Luxembourg had been in economic union since 1921). In imprisonment in Italy in 1941, the renowned anti-fascist and pro-European Altiero Spinelli was writing a manifesto for a free and united Europe (the 'Ventotene manifesto'). The central theme was the awful and inevitable consequences of the existence of separate sovereign states: the global war. Meanwhile in Washington, Jean Monnet (1888–1977), a French businessman, was organizing (as he had also organized in the 1914–18 war) allied war supply. It was Monnet who had inspired Churchill's proposal in 1940 that France, on the brink of military defeat, and the United Kingdom, resolved to fight on, should merge into a single state. Monnet had travelled widely in the family business and in banking, and had become convinced of the essential need for European integration.

After the Second World War he joined the French Planning Commission where he further enriched his experience of organizing and negotiating, in preparation for the unparalleled service he was to render to the unification of Europe.

IDEAS AND DEVELOPMENTS, 1945–54

With democratic governments reinstated in liberated Europe, a series of initiatives was taken to pursue federalist objectives. The structure of post-war Europe had been extensively discussed in resistance movements in the latter stages of the war. This searching phase culminated in a Congress of Europe, held in The Hague in May 1948. It brought together leading figures from France (including twelve former prime ministers and the future president, François Mitterrand), Britain (Churchill, Eden and Macmillan, belonging to the Conservative opposition, all future prime ministers), the Netherlands, Belgium, Germany, Italy and elsewhere. The outcome may have been something of a disappointment or perhaps at most a very

Exhibit 1.1 *Key dates in the history of European integration, 1945–57*

1945 May
End of World War Two in Europe: Britain victorious.

1947 March
Treaty of Dunkirk: Britain and France against possible German aggression.
Truman Doctrine: US ready to provide support to those threatened by communist aggression or subversion.

    June
Marshall speech offering economic aid to Europe if Europeans co-operate with each other.

1948 March
Brussels Treaty: Britain, France plus Benelux states. A treaty of collective defence against Soviets (and initially Germany).

    April
Organization for European Economic Co-operation (1960 OECD) formed by sixteen European states + US/Canada (1960).

    May
Congress of Europe by federalists of the Hague.

1949 April
North Atlantic Treaty signed in Washington by twelve states.

    May
Statute of Council of Europe signed in Strasbourg by ten states.

1950 May
In a speech inspired by Jean Monnet, Robert Schuman, the French Foreign Minister, proposes that France, the Federal Republic of Germany and any other European country wishing to join them should pool their coal and steel resources.

    June
Attack by North Korea on South Korea, leads to proposals for a European army or a European Defence Community.

1951 April
The Six sign the Paris Treaty establishing the European Coal and Steel Community (ECSC).

    May
The Treaty establishing the European Defence Community (EDC) is signed in Paris by ECSC Six.

1952 July
ECSC starts work.

1954 August

The French parliament rejects the EDC Treaty.

 October

Following the London Conference, agreements on a modified Brussels Treaty are signed in Paris, and the Western European Union (WEU) comes into being.

1955 June

The foreign ministers of the Six, meeting in Messina, decide to extend European integration to all branches of the economy.

1957 March

The Treaties establishing the European Economic Community and the European Atomic Energy Community are signed in Rome.
Maudling OEEC talks between Six and other OEEC members.

small beginning for the federalists. While the Congress had called for the constitution of a European parliament, the ensuing negotiations followed the path of the inter-governmental relationships which the British government had favoured: the setting-up of a Committee of Ministers and a non-elected Consultative Assembly, these forming the Council of Europe, founded in May 1949. The Council of Europe aimed only at 'closer unity' as against The Hague demand for 'economic and political union'.

Churchill's speeches in Zurich in September 1946 and at The Hague conference, and his references to 'a kind of United States of Europe', made a powerful impact: although out of office, he was still a great statesman. But he was not offering Britain as a founder member of the union – a friend and collaborator certainly, but a state that also had competing ties to the United States and to the British Empire. (In his Fulton, Missouri speech in March 1946 about the special relationship between Britain and the United States he looked forward to a permanent defence agreement between the United States and the Commonwealth and to possible common citizenship.)

A separate initiative led to the creation of another European body, the Organization for European Economic Co-operation. This was the response to the offer by US Secretary of State George Marshall at Harvard in June 1947 of massive US aid for the rebuilding of Europe (without distinction of East from West) on condition that the beneficiary countries would co-operate with each other in the use of the resources which the United States would make available.

This offer followed the Truman Doctrine of March 1947, in which President Truman had offered to provide American help 'to support free peoples who are resisting attempted subjugation by armed minorities, or by outside pressure'.[22] General Marshall was convinced from a visit to Moscow in April 1947 that the Soviet Union would do nothing to help to build the war-shattered economies of Europe and that it was intent on increasing Soviet influence in Western Europe. The OEEC represented only governments and had no elected or nominated consultative organ. It was a classic inter-governmental operation, acting by consensus or not at all.[23]

These movements, although bold, generous and full of hope, fell far short of the integrationist objectives of those who sought to escape from national rivalries. They also did not touch a number of unresolved problems. There was the question of Franco-German relations, within which the Saar was a specific problem. The Saar was a German province, once again (as in 1918) split from Germany, being administered by France and potentially incendiary. Heavy industry in Germany and elsewhere needed to be restored, but with the guarantee that it would not, as in the past, encourage military production and adventure.

This was the basis of Monnet's plan,[24] which he presented to the French Foreign Minister, Robert Schuman, early in May 1950 and which the latter announced on 9 May in the Salle de l'Horloge in Paris after an anxious wait for clearance from the German government. From this moment the flagship of European integration is the European Communities,[25] of which the Coal and Steel Community was the first. Schuman's stated objective was 'to make war not merely unthinkable but materially impossible'.

The European Coal and Steel Community (Treaty of Paris, signed on 18 April 1951) removed the coal and steel industries of its participants, whether publicly or privately owned, from full national control, placing them under supranational stewardship. The supranational authority was to be the decision centre for production, prices (under certain conditions), investment and social conditions. It was not in the buying and selling business and it was not the negotiator of commercial treaties with non-member countries. France, Germany, Belgium, the Netherlands, Luxembourg and Italy announced their willing participation. The United Kingdom had an option to join but declined to submit itself to supranational authority for reasons which will be examined in Chapter Eleven.[26] This decision was taken under the Labour government; the Conservatives, who came into power in 1951, considered changing it but decided against.

The European Coal and Steel Community Treaty is of federal inspiration. The High Authority, which it created and whose members were designated by the governments of the member states, was a decision-taking body, independent of the member states, save where it needed their assent, which was obtained in some cases by a qualified majority of nationally weighted votes. It consulted an Assembly, but was not bound by its opinions. The Assembly was not in the first instance directly elected but direct election could come.

Outside events combined to hasten progress. The outbreak of the Korean War in June 1950 sharply increased world demand for steel, showing the economic value of co-ordination in production and offering a reminder of the linkage between steel production and war-making. Already in the summer of 1948 the post-war hopes of world co-operation had been broken and the vulnerability of Western Europe had been re-exposed when the Soviet Union sealed off the land routes into Berlin. The North Korean crossing of the 38th parallel in June 1950 was a further reminder, if any were needed, of the artificial post-war cartography where East joins West.

The first Community was regarded only as a starting point. The success foreseen in this sector was confidently expected to spread to others according to the functionalist theory of integration. In particular, the Coal and Steel Community was a selected trial-run for dealing with something far more significant: Western security. The treaty preamble has little to say about coal and steel. It speaks of safeguarding world peace, of establishing an economic community, and of substituting for age-old rivalries and bloody conflicts the merging of the essential interests.

The loss in the first phase of the Korean War of most of the peninsula showed the United States in particular how ill-prepared it was for any kind of war. In 1950 only one complete army division existed in the United States. Setting out to rearm, and assessing its European commitments, the United States called on its allies to follow suit. It also called for German rearmament within NATO command.[27] This was touching the most sensitive of nerves.

Western Europe, although protected by the US nuclear bomb shield, was aware of its own military weakness and of the undesirability of a specifically German contribution to rearmament.

The safest way to assert some military independence and insure against an American withdrawal, or American tactical choices which would leave part of Western Europe less than fully protected, seemed to be the creation of integrated European armed forces obeying no neo-nationalist command. Allowance would be made for out-of-theatre operations which remained in national hands, such as the colonial involvements of France and Belgium. But just as the Coal and Steel Community took the infrastructure of war away from national machination, so the European Army would serve the interests of all of Western Europe.

Here again, as often before, Churchill provided inspiration. On 11 August 1950, at the Fifth Session of the Consultative Assembly of the Council of Europe, he successfully proposed a motion calling for the immediate creation of a unified European Army subject to democratic European control and acting in full co-operation with the United States and Canada. He asked the Assembly to assure the German representative present that if the Germans threw in their lot, 'we shall hold their safety and freedom as sacred as our own'.[28]

It fell, however, to René Pleven, the French Prime Minister, to formulate the corresponding plan for the European Defence Community, presented to the French National Assembly on 24 October 1950 and later to NATO. The plan was in ECSC vein, providing for an Assembly, a common budget and a Council of Ministers as well as for a European Ministry of Defence. The plan received a favourable vote in the National Assembly. A conference was called in Paris, representing the six ECSC states.

The United Kingdom did not attend; its aloofness was later to be criticized by the United States, which for its part, under President Eisenhower, strongly supported the plan. (The Richards Amendment to the Mutual Security Act of July 1953 allocated half of US military aid to Europe to the future EDC.) The EDC Treaty and accompanying protocols with NATO were signed on 27 May 1952, another high point of European integration.[29] A security structure without foreign policy cohesion would have been incomplete. Accordingly, article 38 of the EDC Treaty called on the Assembly which it would set up to evolve a European Political Community (EPC). Taking time by the forelock, this task was pragmatically assumed by the ECSC Assembly, enlarged for the purpose and presided over by Paul Henri Spaak, the Belgian socialist. A draft treaty was prepared providing for a directly elected 'Lower House', a Senate elected nationally, an

Executive, a Court and a Council of Ministers, all common to the ECSC, the EDC and the EPC. The treaty also provided for the establishment of a common market with free circulation of goods, capital and persons.[30] The draft was remitted to ministerial consideration, but they embarked on a virtually new version, less supranational. For example, the Upper House looked as if it would be nominated by governments.

Four member states had ratified the EDC Treaty by April 1954, and in the summer the Italians were close to ratification. In Germany the Socialist Party opposed ratification, as it had also opposed the ECSC Treaty, but was outvoted. In France successive governments, besieged by innumerable problems and of changing political persuasion, either hesitated to press for ratification or lost procedural votes. The US government remained strongly in favour of the EDC. On 14 December 1953, Secretary of State Dulles threatened an 'agonizing reappraisal' of US European policy if the treaty were not ratified. In August 1954 the government of Mendès-France, a Radical who had Gaullist support, demanded a major revision of the treaty but the other participants refused. At the end of the month his government – with no expectation of success – proposed that the ratification debate be placed on the Assembly's agenda, but the Assembly voted to pass on to the next item. It was the end of the European Defence Community and the stillbirth of the European Political Community.

The fast-track to European union was blocked. A fresh start, on a longer path, was needed. European security would pursue its course within NATO and in the Western European Union (WEU), a new creation built on the Brussels Treaty Organization. WEU became a forum in which the United Kingdom met and collaborated with the Six. It later returned to the fore in the context of Maastricht.

THE EMERGENCE OF THE TREATIES OF ROME

Opinion was divided on whether and, if so, how the construction of Europe should proceed. 'Supranational' was for the time being a dirty word, and it was clear that the ECSC and the drafts of EDC and EPC could no longer serve as a model. In Italian government circles there was a preference for the 'OEEC method', inter-governmental and reaching out beyond the Six. In the Netherlands there was a call to proceed with the economic content of integration, a tailpiece of EPC included at Dutch insistence and lost with it. In Germany there was a desire to press forward with policies which gave West Germany a European vocation, although the Economics Minister, Dr Erhard, did not believe in a Europe of the Six, preferring a wider trading structure.

Monnet, President of the High Authority of the Coal and Steel Community, used his contacts and influence in government and private circles to promote a resumption of the dialogue. He persuaded the foreign ministers of the Six to meet at Messina on 1 June 1955. The conference owed much to the sensitive preparatory work of the Benelux countries, and in its conclusions took over much of their argument and language. The governments of the Six resolved that 'the moment has come to go a step further towards the construction of Europe. In their opinion this step must, first of all, be taken in the economic field.'

Specifically, they agreed on objectives for co-ordinating the development of transport and of energy generally and nuclear power particularly and for establishing a European common market free of customs duties and quantitative restrictions.[31] The study of the removal of trade restrictions was also part of the mandate of the OEEC, but in the OEEC it had been more or less confined to the liberalization of quota restrictions. Britain and others considered that tariff-cutting and free trade arrangements belonged properly to the General Agreement on Tariffs and Trade (GATT), where they could be placed in a world trade context. Atomic energy was an inviting and exciting prospect. Europe suffered from a technology gap, possessed (that is, Belgium possessed, in the Congo) uranium resources, and foresaw both shortages of fossil fuels and, unless something was done, undue dependence on the Middle East for essential oil supplies.

The Messina Conference set up a committee of government representatives, under the chairmanship of Spaak and assisted by experts. They invited Britain 'as a power which is a member of WEU and is also associated with the ECSC' to take part. Britain responded by appointing as its representative (not 'observer') on the expert committee R. F. Bretherton, Under-Secretary at the Board of Trade (the precursor of the Department of Trade and Industry).

The work settled down to study a possible Atomic Energy Community and a common market, the second being given lower priority and regarded (even by Monnet himself) as nebulous and too long-term to offer much political dividend. In the atomic energy discussions, which took centre-stage, the position of a non-participant, the United States, was a major factor. The United States led in nuclear know-how. Much of the information needed to build and operate nuclear reactors was classified, because they had been built not to generate power but to produce fissile material for bombs. But there were openings. In a speech at Penn State University on 11 June 1955, President Eisenhower announced the US 'Atoms for Peace' programme. The United States was ready, on appropriate terms, to conclude bilateral agreements which opened up prospects for US exports or, as in the US–Belgian bilateral agreement, ensured a supply of raw uranium. Other European countries were also interested in acquiring US know-how and assistance, and negotiations were prepared. US policy-makers were faced with the problem of balancing their national security interests and their foreign policy objectives. The latter prevailed. Within the State Department the view was taken that:

> the most hopeful avenue for relaunching the movement towards European integration now appears to be the creation of a European common authority, along the lines of the Schuman Plan, to be responsible for the development of atomic energy for peaceful purposes.[32]

In pursuance of this conclusion and in response to rumours that the individual European countries could get a better deal bilaterally than via an Atomic Energy Community, on 30 March 1956 US Secretary of State Dulles authorized his ambassadors in Bonn, Brussels, The Hague, Paris, Rome and Luxembourg to inform foreign ministers that the

> US Government could make available substantially greater resources and adopt attitude of substantially greater liberality towards real integrated community possessing effective common responsibility and authority than would be possible for countries separately.[33]

A difficult issue confronting the negotiators was the insistence by five of them that the member states of a European Atomic Energy Community should forswear the manufacture of atomic bombs. This was unacceptable to France, both on military grounds and because there was thought to be no possibility that the National Assembly would ratify such a self-denying ordinance. The compromise was a provision that no member state would explode a device before 1 January 1961, which was simply a recognition of the lead-time which France would need in its military programme.

The common market discussions in the Spaak Committee took less of the limelight (and gave rise to less debate within the US government). The Six wanted to proceed, as the German states had proceeded eighty years before, to a customs union with no internal tariff barriers but a common external tariff.[34] They also wanted to find a way of including agriculture within the system. The difficulty was that in most of the Six, where mass famine was a vivid recent memory, agricultural production was heavily protected, with the aim of raising self-sufficiency levels (and, historically, of maintaining a rural population which could provide labour for the conscript land army). Various plans for agricultural cross-frontier trade such as 'green pools' had been discussed earlier but had foundered.[35] For Britain, membership of a customs union was out of the question. Under imperial (later Commonwealth) preference it gave (largely) free entry to the raw materials and manufactures of Commonwealth countries and it received a certain amount of tariff preferences for its exports to them.[36] It was not prepared to overthrow this system and subject its imports from Commonwealth countries to 'reverse preferences' – that is, to see them move from free entry towards taxation while imports from the partners in the customs union went the other way.

The alternative to a customs union was a free trade area (without agriculture). There would be no tariffs between the members, but each would maintain its own external tariffs and the origin of goods from outside the area would be controlled. (Origin controls would in any case be necessary in the initial phases of a customs union as members transited to the common external tariff.) Agriculture raised a threat to British cheap food policies. Food imports were largely free of duty and the domestic price was subsidized down to world levels. An increase in food costs would push up the cost of living and unit wage costs in industry.[37] Britain sought to interest the United States in the negative consequences for the United States of a European customs union, but it was not until far on into the negotiations, which the United States had consistently supported, that the latter turned its mind to the possible damage to its agricultural exports. It then looked to the GATT to find a solution.

As the work of the Spaak Committee proceeded, the question of linkage between the two chapters, atoms and common market, became acute. France, for example, wanted progress on atomic energy but lacked interest in the common market. Germany, and especially German industry, thought that a purely national programme of atomic energy (with US help) was likely to be more effective and profitable. On the common market, Germany was decidedly reserved on bringing the African colonies into the arrangements, the proposal being pressed by France.

In November 1955 Spaak asked the non-Messina participants in his committees – Britain, the Council of Europe, the OEEC, the ECSC and the Committee of European Ministers of Transport (a free-standing organization) – to take a position on the arrangements which were emerging. Since Britain was unable to commit itself to any part of the emerging proposals, it effectively ceased from then on to play a part in the preparatory work. Spaak pressed on in 1956, reporting at intervals to meetings of the Six foreign ministers and producing in April the second Spaak Report, which was considered briefly by foreign ministers meeting at Venice in May 1956. Treaty drafting began in earnest after the summer break, and new compromises on disputed points (several remained outstanding from Spaak's reports) were negotiated at foreign minister level and at the meeting of heads of state or government[38] in February 1957. The two treaties, establishing a European Economic Community and a European Atomic Energy Community (Euratom), were signed in Rome on 25 March 1957, although only the EEC Treaty is colloquially known as the Treaty of Rome.

2 The Construction of Europe, 1957–72

The signing of the treaties only resolved some of the questions about the future shape of Western Europe. This chapter examines the initial years of the Communities' experience, the debate about the future shape of European integration, and the developments leading to the first enlargement with the entry of Britain, Denmark and Ireland in 1973.

THE BASIS OF THE EUROPEAN ECONOMIC COMMUNITY

The EEC Treaty takes as its premise that there will be an ever closer union among the peoples of Europe. The treaty stipulates that customs duties and other trade barriers among the member states will be abolished. A customs union will be formed. Cartels, trusts and the abuse of dominant market positions are outlawed. State aids which distort competition are incompatible with the common market. The free circulation within the Community of goods, services, capital and persons is to be secured partly by means of legislation which, by harmonizing divergent rules, standards and practices, will eliminate non-tariff barriers. The agricultural market of the Community is to be organized in accordance with stated principles.[1] The member states transfer to the Community the power to conclude treaties with international organizations and with third countries in matters for which the Community has competence. Provision is made for a special relationship between the Community and the former or existing colonies or overseas dependencies of its member states.

The Community is composed of four major institutions. Their functioning is discussed in Chapters Four, Five and Six.

The Commission is responsible for making legislative proposals, for executing policies which have been decided and which are entrusted to it, and for monitoring member states' compliance with the obligations which they have entered into. This gives rise to the much used characterization of the Commission as the driving force of European integration (because of its right of initiative) and as the guardian of the treaties (because it can intervene with the member states to demand compliance with their obligations).

The Council (often called the Council of Ministers, although this expression is not used in the treaties) is composed of representatives of the governments of the member states, each government deciding on its own representation. The Council decides on Commission proposals. In the more mature Community some decisions were to be taken by a majority vote weighted according to the size of the member: Germany, France and Italy in one band, Belgium and the Netherlands in another, Luxembourg in a third.[2] Broadly speaking, all decisions involving new policies would continue to require unanimity. Although the Commission has some decision-making powers, the Council is the Community's legislator, which is a marked shift towards the recognition of the role of national governments in contradistinction to the Coal and Steel Community where the High Authority was the decision-maker.

The Assembly is consultative. It can, if it musters a sufficient majority, express its non-confidence in the Commission and dismiss it. Its members were initially nominated by national parliaments from within their ranks. It was charged to propose to the Council arrangements for universal direct elections and the Council was to commend them to the member states for adoption under the latter's constitutional procedures.

The Court of Justice is the supreme constitutional authority for giving judgment on the obligations of the institutions, the member states, and legal and physical persons.

The Economic and Social Committee, officially an 'organ' rather than an institution, is consultative. Its members are appointed by the Council on the basis of nominations made by the governments of the member States, and are representative of employers, workpeople and independent persons.

Thus a programme was written and institutions established for the creation of a customs union including agriculture and for the means of reducing or eliminating non-tariff barriers. These went far beyond the intra-European trade liberalization measures adopted and discussed in the OEEC.

The Community was to pass laws binding on its members, who placed themselves unreservedly under the jurisdiction of a constitutional court. This legal order is often called the 'originality' of the European Community. There was a transfer of sovereignty from the member states to the Community. But the member states, meeting in the Council, had the final say on most issues and often could decide only by unanimity. The electorates were not directly represented in the parliamentary body and it was only consultative, its opinion having no binding force. And apart from the high-minded phraseology[3] in the preambles to the treaties, talk of political co-operation, co-ordination or integration was taboo. The parliaments in the member states ratified the treaties and they entered into force on 1 January 1958.

THE REACTION OF OTHERS

One reaction deserves notice: the total opposition of the Soviet Union, which regarded the European Communities as part of the war-making plot against it. It had sponsored its own world (and European) peace initiatives and in March 1957 tried a spoiling manoeuvre. The new Soviet leadership proposed an All-European Economic Agreement.[4] This was swiftly brushed aside.

The prospective coming into being of the European Common Market within the customs union created precisely the situation which the United Kingdom had sought to avoid: a trade split in Europe. Picking up discussions which had begun in the OEEC the United Kingdom embarked on a new objective. It could no longer be a question of a free trade area as the chosen form of economic organization for Europe, but of a free trade area in which the EEC would be a unit, along with the United Kingdom and the other members of the OEEC who wished to belong to it. Accordingly, it was no longer for the United Kingdom to negotiate alongside the Six; the discussions (which the members of the Six desired and for which the National Assembly in Paris had asked in its ratification vote on the EEC Treaty) were within the OEEC – although the

United Kingdom was a leading participant. Prior to the completion of the EEC negotiations and the ratification of the treaty, the free trade area talks could not make much headway. Work began with the publication in January 1957 of the report of the OEEC working party followed by the appearance of a British memorandum setting out proposals for a European industrial free trade area. The United Kingdom's preconditions were formidable. There was to be no agricultural content. The Commonwealth preference system was to be maintained. No significant institutional structure was required. The various compensating insurances built into the EEC Treaty would not be taken up and could be replaced by a complaints procedure. The British cause was not helped by its separate presentation in May 1957 of its 'Grand Design' for rationalising the mushrooming parliamentary-type bodies in Europe. The British proposal, though sound technically, caused suspicion that an attempt was being made to sap the solidarity of the Six and to impose NATO on the neutrals.[5] Another development was to be of more significance: on 1 June 1958, after major political upheaval in France, General de Gaulle returned to power.

At the request of the Six, OEEC ministerial discussions were deferred from July to October 1957. The OEEC Council then agreed to form a ministerial committee to pursue the Council's stated resolve to establish a free trade area. The chairman of the committee was Reginald Maudling, who in August 1957 had been appointed to the non-portfolio post of Paymaster-General in the British government to head up the European negotiations. The Community began to negotiate as one, and the Commission which had taken office on 1 January 1958 began to participate (strictly under article 113 of the treaty it should have been the sole Community negotiator). The Maudling Committee worked through the catalogue of differences with little success until, in November 1958, the French delegation announced to the press that it would not be possible to establish a European industrial free trade area between the Six and the other eleven members of the OEEC. The French had, in fact, concluded that free trade as proposed was a soft option, lacking the rigour which the EEC Treaty imposed on its members. This announcement was seemingly not cleared with the other members of the Community but they did not repudiate it. In a first and very early test, the cohesion of the Community took precedence over other considerations.

Exhibit 2.1 *Key dates in the history of European integration, 1958–72*

1958 January
The Treaties of Rome enter into force and the EEC and Euratom Commissions are set up in Brussels.

1959 January
First EEC tariff cuts.

1960 January
The Stockholm Convention establishing the European Free Trade Association is signed on the initiative of the United Kingdom.
 December
OEEC becomes OECD and includes United States and Canada.

1961 July–August
Ireland, Denmark and the United Kingdom apply for membership of EEC.

1962 July
The common agricultural policy is introduced.

1963 January
General de Gaulle announces at a press conference that France will veto the United Kingdom's accession to the Community.
 July
An association agreement is signed between the Community and eighteen African countries in Yaounde.

1965 April
A treaty merging the excutives of the three Communities is signed in Brussels. It enters into force on 1 July 1967.
 July
France begins boycott of Community institutions.

1966 January
The 'Luxembourg compromise' is agreed, France resuming its seat in the Council in return for retention of the unanimity requirement where very important interests are at stake.

1967 May
Denmark, Ireland and the United Kingdom re-apply for Community membership.
 July
Fusion Treaty takes effect.
 December
Six fail to agree on enlargement.

1968 May
Crisis in France.
July
Remaining customs duties in intra-Community trade in manufactured goods are abolished 18 months ahead of schedule and the Common External Tariff (CET) is introduced.

1969 December
At the Hague Summit the Community's heads of state or government decide to bring the transitional period to an end by adopting definitive arrangements for the common agricultural policy and agreeing in principle to give the Community its own resources. They also paved the way for enlargement, EPC and discussion of EMU.

1970 April
A treaty providing for the gradual introduction of an own resources system is signed in Luxembourg. It also extends the budgetary powers of the European Parliament.
June
Negotiations with four prospective member states (Denmark, Ireland, Norway and the United Kingdom) open in Luxembourg.

1972 January
The Treaty on the Accession of Denmark, Ireland, Norway and the United Kingdom is signed in Brussels.
April
The currency 'snake' is set up, the Six agreeing to limit the margin of fluctuation between their currencies to 1.25 per cent.
September
Norway withdraws its proposed membership following a referendum.

In the sequel, a series of proposals were made inside the Community and in the OEEC for averting the discrimination (although the use of this word was contested) which the Six would practise when they began on 1 January 1959 to implement cuts in the intra-Community tariffs and increases in quotas, and which would worsen so far as the low-tariff EEC countries were concerned when they began on 1 January 1962 to move to the Common Customs Tariff. None of the proposals stood up to the scrutiny to which it was subjected. Seven OEEC countries – Britain, which took the lead, Denmark, Norway, Sweden, Switzerland, Austria and Portugal – then decided to form a free trade area. The Stockholm Convention founding the European Free Trade Association (EFTA) was worked out at Saltsjöbaden near Stockholm in July 1959. The parties planned and expected to:

- obtain trade benefits for themselves;
- keep in step with the 'intra'-tariff reductions among the Six;
- continue to work for an agreement with the Community (an activity known as 'bridge-building').

The United Kingdom strictly and formally opposed the journalistic phraseology which spoke of the 'Inner Six' and the 'Outer Seven'. But after almost a decade of negotiations, the three European Communities were in business and Western Europe was divided into two trading groups.

THE COMMUNITIES START WORK

Within the Communities a vast work programme had been laid out. One primary task was to put flesh and bones on the general provisions of the EEC Treaty relating to agriculture. This work was inaugurated by the holding of a conference of all interested parties at Stresa on 3 July 1958. The ensuing Commission proposals provoked the first of the 'marathon' meetings which, for the next thirty years, were to be a feature of Community life. (Initially, the meetings were of foreign ministers; later agricultural ministers took over.) The guiding principles that emerged and that determined subsequent agricultural legislation were:

- common prices;[6]
- common financing (that is, an agricultural budget);
- Community preference (over imports).

As a major world trader, and with commercial policy as a Community competence rather than one within the sovereign control of the member states, the Community was sought after by other trading states which wished to establish or improve their commercial relations. The Commission became the Community's spokesman in GATT discussions and was immediately involved in defending the Community against claims that the tariff changes arising from the customs union should give rise to compensation for third countries. The Community had its own commercial relations agenda, notably the question of the African territories linked to member states. Following decolonization, eighteen African countries took the 'European option' and entered into negotiations which resulted (in July 1963) in the Yaoundé Convention.[7] This gave them tariff freedom in the EEC. In return they were required to give duty-free and quota-free access to EEC exports, subject to maintaining duties and quantitative restrictions to meet their development needs, including revenue. The African countries used this right, but the principle of reciprocity for imports from the EEC was established. The Convention was also a vehicle for aid in the form of the European Development Fund (EDF).

In the Coal and Steel Community, however, the situation was unpromising. By the end of the 1950s demand for coal was being squeezed by the rapid increase in oil consumption. The international oil companies, responding to the nuclear challenge, marketed vigorously and successfully. Moreover, coal was being imported into the Community (especially into Belgium) at a price which Community producers could not match. The High Authority judged that this was a 'manifest crisis' in the terms of the treaty, and it proposed a limitation on Community output as well as restructuring measures. For diverse reasons, France, Germany and Italy demurred. France considered that the crisis was not of its making: measures had already been taken to modernize coal production and the closure of French coal mines was economically and politically unacceptable, especially if done at the insistence of an external authority. In the free market of the German economic miracle nurtured by the Economic Minister Dr Erhard, there was resistance to interventionist measures and a conviction that Germany could find its own best way forward.

At a specially convened meeting on 15 May 1959 the High Authority's proposals for introducing production quotas were rejected by France, Germany and Italy. Although Belgium accepted and was paid for mine closures under the High Authority Plan, other coal producers successfully pressed the High Authority to approve national measures, including subsidies. This was a serious reverse for European integration and for the standing of the High Authority.

Euratom, once also seen as the great hope of European construction, did not take long to run into difficulties at the hands of the member states. Although, with some German hesitations, they had felt the need to come together to establish a civil nuclear industry, they found that the propects for nuclear power were less promising than they had appeared. Considerable difficulties arose over the allocation by the Brussels authorities of research contracts among the member states, each of which had its own ideas of what constituted a fair share (*juste retour*). Euratom was financed by national contributions and these gave the measure of what contributors expected to get back. The sign of crisis and of the diminishing authority of Euratom was the French refusal to renew the terms of office of Etienne Hirsch of France, President of the Euratom Commission and a convinced European, when his appointment expired at the beginning of 1962. It was perhaps from this moment, only shortly after the entry into force of the EEC and Euratom Treaties, that the creation of the common market of the EEC assumed primary importance and that the other Communities were relegated to a secondary status.

CONTRASTING STRATEGIES ON THE FUTURE OF THE COMMUNITY SYSTEM

It remained the strategy of Monnet, President of the Action Committee for the United States of Europe, which he had founded when he resigned from the presidency of the Coal and Steel Community, that economic Europe should be the path to political Europe, to European Union. This view was not shared by President de Gaulle. He had already made a major contribution to economic Europe by the economic and monetary reforms that he had carried through in France and by insisting on the creation of the Common Agricultural Policy, but he did not wish to see a structure that was divorced from governments become the gathering point for political union. His own European plan was for a 'Europe of the states'. He regarded all else as an illusion or delusion. He envisaged a Europe which proceeded by co-operation, which took its decisions by unanimity, which would become less dependent on the United States and which would engage in dialogue with the Soviet Union on equal terms, and under French leadership.

At his first meeting in 1958 with Chancellor Adenauer, whom he otherwise assured of his attachment to the Alliance and to the Communities, de Gaulle proposed regular meetings of foreign ministers, assisted by a small secretariat. When this proposal was put out more widely among the Six it provoked opposition, notably from the Netherlands, which saw it as further weakening the Atlantic community. Other EEC members also feared a weakening of the role of Community authorities. After some exchanges with his EEC partners, on 5 September 1960 de Gaulle held one of his dramatic press conferences at which he launched his plan for Europe. Although his downgrading of the European institutions caused alarm, the principle of a new drive for union was welcomed by Monnet as opening up a prospect for progress. The heads of state and government of the Six met in Paris on 10–11 February 1961. In their communiqué,[8] they declared their intention to lay the foundation of a union which would develop progressively, and they spoke of a new type of relationship based on the development of the common market and on political co-operation. At the follow-up meeting in Bonn on 18 July 1961, they agreed that they would meet regularly 'to compare their views, to concert their policies and to reach common positions in order to further the political union of Europe, thereby strengthening the Atlantic Alliance'. They also called on the committee, which they had established at their earlier meeting, to 'submit proposals on the means which will, as soon as possible, enable a statutory character to be given to the union of their peoples'.[9] The French representative and chairman of the committee was Christian Fouchet, a career diplomat. On 2 November, Fouchet presented to the committee a French draft treaty (Fouchet I). This provided for a 'union of the states' working through the adoption of a common foreign policy and a common defence policy. The Council of the Union was to take decisions by unanimity. Meetings of the Council would be prepared by a European Political Commission consisting of senior officials from foreign offices. After three years there would be a review, having as its main object the introduction of a unified foreign policy and 'the gradual establishment of an organization centralizing, within the Union, the European Communities referred to in the Preamble to the present Treaty' (article 16).

The draft provoked adverse comment among the other committee members and elsewhere. In particular the Assembly, in an opinion prepared by René Pleven, while approving the idea of regular summit meetings, insisted that nothing in the new treaty should call in question the existing institutions. It criticized the reference to a 'union of the states' and asked for a return to the 'union of the peoples' used in the Bonn communiqué. It disapproved of the Political Commission, advocating instead an independent secretary-general (who could be dismissed by the Assembly). It also opposed the unanimity rule.

On 18 January 1962 Fouchet presented a new draft to his committee (Fouchet II). This maintained all the disputed provisions of the first draft and added that the union was to act also in the economic field. Inter-governmental co-operation was to become the apex of the work of the three European institutions. The aim of the modified revision clause was to strengthen the union in general, 'or, in particular, for simplifying, rationalizing and co-ordinating the ways in which the Member States co-operate' (article 16).

The reception given to this proposal was even colder. Negotiations continued, especially between France, Germany and Italy. Foreign ministers met in Paris on 17 April 1962 to make a final attempt at agreement, and failed. Spaak, the main opponent of Fouchet II, along with Luns of the Netherlands, proposed that discussion should be adjourned until Britain had joined the EEC, and they were able to cite a speech by Edward Heath on 10 April 1962 in which, changing front from an earlier position, Britain had asked to take part in the discussion of political union. The subject was dead and de Gaulle, in a further press conference on 15 May 1962, poured scorn on his opponents and their 'Europe of the stateless' (*apatrides*) and said disobliging things about the Atlantic Alliance, thereby provoking the resignation from his government of Maurice Schumann, Pierre Pflimlin and other members of the pro-European Mouvement Populaire Républicain which was in coalition with the President's own party. (Twenty-two years later Pflimlin became president of the second directly elected European Parliament.)

The sequel was the consolidation of the Franco-German entente. A Treaty of Franco-German Co-operation was signed on 22 January 1963 and instituted regular joint meetings of the ministerial teams.[10] The regular meetings of the foreign ministers of the Six which had begun, on French initiative, in 1959 were now abandoned.

Thus the first attempt at a European Political Community (via the Pleven plan) failed because France could not fall in with it. The second attempt failed because the Five could not follow the Fouchet plans. Given British attitudes to European integration, (as discussed in pp. 245–63), Britain had no difficulty with Fouchet II. But the staunchest supporters of British entry into the Community were also the strongest opponents of both Fouchet plans. Meanwhile, the British themselves had lost the initiative. Installed in the EFTA camp they now had no leverage to obtain the wider European free trade area which they had been promised after the formation of the EEC and which, they claimed, was the basis of their support for it. Worse, the context of the negotiations had changed. First the Commission and later the Six reasoned that alleged tariff discrimination was not a European but a world-wide problem. Solutions should be pursued in the world forum, the GATT. 'Globalism' was supported by the United States, which also continued to back the European integration process. In doing so it parted company with Britain, which opposed the EEC plans to accelerate the tariff adjustments towards the customs union, which the United States supported. Time was also running out. Throughout 1960 the Six, at French insistence, were hammering out their common agricultural policy, an incubus for the United Kingdom in its economic relations with the Six.

THE FIRST BRITISH APPLICATION

The fresh start came in the decision to apply for EEC membership announced by the British Prime Minister, Harold Macmillan, on 31 July 1961. The leader of the UK negotiating team was Edward Heath, appointed Lord Privy Seal but also acting as Foreign Office minister (when Reginald Maudling embarked on the free trade negotiations his base was not in the Foreign Office). British government spokesmen made it clear that the decision was primarily political. Denmark applied for EEC membership on 10 August 1961 and Norway on 30 April 1962. Ireland, not an EFTA member but in free trade with the United Kingdom,[11] applied on 30 July 1961. Austria, Sweden, Switzerland and Portugal applied to become associates. The focus of the discussion was on the UK negotiations.

On 15 December 1962 Macmillan visited de Gaulle at Rambouillet. They discussed the accession negotiations and defence. Macmillan explained that he was shortly to meet President Kennedy to discuss the implications of the expected US discontinuation of the Skybolt nuclear missile development. Britain depended on this weapon following the cancellation of its national project, Blue Streak. In the event, Britain and the United States agreed on the Polaris programme. The United States would provide the missiles for the

British-built launchers (submarines) and warheads. Kennedy offered Polaris missiles on the same terms to France as he had already negotiated with Britain. The offer was declined (France had no launchers or warheads)[12] and was seen in Paris as part of a US strategem to dominate the European nuclear weapon capability. A second controversy arose over whether Macmillan had rebuffed de Gaulle by not evoking the possibility of Anglo-French collaboration on nuclear weapons.

On 14 January 1963, the day before Heath was due to begin one of two scheduled marathon sessions with the Six in Brussels, de Gaulle announced at a press conference that in the French view the United Kingdom was not ready to accept the conditions of EEC membership. He answered in the negative the (planted) question of whether:

> Great Britain can at present place itself, with the Continent and like it, within a tariff which is truly common, give up its preference with regard to the Commonwealth, cease to claim that its agriculture be privileged and, even more, consider as null and void the commitments it has made with the countries which are part of its free trade area.

Despite the French veto administered in Paris, the accession negotiations continued in Brussels until 29 January 1963. Spaak, whose European credentials were beyond dispute, pronounced judgement:

> On 14 January we were faced with a spectacular reversal of French policy . . . without being forewarned . . . and without even being permitted to discuss the reasons. . . . It will be extremely difficult, I am convinced, to continue to develop the economic Europe. As for the political Europe about which we had dreamed as a necessary consequence of economic organization, I do not know when it will be possible to speak of this again.

THE MERGER OF THE INSTITUTIONS

Thereafter the EEC and EFTA remained apart as the other EFTA countries and Ireland also abandoned their negotiations. The EEC proceeded to implement the treaty.

One organizational matter required attention. For the three Communities there was a single Assembly, a single Court of Justice and in practice a single Council, but three different executives each with a president. The Assembly and several member states were in favour of the fusion of the executives, in order to enhance the authority of a single new Commission. France agreed, subject to the later fusion of the treaties (which never occurred). The Fusion Treaty – which also legally created a single Council – was signed in Brussels on 8 April 1965. It innovated by referring specifically in article 4 – the only treaty reference – to the Committee of Permanent Representatives (COREPER), responsible for preparing Council meetings. The new Commission was transitionally composed of fourteen members, then reducing to nine, which gave France, Germany and Italy two members each. Fusion brought with it the problem of the seat. The ECSC High Authority had its seat in Luxembourg. The new Commission was in Brussels, which exerted a centripetal force. The Assembly had its headquarters in Luxembourg but also met in Strasbourg, sharing premises with the Consultative Assembly of the Council of Europe. The transfer of the Assembly (now the European Parliament) to Brussels, was urged by a majority of its members.

CRISIS

The actual installation of the new Commission was hit by a rift within the Council, nominally over budgetary matters, but reaching out to the whole span of Community activity. The budgetary question concerned the financing of agricultural expenditure, which was likely to rise from 1964, when according to a Commission proposal, there would be a single cereal price across the Community. According to the EEC Treaty (article 200) the Economic and Euratom Communities are financed by national contributions which the member states vote in their own national budgets. (The ECSC was financed by a levy on production.) Article 201 of the EEC Treaty enjoined the Community to replace the national contributions of article 200 by the creation of 'own resources'. The Commission accordingly proposed on 31 March 1965 that the Community should possess, as its own resources, the agricultural levies (on imports) and customs duties collected by the member states and hitherto retained by them as national revenue. In parallel the Commission proposed a treaty amendment which would make the Assembly a joint budgetary authority with the Council – a logical development since national parliamentary control over the sums in question would come to an end. The proposal was, however, ahead of its time. In addition, the German President of the Commission, Dr Hallstein, unveiled the proposal before the Assembly, to the irritation of member states. In discussion France proposed the continuation of the existing national contributions system for a period of years; others proposed shorter periods and there was a blockage. France, in the chair, closed the meeting down on 15 June 1965. It then boycotted Community meetings[13] and listed its grievances.

Under the EEC Treaty, from 1 January 1966 a large number of Council decisions were to come under the rule of majority voting. This was not acceptable to the government of President de Gaulle. It was only in January 1966 – after de Gaulle had failed to obtain a sufficient majority in the first round of the presidential elections in December 1965 – that France agreed to attend a meeting with the five foreign ministers. This was held in Luxembourg rather than Brussels to show that it was not a normal meeting. The French Foreign Minister presented his country's demands: unanimity was to be required when a country had major interests at stake, there should be a code of good conduct for the Commission ('the Decalogue') and a work programme was to be agreed.

The first point gave the greatest difficulty to the Five united against France – although France had not been alone in opposing the original 'own resources' proposal. The outcome of a second meeting held on 28–30 January and largely shaped by Spaak was the Luxembourg Compromise:

I Where in the case of decisions which may be taken by a majority vote on a proposal of the Commission very important interests of one or more partners are at stake, the Members of the Council will endeavour, within a reasonable time, to reach solutions which can be adopted by all the Members of the Council, while respecting their mutual interests and those of the Communities, in accordance with Article 2 of the Treaty.

II With regard to the preceding paragraph, the French delegation considers that where very important interests are at stake the discussion must be continued until unanimous agreement is reached.

III The Six delegations note that there is a divergence of views on what should be done in the event of a failure to reach complete agreement.

IV The Six delegations nevertheless consider that this divergence does not prevent the Community's work being resumed in accordance with the normal procedure.[14]

Often described as an agreement to disagree, the Luxembourg Compromise was, on the contrary, determining. The Council did not proceed to majority voting on those issues to which it applied according to the treaty and the normal procedure became a search for unanimity achieved through the Council and its preparatory bodies negotiating within themselves to amend Commission proposals.

With the 'empty chair' again occupied, the Council had to catch up with its arrears including the adoption (on 11 May) of a financial regulation and the nomination of the new (single) Commission. Hallstein, who had been President of the EEC Commission since its inception, was not reappointed. Jean Rey of Belgium was the new President.

THE SECOND BRITISH APPLICATION

In October 1964 the Labour Party, led by Harold Wilson, came to power in Britain. The new government felt it necessary to impose a 15 per cent import surcharge, a move which was contrary to EFTA rules and which upset Europe in general. It took some time to repair relations with both. However, an apparently profound change in British attitudes, examined in Chapter Eleven, resulted on 11 May 1967 in the United Kingdom applying for membership of the European Communities. Ireland and Denmark applied on the same day; Norway on 24 July.

As required under article 237 of the EEC Treaty, the Commission gave an opinion – generally favourable – on the UK application and the Five prepared to proceed towards negotiations. De Gaulle, however, demurred. At a press conference on 10 May 1967 he administered the 'velvet veto', and on 27 November 1967 he commented on the weakness of the UK economy (the pound had been devalued on 19 November) and predicted that the entry of the United Kingdom would damage Community structures and would transform the Community into a simple free trade area. In internal discussion in Brussels, France maintained its position: there could be no entry negotiations until the United Kingdom took the necessary measures to repair its economic weaknesses, as France had done before the entry into force of the EEC Treaty. Franco-British relations were set back by the 'Soames Affair' in February 1968.[15] In discussion with the British Ambassador, Sir Christopher Soames, de Gaulle spoke of his own concept of Europe. Specifically, he reportedly envisaged replacing the Community system by a more flexible arrangement, embracing all the EFTA states, and with long-term bilateral agreements for agricultural trade. Politically, Europe would assert its independence under a Directorate consisting of France, Germany, Italy and the United Kingdom. The British, embarrassed by these proposals, with which they in any case could not agree, decided to inform the Five – although France disputed the Foreign Office version of the conversation (Soames had taken the precaution of showing his reporting telegram to the French foreign minister) and although Wilson himself was against disclosure. The upshot was that the Six were unable to agree on the opening of negotiations with the applicant countries. The United Kingdom announced that 'it did not take no for an answer' and that its application, to which it had received no response, remained on the table of the Community.

THE FIRST ENLARGEMENT

President de Gaulle resigned on 28 April 1969, after losing the referendum he had called on the reform of the regions and the Senate. The successful Gaullist candidate in the ensuing election was Georges Pompidou, a former prime minister under the General, who defeated the ardent European, Alain Poher. Pompidou moved in short order to obtain a meeting of Community heads of state and government. The agenda could not possibly have left unmentioned the dormant applications for membership. Many straws were in the wind, including Pompidou's remark at his first press conference on 10 July 1969, 'We have no objection of principle against a possible UK accession.' The summit meeting took place at The Hague on 1–2 December 1969. Apart from launching the initiatives for European Political Co-operation, which are examined in Chapter Ten, it came out with the triptych: completion (which meant at the time securing the financing of agricultural expenditure), deepening and widening (the admission of more members). It was understood that the negotiations should open in the first half of 1970, and 30 June became the date. In February 1970 the Labour government published as a White Paper an economic assessment of membership (Cmnd. 4289) which was generally objective but reaffirmed the government's commitment to reaching a successful conclusion. Eight days before 30 June 1970 the Conservative Party won a general election in Britain and Edward Heath formed the new government. It inherited (and accepted) the preparations which its predecessor had made for the entry negotiations. Ireland, Denmark and Norway also prepared to negotiate.

In the Maudling days, the negotiations had the appearance of being among seven states. In the first Heath negotiations it was the Six (aided by the Commission), plus one. Third time round it was to be the Six as one, plus one. The Six arranged that, with the help of the Commission, they would speak only through the President of the Council – although the Six would all be present at negotiating sessions, silently observing and on hand to caucus if the session needed a new contribution from them. For the Six the ground rules were that the applicants accepted the treaties and the *acquis* (translated as 'what the communities have achieved'), and that there would be transitional arrangements, but that their purpose was solely to allow for the adhering states to adjust to the conditions of membership. It was also perhaps in the mind of all that this time round there were not to be discussions at the level of what to do about kangaroo meat – but in the event, matters such as tariff arrangements for mimosa wattle had to be discussed and agreed. By early 1971 the negotiations were running into log-jams which made recourse to bilateral diplomacy at all levels necessary. (The leader on the UK side was Geoffrey Rippon, in another non-portfolio post as Chancellor of the Duchy of Lancaster, and having his base in the Foreign and Commonwealth Office, as it had come to be called following the post-1965 reorganization of the Diplomatic Services.) From 19 to 21 May, Heath met Pompidou in Paris. At the close, Pompidou was able to conclude that: 'it would be unreasonable to believe that agreement is impossible at the Conference in June.'

So it was in Luxembourg in June that the last four big issues were settled. The first was the UK budgetary contribution, where the

United Kingdom opened with a (knowingly) low bid. The solution was a relatively low starting position, a growth formula and an anti-surge rule for the last year of the transition. The second was the transitional period. The British opener had been a longer period for moving to agricultural prices than for abolishing internal tariffs, regarded by the Six as having the cake and eating it. The solution was to make the periods approximately the same. The third divide was over Commonwealth sugar, which had contractual access to the British market and a favourable price there for 1.4 million tons. The United Kingdom wanted the equivalent to become a Community obligation and demanded 'bankable assurances', but finally accepted that the enlarged Community *'aura au coeur'* the interests of Commonwealth producers, including sugar producers, especially in the forthcoming association negotiations with Caribbean, African and Pacific countries.[16] A fourth problem was New Zealand dairy produce, resolved in a protocol fixing access and price for an import quota which gave satisfaction to the New Zealand representative, John Marshall, who was on hand in the building, and his government. The complete results of the negotiations were set out in a White Paper in July 1971 (Cmnd. 4715).

Denmark, Norway and Ireland concluded their negotiations, and the Accession Treaties were signed in Brussels on 22 January 1972. They provided for the four new members to join on 1 January 1973. One immediate task for the Ten was to establish a relationship with what would be left of the European Free Trade Association EFTA when three of its members left it. All had accepted the proposal of the Six that bilateral free trade agreements should be negotiated with each of the EFTA members, not with EFTA as a bloc. Such agreements were signed in July 1972 with Sweden, Switzerland, Austria, Portugal and Iceland. Signature of an agreement with Finland was deferred to October 1973, pending Finland's discussion of its European relations with the Soviet Union. In Ireland and in Denmark referendums were held on the terms of membership (Ireland 83 per cent yes; Denmark 63.3 per cent yes) and parliamentary ratification followed. In the United Kingdom the European Communities Bill was enacted. At third reading in the Commons on 13 July 1972 the vote was 301 for, 284 against. In Norway the consultative referendum went against membership (53.49 per cent no)[17] and Norway concluded a Free Trade Agreement with the enlarged Community in May 1973.[18]

This then redrew the economic map of Western Europe so far as those states were concerned that had, since the Second World War, wanted to create a new structure, or had been obliged by those who wanted it to find their place in it.

3   The Construction of Europe, 1973–86

This period was initially one of great strain in the Community, and yet it also saw a number of initiatives for the development of the Community and culminated in both the Single European Act and further enlargement.

Early in its existence the new structure came under a strain which was to prove too much. In October 1973 the Arab oil producers embargoed exports to the Netherlands, which they regarded as pro-Israel, and began to drive up oil prices. Community solidarity was not enough to defend a member state (although the oil majors did so). The United Kingdom and France were quick to make oil deals with Arab states, and the Community was seen to show little backbone when Arab ministers showed up in Copenhagen at a summit meeting in December 1973.

With the return of a Labour government to power in the United Kingdom on 28 February 1974, the Community was propelled into further difficulty with the renegotiation of the terms of British membership (see Chapter Eleven). This culminated in the positive vote in the British referendum of 5 June 1975. With membership questions thus settled the Communities could turn to an institutional problem, although some of the old problems soon came back.

INSTITUTIONAL DEVELOPMENT

Each of the three treaties creates an Assembly; the Convention on

Certain Institutions Common to the European Communities provides that the same Assembly serve each of the three. Each treaty stipulates that the Assembly:

• Consists of delegates who shall be designated by the respective Parliaments from among their members – between 1973 and 1975 the Labour Party did not designate members, showing its opposition to Britain's membership.
• Shall draw up proposals for elections by direct universal suffrage in accordance with a uniform procedure in all member states – the Council shall, acting unanimously, lay down the appropriate provisions which it shall recommend to member states for adoption in accordance with their respective constitutional requirements.

In 1960 the (single) Assembly drew up and adopted a draft convention for direct elections. The Council did not act on it. There was disagreement over details and reservation on the principle of creating a body which would have supranational status and which would rival the democratic legitimacy of the parliaments and governments of member states. Italy, which did not share these hesitations, at one point initiated measures to secure the direct election of Italian members.

The heads of state and government meeting in Paris on 9–10 December 1974 took two institutional decisions. One was to create and arrange for meetings of the European Council in which they would come together regularly in future. The other was in favour of universal direct elections to the European Parliament. Some commentators saw a trade off between the two. The United Kingdom and Denmark reserved their position on direct elections.

The Assembly itself had campaigned for direct elections at every opportunity and on 14 January 1975 it adopted a new draft convention (the Patijn Resolution, from the name of its draftsman). The draftsman had concluded that a uniform procedure, exactly the same in every member state, created too many problems. The European Council majority in 1974 had spoken of direct elections in 1978 but the United Kingdom needed more time for 'internal consultations', including difficulties with the Conservative opposition. In the event, the first European direct elections were held in June 1979. The turn-out was generally low, except where voting is compulsory,

Exhibit 3.1   *Key dates in the history of European integration 1973–86*

1973   January
Accession of Denmark, Ireland and United Kingdom.
October
Yom Kippur war in Middle East leading to oil and economic crisis in Europe and elsewhere.

1974   April
First Gymnich informal meeting of foreign ministers.
December
At the Paris Summit the Community's heads of state or government decide to meet three times a year as the European Council, give the go-ahead for direct elections to the European Parliament and agree to set up the European Regional Development Fund (ERDF).

1975   February
A first Convention between the Community and 46 states in Africa, the Caribbean and the Pacific is signed in Lomé.
March
Dublin – First European Council meeting.
June
Yes to continued membership in United Kingdom referendum; Greece applies for membership.
July
A treaty giving the European Parliament wider budgetary powers and establishing a Court of Auditors is signed. It enters into force on 1 June 1977.

1977   March
Portugal applies for Community membership.
July
Spain applies for Community membership.

1978   July
At the Bremen European Council, France and the Federal Republic of Germany present a scheme for closer monetary co-operation (the European Monetary System) to replace the currency 'snake'.

1979   March
The EMS starts to operate.
May
The Treaty on the Accession of Greece is signed.
June
The first direct elections to the European Parliament are held.

October
A second Convention between the Community and 58 states in Africa, the Caribbean and the Pacific is signed in Lomé.
December
European Parliament for first time does not approve proposed Community budget.

1981 January
Greek accession to Community.
October
'London Report' on EPC.

1983 June
Stuttgart 'Solemn Declaration on European Union'.

1984 February
European Parliament Draft Treaty establishing the European Union.
June
Direct elections to the European Parliament are held for the second time. At the Fontainebleau European Council, the Ten reach an agreement on the compensation to be granted to the United Kingdom to reduce its contribution to the Community budget.
December
A third Lomé Convention between the Ten and the ACP states, now numbering 66, is signed in Togo.

1985 June
Commission publishes its White Paper 'Completing the Internal Market'. Milan European Council accepts Commission White Paper and calls an Inter-Governmental Conference.
December
At the Luxembourg Council the Ten agree to amend the Treaty of Rome and to revitalize the process of European integration by drawing up a 'Single European Act'.

1986 January
Spain and Portugal join the Community.
February
The Single European Act is signed in Luxembourg.

and the campaigns were largely fought on national issues. The House elected as its first president Mme Simone Veil, a French member of the Liberal group and former minister, and for the second half of its mandate Piet Dankert, a Dutch socialist. When Greece acceded to the Community, its members were initially designated by the Greek parliament, pending direct elections. The second direct elections (still conducted on national lines) were held in June 1984. The first Spanish and Portuguese members in 1986 were designated but direct elections were held shortly afterwards in both states.[1]

The holding of direct elections made no formal differences to the Assembly's advisory and supervisory functions. But it could speak with greater authority – for example, in rejecting the budget – and could reinforce its demand to be given legislative or co-legislative functions. On 30 March 1962 the Assembly had decided to change its name to European Parliament, although this name was not used in legislation. The Single European Act of 1986 formally changed the name.

THE UK/EC BUDGETARY PROBLEM

It was said above that some old problems soon came back. The problem of budgetary imbalance – the net amount transferred by the United Kingdom to the Community budget – did not go away after renegotiation and the British referendum of 1975. It had been to some extent tempered by transitional arrangements, but with continuing growth in agricultural expenditure it became a major issue for Britain – and for the Community – when the Conservative government under Margaret Thatcher came to power in Britain in 1979. Britain pressed with some vigour its argument that seven of the nine member states, including five more prosperous than the Community average, were net beneficiaries of the budget. In fact, the budget transferred resources from member states with relatively small agricultural sectors to those which are net exporters of agricultural products regardless of their relative prosperity. Two member states, Britain and Germany, were left to make transfers to the others. After a stormy session of the European Council in Dublin on 29–30 November 1979, it was agreed that there should be 'complementary measures' in favour of Britain, in the form of additional projects financed by the Regional and Social Funds. In May 1980, after difficult discussion of a series of issues in the Council, the Commission was given a mandate to produce the proposals which would enable the Community to fulfil its pledge to resolve the problem by means of structural change. The new Commission (under the presidency of Gaston Thorn, former Foreign Minister of Luxembourg) responded to this mandate in June 1981. Meanwhile the complementary measures continued and became a dispute between the Council and the European Parliament, which as a budgetary authority had the right to scrutinize them, to vote on them and to subject them to budgetary control. As the debate on lasting solutions to the Community's financial problems was pursued from Council to Council and European Council to European Council – including the failure of the European Council in Athens in December 1983 to adopt any conclusions at all – *ad hoc* refunds in Britain's favour were agreed for 1983. For 1984 a new correcting mechanism was established as a fixed amount for that year and, for future years, as relief in the amount of VAT which Britain was due to pay into the budget. This changed from one which compensated Britain by channelling additional Community expenditure there to one which reduced the amount transferred by Britain to the Community budget. It was accompanied by a decision to increase the total size of the budget (in revenue and expenditure) and was to be examined *ex novo* before the new revenue ceiling was reached (European Council, Fontainebleau, 25–26 June 1984). This examination was integrated into the task of 'making the Single Act succeed', which was brought to a conclusion at the European Council meeting in Brussels, under German presidency, in February 1988.

The two major rounds of financial negotiation, pre-Fontainebleau 1984 and pre-Brussels 1988, covering the future financing of the Community, the development of new policies, problems of enlargement, budgetary discipline, 'budgetary imbalances' (the UK problem) and the cost of the CAP took a heavy toll of eight years of the Council's time and negotiating capacity, as well as touching off acrimony among members of the Council and between it and the parliament. In particular, the protracted and sometimes sterile negotiations could not but delay progress in the Community's further enlargement. The applicants wished to see what kind of Community they were applying to join, and the member states had to find time to address the problems of the enlargement negotiations.

MAJOR CONSTITUTIONAL REFORM?[2]

The early 1980s

A new round of constitutional and institutional reform opened at the meeting of the European Council in London in November 1981, when the German and Italian delegations, acting jointly, gave notice of a new plan to promote European union. The German side elaborated its ideas at an internal meeting on Epiphany. The plan was for the adoption of an Act of European Union and was known as the Genscher–Colombo initiative. The plan took as its principles the need to provide a firmer orientation to political objectives, a more effective decision-making structure and a comprehensive political and legal framework capable of development. The detailed provisions included an organization which placed the European Council at the apex both of the work of the Communities and of political co-operation and which recognized the central importance attached to the work of the European Parliament in the development of European union.

An attempt was made to define the use of the notion of 'vital interest' in the invocation of the veto. A state claiming that its vital interests were at stake would be required to give its reasons in writing. The Council would defer its decision until its next meeting. If, at the meeting, the member state concerned again invoked its vital interests (in writing), a decision would again not be taken. There was to be a review of the European Act after five years with a view to preparing a treaty on European union. An accompanying statement on economic integration called for a functional internal market, an adjustment of the Common Agricultural Policy, an improvement in budgetary structure and closer co-ordination of economic policy.

The Council found it hard going to discuss a paper which had not come to it from the Commission or from its own presidency and progress was slow and difficult. Having taken a forward public position, the authors found it difficult to compromise. Even when the incoming German presidency in January 1983 began to compile a final version, the text which emerged from the European Council meeting in Stuttgart on 19 June 1983 – no longer an Act but a Solemn Declaration of European Union, not involving constitutional procedures in member states – was subject to reservations set out in footnotes. Five out of the Ten (Denmark, Greece, France, Ireland and Britain) upheld the Luxembourg Compromise; Denmark opposed any extension of the Council/Parliament conciliation procedure; Greece did not accept the desirability of reaching more rapidly common positions in political co-operation. The Solemn Declaration did not achieve what the Genscher–Colombo plan wanted and the outstanding problems had to be faced again two years later.

From 1980 to mid-1984, spanning the Genscher–Colombo initiative, the major preoccupation within the Community was 'budgetary imbalance', the catchword for the British demand for relief from what it regarded as its excessive gross and net payment to the Community budget. This was linked with the (generally) rising cost of agricultural guarantee expenditure. By a quirk of nature, agricultural spending in 1980 was relatively low. In 1982, when the Council came to fix agricultural prices for the coming season, Britain was at war in the Falklands and was seeking and obtaining support from Community institutions and from the governments of member states for economic measures against Argentina.[3] It opposed the proposed price increases and invoked the Luxembourg Compromise. This was not accepted by a majority of member states, on the grounds that the British objection was not intrinsic to the matter for decision but belonged to its attempt to obtain budgetary reform. By majority vote substantial price increases were agreed. Agricultural spending continued to rise. As described above, at the European Council meeting in Fontainebleau in June 1984 the French presidency successfully put through a series of measures which took the sting out of the budgetary problem and laid a basis for the further development of the Communities.

From Fontainebleau (June 1984) to the SEA (1986)

Apart from budgetary issues, the European Council at Fontainebleau decided to set up two new committees to prepare reports on the future of the Communities. Each took the name of its chairman: Dooge, an Irish Senator who had been Minister of Foreign Affairs, presided over the *ad hoc* Committee on Institutional Questions, and Adonnino, a former Italian member of the European Parliament, took the Committee on 'Citizen's Europe'.[4] Although the passage in the European Council conclusions appointing the Dooge Committee likened it to the Spaak Committee of foundation days, there was a major difference. Dooge had a completely open mandate because nothing had been decided. Spaak had worked on the commitments entered into at Messina. The Dooge Committee did not set out to be consensual, and its report is qualified by dissent. In all there are thirty-seven reservations and two closing unilateral declarations. The mainstream report (March 1985) looks towards a single market by the end of the decade; the improvement of competitiveness; the promotion of common values (including cultural); the search for external identity (including security and defence); more regular recourse to voting in decision-making (with a saving for very important national interests); the strengthening of the role of the Commission; the participation of Parliament in legislating (including co-decision in defined matters); and operationally the convocation of a conference to draft a treaty of European union (Danish, Greek and British disagreement).

The European Council meeting in Milan in June 1985 did not follow mainstream Dooge. A series of further proposals were on its table (including British and Franco-German ideas about political co-operation), but the Council confined itself to an agreement in principle, taken for the first time in a European Council by vote – Denmark, Greece and Britain being outvoted – to convene a conference under article 236 of the EEC Treaty to discuss treaty amendment.[5]

THE SINGLE EUROPEAN ACT

It fell to the ensuing Presidency, Luxembourg, to organize the conference and to discharge the preparatory procedures under article 236. All this could be done by qualified majority, but the final outcome needed common agreement and ratification by each member state. This was the genesis of the Single European Act, which emerged after less than six months, to be signed on 17 February 1986 by nine member states, followed on 28 February by Denmark, Italy and Greece. The Danish government had been required by its parliament, the Folketing, to ascertain whether a revision of the Act was possible and had done so. It was not. It then held a referendum in which the electorate voted in favour of acceptance of the Single European Act.

'Single' recalled that the Act concerned both the revision of the three treaties under article 236 of the EEC Treaty and corresponding clauses of the other treaties, *and* contained separate (and for the first time) treaty provisions on political co-operation, including the establishment of a small secretariat consisting of officials temporarily seconded from foreign ministries.[6]

Exhibit 3.2 *SEA revisions to the Treaty of Rome*

The Treaty revisions contained in the Single European Act, which came into force in July 1987, expanded the scope of majority voting within the Council of Ministers. It thereby restricted the requirement for unanimous agreement to sensitive issues such as taxation, the dismantling of borders and workers' rights.

The Single Act also extended the powers of the European Parliament in the decision-taking process and codified procedures on foreign policy co-operation for the first time. The authority of the Community was broadened to cover aspects of energy, environment, monetary and social policies as well as research and technology. Priority was to be given to strengthening the economic and social cohesion of the Community.

In the Community section, Title II, the Single European Act made four main innovations:

1. It provided that certain decisions hitherto subject to unanimity (for example, article 100 of the EEC Treaty, harmonization of standards) were brought under the qualified majority rule (for example, new article 100A).
2. It formalized Community concern with research and development and with the environment, hitherto actively pursued in the Community but under general enabling provisions (for example, article 235).
3. It devised a 'co-operation procedure' between the Council and the Parliament which gave Parliament more say but without co-decision. The procedure applied to measures aimed at creating the single market. The Commission retains the monopoly of legislative initiative. The Parliament gives an opinion on the Commission proposal. The latter may, but is not obliged to, modify its proposal accordingly. The Council takes, by qualified majority, or by unanimity if it amends the (possibly revised) Commission proposal, a 'common position'. The Parliament then examines and votes on the common position, needing a qualified majority (of at least half its members) to propose amendments. The Council considers Parliament's second reading and decides. Parliament and Council have three months each for their second

readings (extendable by common agreement to four months) and the Commission has one month in which to express an opinion on the Council's 'common position'. If at the end of the period the Council has not decided, the proposal is dead.

4. It gave the Parliament the right to grant or withhold assent when consulted by the Council on the entry of new member states into the Community (article 237) or new agreements with third countries for association with the Community (article 238).

The majority in the European Parliament regarded the Single European Act as disappointingly meagre compared with its own aspirations but resolved to 'exploit it to the limit'. Full ratification was delayed when, in Ireland, a private citizen, Raymond Crotty, obtained a judgment on 9 April 1987 that the political co-operation part of the Single European Act could not be ratified without a constitutional amendment. A referendum was held to change the Constitution. Turnout was 44 per cent, and 69.9 per cent of votes cast were in favour. The Act entered into force on 1 July 1987.[7]

A negotiation which had opened in disagreement ended in consensus. The final package had the required 'something for everyone' character. For example, new article 100A, paragraph 4, provides that if following Council decision a member state needs (stronger) national measures, for the reasons adduced in article 36 (the escape clause of the EEC Treaty) or for the protection of the environment or the working environment, it can be authorized by the Commission to keep them in being. This was intended to be helpful to Denmark, which had difficulties over the years with what it regarded as the low standard of Community environment legislation. The Single Act explicitly provides for economic cohesion, on which Greece, as a country below average GNP, had insisted in its note of dissent in Dooge. For the United Kingdom a major preoccupation, new in the negotiations, was the programme for the completion of the Single Market. This gave treaty effect to the White Paper which the Commission had produced in June 1985 under the leadership of Vice-President Lord Cockfield,[8] setting out an annotated, precise and timed programme for the completion of the Single Market in 1992.

The Single Market was predicated on the elimination of all controls at frontiers, such that the circulation of goods, services, capital and people across frontiers would be as free as circulation within national frontiers. The White Paper set out proposals for Community decisions which would replace nationally divergent rules such as those concerning product standards, pharmaceutical and phyto-pathological controls, financial services, professional qualifications, company law, indirect tax rates (VAT and excise) and passport control. Although the member states strongly backed the programme (without committing themselves to accept every measure exactly as the Commission proposed it), several of them had major reservations about the fiscal proposals and about abolishing all frontier controls on travellers, mingled among whom are terrorists, drug traffickers and international criminals.

The Single European Act needed accompanying financial measures, to cost the programmes and to arrange for their financing by curtailing the growth of agricultural expenditure and increasing the resources available to the Community budget. The Commission filled in this part of the mosaic in the documents (COM)100 and (COM)101, which it published in February 1987 under the headline 'Making the Single Act Succeed'. This set the member states off on a new round of negotiations, first with each other and the Commission and then with the European Parliament, the joint budgetary authority.

To bring agricultural spending under control the Commission proposed a maximum annual growth rate (modelled on one already in use), a reserve fund for fluctuations in the exchange-related price of agricultural produce, and the introduction or extension to other products of stabilizers, which limit the quantities to which Community price guarantees apply. For additional revenue the Commission proposed a new resource, proportionate to member states' GNPs. Under the principle of cohesion, it proposed the doubling of the structural funds (Regional, Social and Agricultural Guidance), along with new objectives for backward and declining areas. Finally, it proposed that budgetary expenditure should be programmed five years ahead. At European Council meetings in Brussels (June 1987, Belgian presidency) and Copenhagen (December 1987, Danish presidency) the member states inched towards agreement. At Brussels in February 1988 the German presidency carried through a package, subject to reaching an inter-institutional agreement with the European Parliament, on what could be variously regarded as containing expenditure ('budgetary discipline') or planning its growth. Such an agreement, almost the last piece in the jigsaw, was signed at the European Council meeting in Hanover in June 1988. It remained for the governments to obtain national parliamentary ratification of the decision to increase the Communities' 'own resources'.

GREECE, SPAIN AND PORTUGAL BECOME MEMBERS

For six states which are European in the sense of article 237, and were therefore eligible for membership of the Communities, relations limited to trade or to association have been found insufficient. Greece had been quick to establish a relationship with the Communities. An Association Agreement under article 238 of the EEC Treaty was concluded in July 1961 and came into force on 1 November 1962. It looked to later membership.[9] On 21 April 1967 units of the Greek armed forces rebelled and assumed power in what was known as the 'Rule of the Colonels'. The Community thereupon 'froze' the Association Agreement, confining its operation to day-to-day matters. On 24 July 1974, following the ill-fated intervention by the Colonels in Cyprus, democracy (but not monarchy) returned to Greece. The Association Agreement was brought out of the cold. On 12 June 1975 the new Greek government applied for EEC membership, the first time that an associate had done so. For the Council, there was no question of turning down the application, which was regarded as an expression of Greek desire to consolidate democratic government. On 28 January 1976, however, the Commission noted that in its opinion Greece and Turkey had hitherto been on an equal footing, as associates. It proposed that the rights guaranteed to Turkey by its associate status should not be affected by the examination of the Greek application. The Greek Accession Treaty was signed in Athens on 28 May 1979. Greece became the tenth member state on 1 January 1981.

Spain, under General Franco, stood aside from the democratic movements of post-war Europe. In 1962 Spain proposed to the EEC that it should become an associate, but the proposal languished in Brussels. At the end of the 1960s, the Community became concerned to develop what it called an 'overall Mediterranean approach'. Some member states had important interests in the Mediterranean area and there were loose ends in the EEC Treaty, which had special and now outdated provisions for Algeria. Within the overall approach a Trade

Agreement (article 113 of the EEC Treaty, not article 238) was concluded between the EEC and Spain in 1970. It did not envisage membership. From 1975, when King Juan Carlos ascended to the vacant throne, Spain set out to improve and strengthen its relations with its European neighbours. It submitted an application for membership on 28 July 1977. The negotiations were long drawn-out, less because of the problems intrinsic to them than because of the Community's preoccupations with its own internal problems, especially of finance. It fell to the Italian presidency, in the first half of 1985, to give a new impetus. The Accession Treaty was signed in Madrid on 12 June 1985 and Spain entered the Community on 1 January 1986.

Portugal, a member of EFTA, concluded a Free Trade Agreement with the EEC in 1972. Democracy was restored to Portugal in 1974. On 28 March 1977 Portugal applied for membership of the Communities. In its opinion on the application the Commission said that there was no choice, 'The Community cannot leave Portugal out of the process of European integration.' The Portuguese and Spanish negotiations proceeded in parallel. The Accession Treaty was signed in Lisbon on 12 June 1985 and Portugal entered the Community on 1 January 1986.

PROGRESS TOWARDS UNION?

The long march of European Councils from Stuttgart to Hanover via every other state in the Community of Ten had provided the Community's new statutory and budgetary base – and had taken it to within a few months of the appointment of a new Commission (of which Jacques Delors had been redesignated President) which would be responsible for transforming the common market into the single market of twelve members (for goods, capital, services and people) by the end of its mandate in December 1992, and which now included Spain and Portugal, making a Community of Twelve.[10]

In this march the idea of European union had been frequently appealed to, even if as seen little progress was made in giving it concrete effect. European Union is a concept with many connotations. Whatever else it means in the minds and sayings of those who use it, it usually implies that some of the powers and functions of the governments of the member states will pass to the organs of the

Union. It usually also means that the Union will undertake a wider range of responsibilities than those exercised by the Communities.

When the shortcut to 'political union' was blocked in the mid-1950s, the approach to closer integration became circuitous. Some of the milestones were the first modest revisions of the EEC and Euratom Treaties in 1970 and 1975 to give the (nominated, not elected) Parliament budgetary power, a characteristic of most parliaments. On 19–20 October 1972 the heads of state and government at their meeting in Paris (including the new member states) set themselves the major objective of transforming, before the end of the 1970s, the whole complex of the relations of member states into a 'European union'.[11] The strain placed on the Community in the oil crisis of 1973 put paid to such intentions. The European Council meeting in Paris in December 1974 asked its Belgian member, Leo Tindemans, a Flemish Christian Democrat, to write a report on European union and his report (*Bulletin of the EC*, Supplement 1/76) was considered at the meeting in The Hague in 1976. In a 'high road to European Union'[12] Tindemans proposed a common foreign policy, on a legal basis; a monetary policy within an economic policy; a 'citizen's Europe'; and a reform of the institutions (including direct elections, majority voting in the Council, an annual Council Presidency, delegation of powers to the Commission and the right of the president of the Commission to choose his or her team). Tindemans' report was not followed up at the time, but many of the ideas came back strongly later.

Another report on Community institutions by 'three wise men', Biesheuvel of the Netherlands, Dell of the United Kingdom and Marjolin of France (OOP, 1980), was examined at the European Council meeting in Brussels in December 1978, without significant effect. The holding in June 1979 of the first direct European elections was a landmark, and strengthened the already dominant European spirit of the body. While the Council proceeded via the Solemn Declaration of European Union of Stuttgart in June 1983 towards the Single European Act, the new Parliament tried a more direct route. It appointed on 9 July 1981 a Committee on Institutional Questions, charged with producing proposals for establishing a European union. The Committee, led by the late Altiero Spinelli, set to work to prepare a draft treaty. (Spinelli had been expelled from the Italian Communist Party in 1937 but was an affiliate of it in the European Parliament. He was a Commissioner from 1970 to 1976.)

On 14 February 1984 the European Parliament (membership of 434) adopted by 237 votes for, 31 against and 43 abstentions the Draft Treaty Establishing the European Union.[13] Parliament sent the draft treaty to the parliaments and governments of member states, and charged the new Parliament (from the elections of 17 June 1984) to pursue contacts with national parliaments.

The issue of European Union was clearly not settled in this period, and it came back on to the agenda soon after the Single European Act was agreed.

Part One: Further Reading

Archer, C., *Organizing Western Europe*, London, Edward Arnold, 1990.

Brugmans, H., ed., *Europe: dream, adventure, reality*, Brussels, Elsevier, 1987.

Burgess, M., *Federalism and European Union*, London, Routledge, 1989.

Camps, M., *Britain and the European Community 1955–1963*, Oxford, Oxford University Press, 1964.

Camps, M., *European Unification in the Sixties*, Oxford, Oxford University Press, 1967.

Cecchini, P., *1992: the benefits of a single market*, Aldershot, Gower, 1988.

Haas, E., *The Uniting of Europe: political, social, and economic forces, 1950–1957*, Stanford, Stanford University Press, 1958.

Hallstein, W., *Europe in the Making*, London, Allen and Unwin, 1972.

Heater, D., *The Idea of European Unity*, London, Leicester University Press, 1992.

Laffan, B., *Integration and Co-operation in Europe*, London, Routledge, 1992.

McAllister, R., *The European Community: an historical and political survey*, Hemel Hempstead, Harvester Wheatsheaf, 1992.

Milward, A. S., *The Reconstruction of Western Europe 1945–51*, London, Methuen, 1987.

Monnet, J., *Mémoires*, 2 vols, Paris, Fayard, 1969.

Morgan, R., *West European Politics since 1945: the shaping of the European Community*, London, Batsford, 1972.

Nicolson, F. and East, R., *From the Six to the Twelve*, Harlow, Longman, 1987.

Pryce, R., *The Dynamics of European Union*, Beckenham, Croom Helm, 1987.

Urwin, D., *The Community of Europe: a history of European integration since 1945*, Harlow, Longman, 1991.

Vaughan, R., *Postwar Integration in Europe*, London, Edward Arnold, 1976.

Weigal, D. and Stirk, P., eds., *The Origins and Development of the European Community*, London, Leicester University Press, 1992.

The Institutions at Work

4 Commission and Council

Although there are four major institutions and a number of 'lesser institutions' in the Community system, a key dynamic in the system and in the development of the Community is the relationship between the Commission and the Council. This initial chapter on the institutions, therefore, explores that relationship and the component parts of these institutions.

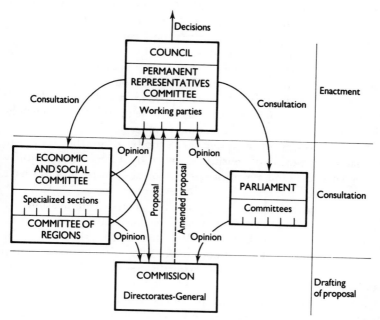

Figure 4.1 *The Community's decision-making process*

THE COMMISSION

The Commission, sometimes called the European Commission, more formally the Commission of the European Communities, consists – in the Community of twelve member states – of seventeen Commissioners. Two come from each of Germany, Spain, France, Italy and Britain, and one from each of the other member states. Those with two can share the appointments among political parties (as Britain has always done). Commissioners must be nationals of member states. They have mostly been active politicians.

Commissioners are appointed by common accord of governments, but in practice this agreement is taken for granted and each government announces its choice unilaterally and in its own time.[1] The original appointment is for four years and is renewable. In the Treaty on European Union, the term is changed to five years with effect from 1994 in order to bring the renewal of the Commission roughly into line with the life of the Parliament.

Several Commissioners have had several terms but many have had only one. In performing their duties Commissioners are required to be independent and neither to seek nor to take instructions from any quarter.[2] Once appointed, a Commissioner can be dismissed only if the Court of Justice, on application by the Council or the Commission, retires him or her. If a vacancy occurs, a successor can be appointed on the same conditions, or the Council may decide that the vacancy need not be filled, as happened in 1992, when Ripa di Meana resigned to join the Italian government, and his responsibilities were assumed by another Commissioner.

Commissioners must resign as a body if in the European Parliament a motion of censure is carried by a two-thirds majority of the votes cast and a majority of members. Censure motions have been proposed but no such vote has ever carried.

The President[3] and Vice-presidents of the Commission are appointed by common accord of the governments for a period of two years, renewable. The European Parliament is consulted before the name of the President is announced. One of the Commissioners from the five dual-member countries normally becomes a Vice-president (unless the President comes from that country). Other Vice-president posts rotate between the other member states. Until 1989, when Greece appointed Madame Papandreou and France Madame Scrivener (re-appointed in 1993), all Commissioners had been men.

The Commissioners meet weekly (47 meetings in 1991), and in principle take their decisions by simple majority – nine out of 17.[4] In 1991 the Commission adopted 6,130 instruments and sent the Council 652 proposals and 208 other communications.

The Commission's proposals may be the brainchild of a Commissioner. They may flow from the treaties, or from legislation already adopted under them. They may be consequent upon a judgment of the Court. They may respond to a demand of the Parliament, or of the Council, or of a member state, or of an interest group. They may have their origins in the Commission staff, following a study or a piece of research or participation in a programme run by an outside body. Wherever they come from, they must be accompanied by a budgetary statement (of their cost to the Community) and a statement, in the name of deregulation, on their effect on small and medium-sized firms. In future there will be a justification under the principle of subsidiarity. They must also come in all nine official languages.

Each Commissioner has a portfolio of subjects for which he or she is responsible, but decisions are collegiate and all Commissioners keep themselves informed of the whole of the work of the Commission. They travel extensively, meeting their ministerial counterparts in the member states, political personalities in their home countries, and individuals and groups who have points to make or to whom points are to be made. Commissioners also attend plenary sessions of the European Parliament and its committee meetings to answer questions, present Commission proposals and take part in debates.

Each Commissioner has a private office, or *cabinet* (the French word). The *cabinet*, which has a *chef*, consists of four or five people selected by the Commissioner as his personal staff. Some come from the institutions, especially the Commission itself. Others come from outside, often from national government service, and hold temporary appointments. Between them, the *cabinet* members help their Commissioner to cover the whole of the work of the Commission and to run his or her particular responsibilities. The *chefs de cabinet* meet weekly under the President's *chef* to prepare the weekly Commission meeting. The *chef de cabinet* has more onerous responsibilities and a higher public profile than a typical private secretary in a British minister's private office.

Before or on taking up office, the incoming Commission meets to

Exhibit 4.1 *Composition of the Commission, 1993–4*

Jacques Delors	Secretariat General
	Forward Studies Unit
	Inspectorate-General
	Legal Service
	Monetary Matters
	Spokesman's Service
	Joint Interpreting and Conference Service
	Security Office
Henning Christophersen	Economic and financial affairs
	Monetary matters (in agreement with President Delors)
	Credit and investments
	Statistical Office
Manuel Marin	Co-operation and development
	● economic co-operation with the countries of the southern Mediterranean, the Middle East, the Near East, Latin America and Asia
	● Lomé Convention
	European Community Humanitarian Aid Office
Martin Bangemann	Industrial affairs
	Information and telecommunications technology
Sir Leon Brittan	External economic affairs (North America, Japan, China, Commonwealth of Independent States, Europe, including Central and Eastern Europe)
	Commercial Policy
Abel Matutes	Energy and Euratom Supply Agence
	Transport
Peter Schmidhuber	Budgets
	Financial control
	Fraud prevention
	Cohesion Fund: co-ordination and management
Christiane Scrivener	Customs and indirect taxation
	Direct taxation
	Consumer policy

Bruce Millan	Regional policy Relations with the Committee of the Regions
Karel Van Miert	Competition Personnel and administration policy, translation and informatics
Hans van den Broek	External political relations Common foreign and security policy Enlargement negotiations (Task Force)
João Deus de Pinheiro	Relations with the European Parliament Internal relations with member states with regard to openness, communication and information Culture and audiovisual Office for official publications
Padraig Flynn	Social affairs and employment Relations with the Economic and Social Committee Questions linked to immigration, internal and judicial affairs
Antonio Ruberti	Science, research and development Joint Research Centre Human resources, education, training and youth
René Steichen	Agriculture and rural development
Ioannis Paleokrassas	Environment, nuclear safety and civil protection Fisheries
Raniero Vanni d'Archirafi	Institutional questions Internal market Financial institutions Enterprise policy: small and medium-sized enterprises, trade and crafts

allocate the portfolios. This used to be a 'night of the long knives', but more recently has been arranged in a more gentlemanly manner. Each Commissioner (sometimes including the President) acquires responsibility for a range of subjects, which are handled by the Directorates General of the Commission. The number of Directorates General varies, but is usually around twenty. In addition, there is a Secretariat General, under the Secretary General of the Commission, which holds the operation together, ensures co-ordination and under that heading is specifically responsible for data processing; a Legal Service; a Spokesman's Service, centralized under the President and replacing the arrangements for media liaison which each Commissioner used to make; a Joint Interpreting and Conference Service, which also provides interpreters for the Council and the Economic and Social Committee; and a Statistical Office. The Directorates General and the services plus the College of Commissioners is often collectively described as 'The Commission'. Most of the Commission staff are in Brussels but there are some in Luxembourg and in the Joint Research Centre at ISPRA in Italy. The Commission maintains information offices in each member state and delegations in some eighty-five countries and to four international organizations.

The terms of employment of the staff of the Commission (and of all the institutions) are governed by the Staff Regulations, which have legal force and are much invoked in proceedings before the Court of Justice.[5] Staff are subjects of member states. The institutions are required to recruit on the widest possible geographical basis and they seek to maintain a geographical balance among the nationalities. The Commission is responsible for all appointments to its staff. Recruitment at the entry grade is by open competition, usually involving both written work and interview. Candidates must have a working knowledge of a Community language other than their own. Although there is a good deal of mobility within the Commission, and rather less between different institutions, there is a tendency towards specialization, and some staff, such as scientists, are recruited for their skills. Redundancy is rare: the staff of the Commission (and of other institutions) grows steadily. At the higher ranks, and usually after informal consultations with member states, some staff are appointed from outside ('parachuting'), often from national government service. As in the other institutions, a very large part of the staff is concerned with the translation (into eight languages from an original) and physical production and distribution of papers. The remuneration of staff of the institutions is exempt from national income taxes but subject to a Community income tax, which accrues to the Community budget.[6]

The Commission is often criticized, and vocally in the crisis of confidence in 1992, as being a monster. Its payroll is about 15,000.

Comparisons are odious, because functions differ, but this is smaller than the staff of the Scottish Office.

THE COUNCIL

The Council of the European Communities is theoretically a single body but in practice it meets in different compositions. Its members are representatives of governments, normally ministers. The presidency rotates among the member states for six-month spells in the alphabetical order of the countries' names in their own language. With an even number of member states, this means that each would have the same semester every six years, although the burden of work is not evenly distributed throughout the year. (August is not a working month. The budget falls in the second half. Farm prices are a heavy responsibility in the first half.) For the cycle 1993–8, the annual order is reversed: Denmark, Belgium, Greece (Ellas), Germany, France, Spain, Italy, Ireland, the Netherlands, Luxembourg, the United Kingdom, and Portugal.

The Foreign (or General) Affairs Council, the Agriculture Council and the Economic and Finance Council (ECOFIN) meet monthly. The Internal Market Council meets four or five times a year. The Fisheries and Budget Councils meet three or four times, Councils such as Industry, Research, Steel, Transport, Energy, Education, Development, Environment, Culture and Social Affairs meet two or three times, and those such as Consumer Affairs, Tourism, Health, Telecommunications once or twice. Council meetings are held in Brussels, and in Luxembourg in April, June and October. The Budget Council sometimes meets in Strasbourg in December, during a parliamentary session. The work of the Council(s) is prepared by meetings of officials of the member states. According to article 4 of the treaty creating a single Council and single Commission (1965, as amended) the work of the Council is prepared by a committee consisting of Permanent Representatives. By use and wont, this rule does not apply to the Agriculture Council, where the same task is performed by the Special Agricultural Committee (CSA).

The Committee of Permanent Representatives (COREPER) is split in two. Part II, consisting of Ambassadors, works (broadly speaking) for the Foreign (or General) Affairs Council, for ECOFIN, for the Energy Council, for the Research Council and via the Foreign Affairs Council for the European Council. The work of COREPER II is itself facilitated by the 'Antici Group' of Ambassadors' assistants, with whom the presidency discusses agenda planning, work programming and procedural matters. Part I of COREPER consists of deputy permanent representatives and works for the other ('specialized') councils.[7] The preparation of a Council meeting is the process of agreeing on the matter to be submitted to the Council and in what terms.

In the 'Community method' the starting point is a Commission proposal, sent to the Council. The Commission has a monopoly, under the treaties, of the power to make proposals. As a general rule, the Council can take decisions only on Commission proposals. Every proposal (and decision) rests on a legal base – an article of the treaty concerned. The choice of legal base determines:

- the majority required for the proposal to pass;
- the procedure to be followed with and in the European Parliament.

The Council's voting rules provide for simple majorities (mainly for procedural questions), qualified majorities (for the infilling of existing policies) or unanimity (for new policies, or if the Council wishes to change a Commission proposal without the latter's agreement). A qualified majority is made up of 70 per cent of the votes of the member states, weighted by size. In the Community of twelve the weighting is 10 votes each: Germany, France, Italy, the United Kingdom; 8 votes: Spain; 5 votes each: Belgium, Greece, the Netherlands, Portugal; 3 votes each: Denmark, Ireland; 2 votes: Luxembourg. The qualified majority is 54.

Conversely the blocking minority, which will prevent a positive vote, is 23. Unanimity can be obtained with abstentions. In qualified majority voting, however, abstentions have the same effect as votes against. The Council needs a quorum of six members. A member may give its proxy to another.

Although the Luxembourg Compromise was a note of disagreement, and although the European Council decided in Paris in 1979 that there should be more regular recourse to voting, up to the mid-1980s Councils generally preferred to reach consensus. This took time, usually involved amending the Commission's proposal, and could result in no decision being taken. The successive enlargements, adding to the spectrum of interests, further complicated the attempts to find solutions acceptable to all. This is the principal task of the 'Council bodies'. Their work consists of examining a Commission proposal, first of all to ensure that there is a common understanding of it and then to establish whether it can be accepted – and if not, what changes or glosses might make it acceptable.[8]

This kind of preparatory work is organized hierarchically. It begins in the 'working groups'. These meet under the serving presidency and with the Commission present. They consist of member states' officials. Some are manned by Brussels residents, members of the 'permanent representations'. A permanent representation typically has 30–40 staff with diplomatic status (more during a presidency), plus support services. The staff are either members of the national diplomatic service or are seconded to it from national ministries. They receive their instructions from capitals, where the different agencies co-ordinate national positions. In some working groups the Brussels residents are supplemented or replaced by visitors from capitals (often referred to as 'experts') who come with instructions.[9] An 'Attachés Group' consists exclusively of members of permanent representations. It can be convened at short notice and is sometimes deployed to find a way through when 'experts' are bogged down. The 'Friends of the President' is a special kind of Attachés Group, consisting of people from permanent representations who know each other and the subject and can spend more time on tricky points than Ambassadors can find for them.

The working group sets out to prepare a report which will show what can be agreed and what remains disputed at its level. The chairman, Commission representative and individual delegates may also seek to devise compromises or otherwise to act as brokers between different viewpoints. This includes bilateral negotiations outside the conference room,[10] and negotiations between delegations and the Commission. On major points such negotiations may be taken over by senior officials and ministers in capitals, telephoning their opposite numbers or travelling to meet them.[11] In the search for compromise, the Council has the help of its Secretariat General. This body had no treaty basis prior to the Treaty on European Union, its only official manifestation being its administrative budget, incorporated in the general budget. It numbers some 2,000 staff, the larger part being translators and services for providing conference facilities, printing and distribution. Some 150 staff are recognizably committee secretaries, whose responsibilities are to record the result of discussions, to brief presidents and to help them in any initiatives they want to undertake, including the search for compromise. This search goes on at all levels: Council, COREPER, committee. Only the Council has the power of decision. What is done at the lower level is informal and rests on the understanding that the Council will, in due course, endorse it. The Council infrastructure is substantial. Each presidency has to find chairmen or women for some 150 working groups. The number of 'meeting days' is shown in Table 4.1.

As long as the Council wanted consensus (and in its absence, refrained from deciding) the work of 'Council bodies' was devoted to this aim. This in turn led to the charge that the bureaucrats had captured the Council and prevented or discouraged ministers from taking decisions which required political will.

In the Single European Act the member states agreed that a number of key treaty articles, and especially those concerned with the completion of the single market, should be modified to provide that decisions on proposals made under them should be taken by qualified majority voting. This does not, of course, mean that the Council has no choice but to vote for or vote down a Commission proposal. It can still, if it wishes, and acting by unanimity, modify the Commission proposal, and it can still find itself without a qualified majority for a proposal. But it can also find that a qualified majority can be obtained if, after hearing the arguments, the Commission is ready to change its proposal. Such a qualified majority is what would often have been unanimity in a smaller Community. Consequently, the readiness of the Council to vote does not at a stroke eliminate the preparatory work. It is still necessary for the member states to make sure that they have a common understanding of the Commission proposal, to explore at working level whether it is generally acceptable, or what changes would make it so, to test

Table 4.1 *Number of days spent on Council meetings and meetings of preparatory bodies: selected years*

Year	Ministers	Ambassadors and ministerial delegations	Committees and working parties
1958	21	39	302
1968	61	132	1,253
1978	76.5	104.5	2,090
1988	119.5	104	2,000.5

whether the Commission may be prepared to make changes and, where there is disagreement, to report to ministers the reasons for it. In the light of their discussion, and under the political responsibility of their president, ministers decide whether they wish to vote, to negotiate for compromise at their level, to allow time for reflection, to remit the matter for more work at official level or, where major questions are open, to involve the European Council.

To create the material conditions for greater use of voting, the Council modified its internal rules of procedure in 1987. The Commission or a member state can now ask in Council for a straw poll to be taken on the procedural question of whether the Council should now vote on a proposal. This procedural question is settled by a simple majority (seven member states for) and, if it passes, the Council then votes on a qualified majority basis. If no qualified majority exists, the Council does not regard the proposal as lost and it may return to its search for a compromise. The Council also cleared the way for voting by marking on its agenda notices, sent out in advance of meetings, the points on which a vote could be taken.

No exact statistics exist to mark the evolution, since about 1983, towards the use of voting. This is because the Council does not, and did not in the past, always need to record votes cast. A chair can infer from discussion that agreement exists without polling delegates. If he or she concludes that it does, and this conclusion is not challenged, the decision-making process has worked. It was agreed at the meeting of the European Council in Edinburgh that formal votes taken in Council will be recorded in the press communiqué along with any explanations of vote. This should mean that whenever a decision is attributed to a majority vote, the voting record should be published, showing which member state voted for, which against and which abstained.

Council agendas are divided into two parts. 'A' points are those on which delegations, acting under instructions, have found that there is agreement and Council discussion is not required. 'A' points are formally approved in Council meetings and can relate to matters which are not within the ambit of the Council approving them. 'B' points are those which require ministerial discussion.

The Budget Council was always an exception to the consensus rule. In article 203 of the EEC Treaty an annual timetable is laid down. The draft budget has to reach Parliament from the Council by 5 October. When it returns from Parliament in early November, the Council has fifteen days to make any changes. Because of this time constraint and perhaps because the Council can, in this sole case, change the Commission's preliminary draft by qualified majority, not by unanimity, the draft budget has always been voted in the Council. This does not always guarantee a result: in 1987 the Council, under the Danish presidency, was unable to find a qualified majority for any budgetary proposal, despite 15 presidency proposed compromises.

There were eighty Council meetings in 1991. The Council adopted 72 directives, 335 regulations and 174 decisions. In addition to these meetings there are two variants on 'normal' Council meetings. Councils sometimes meet 'informally', and then usually in the presidency country at the invitation of the presidency. At informal Councils there is no set business, rather general discussion and no intention of reaching decisions. The presidency may take the opportunity to prefigure ideas which it may have for the agenda and handling of the next formal meeting. Some presidencies (and individual presidents) set more store by informal Councils than others.

Exhibit 4.2 *Danish presidency, January–June 1993: Calender of Council meetings.*

Date	Council	Other meetings
Jan. 18	ECOFIN	
18 (poss.)	Fisheries	
18–19	Agriculture	
Feb. 1–2	General Affairs	
8	Internal Market	
9		Informal, Education Ministers (Copenhagen)
9–10	Agriculture	
15	ECOFIN	
Mar. 2	Consumers	
8–9	General Affairs	
15	Transport	
15	ECOFIN	
16–17	Agriculture	
18	Fisheries	
23	Environment	

Apr. 5–6	General Affairs	
5	Internal Market	
6	Social Affairs	
19	ECOFIN	
19	Energy	
23–24		Foreign Ministers/RIO Group (Copenhagen)
26–27	Agriculture	
29	Research	
May 3–4		Informal, Ministers of Employment (Nyborg)
4	Industry	
4–5		Informal, Ministers of Justice/Home Affairs (Kolding)
6–7		Informal, Ministers of Immigration (Kolding)
10	Telecommunications	
10–11	General Affairs	
10–11		Informal, Ministers of Fisheries (Esjberg)
14		Informal, Internal Market (Vejle)
17	Cultural Affairs	
21–23		Informal, ECOFIN (Kolding)
24–25	Agriculture	
25	Development	
27	Health	
Jun. 1–2		TREVI/Immigration Ministers (Copenhagen)
1	Social Affairs	
7	ECOFIN	
7–8	Transport	
8	General Affairs	
11	Education	
14	Internal Market	
14–15	Agriculture	
21–22		European Council (Copenhagen)
24	Fisheries	
28–29	Environment	
30	Research	

Purists are wary of meetings which are not conducted in accordance with the formal rules, but may seek to reach decisions. In exceptional cases, informal Council meetings may result in published conclusions, as at the informal meeting of finance ministers in Bath, England in September 1992, in the middle of the currency crisis.

There are also meetings of 'The Council and Ministers of . . . meeting within the Council'. This indicates that there was discussion of matters which are not within the competence of the Community, or on which Community competence is accepted by some but opposed by others.

THE EUROPEAN COUNCIL

Meetings of the European Council have become formidable affairs, far removed from the fireside chat which may have been their original conception. Usually held in the custom-built Conference Centre with which every presidency equips itself, sometimes held away from the capital city, they bring together the large entourages which accompany each head of state or government. The media and the police are present in strength. Hospitality is customarily lavish.

Despite media attention and the various public ceremonies as dignitaries arrive or gather for the 'family photograph', not much is known about the happenings inside the tightly guarded rooms in which the European Council meets.

With the heads of government are their foreign ministers (for some of their sessions), the President of the Commission and a Vice-President (varying according to subject). In a Declaration annexed to the Treaty on European Union it is provided that economic and finance ministers will be invited to European Council meetings when their subjects are under discussion. Whereas in Council meetings, delegations include officials, only the Secretaries General of the Council and of the Commission are present. In the background is a rotating company of middle-ranking officials from the Council Secretariat known (in French and English) as 'note-takers'. Their task is not to prepare an official record, but, after 20 minutes or so in the room, to emerge to tell the Antici Group what has been said. This is relayed to delegations in the outer rooms and the latter brief the press informally as time passes. Rumour, that lying jade, also circulates like wildfire.[12]

Before a meeting of the European Council,

- Its President writes round to colleagues suggesting what they and their foreign ministers should talk about, in the formal sessions and at mealtimes.
- Papers may appear, especially reports from the Commission; and other heads of state or government may give notice of matters they would like to raise.
- The Permanent Representatives, and separately the Political Directors, study possible draft conclusions which have been prepared by the presidency staff in conjunction with the Secretary General of the Council.

It appears that although it is not a cosy chat, members of the Council have grown away from the style of setpiece *tour d'horizon* and address themselves directly, and at appropriate length, to the points which the presidency has focused on, in the knowledge that they are expected to reach substantive conclusions.

In the light of the debate and of the president's running summing-up, the authors of the draft conclusions embark on revision. Early copies pass to delegations, who may want amendments after consulting their leader. Heavily reworked versions are presented by the President to his colleagues, and discussed at a final session, often it appears, under great pressure of time, with a famous final 'five minutes' in which agreement is reached, or not, as has happened more than once.

The published conclusions – in a *tour de force* of Council services they exist in all languages within moments of the end – are known as 'presidency conclusions'.[13] In other EC meetings this label can mean that the conclusions do not necessarily bind all the participants, but this subtlety does not apply to the European Council. There are usually several 'Declarations' about foreign affairs. European Council conclusions are far more substantial than the guarded and cryptic press communiqués which come out of Council meetings. They are the Holy Writ for future work in the Council.

The European Council is not an institution of the European Communities or European Union.[14] But the Heads of State and Government can act as a Council in the treaty sense and take formal decisions, provided the conditions are met (a Commission proposal exists, the required parliamentary opinion has been obtained, the

Commission and the quorum are present, the relevant voting rules are respected). Its task and composition are described in article D of Title I of the Treaty on European Union, but this title does not create any Union institutions. According to the same article, the European Council meets at least twice a year. Recently, it has held extra meetings (three in 1991 and in 1992) devoted to current pressing problems.

THE COUNCIL PRESIDENCY

The rotating presidency, serving for six months, has acquired increasing responsibilities. Its elementary function is to arrange dates of meetings, provide people for them and propose agendas. But a presidency would not be human if it discharged these functions mechanically. In its planning the presidency may decide to take initiatives on subjects which it finds of special importance and which, for given reasons, it prefers not to leave to the Commission to initiate. Every presidency brings its own input and has its own ideas about the purpose of its work programme. This purpose will show a blend of national and Community interest.

The presidency therefore sets certain priorities and tries to do so in concert with the Commission. More especially, each presidency plans for and proposes the decisions to be taken at the European Council meeting which it will host and which will be a political and media event. Some priorities are more or less dictated to it: business of the Community which is spread over several presidencies and needs to be kept going by each. To provide some continuity, and to improve Council support for its programme, presidencies may use the 'troika' system. This brings together the last presidency, the serving presidency and the next presidency. It is used in Political Co-operation, and in the Economic Community it was used to overhaul the 'rolling programme' of Council work connected with the realization of the Single Market.

When discussion is joined and when difficulties emerge, there is an expectation that the presidency will bring out a compromise, to the point that this is now regarded as a presidency duty. The Commission may also propose compromises, but is to an extent inhibited by the fact that a compromise (the noun is used positively) may compromise (the verb is used negatively) its original proposal and any arrangement which it has made with the Parliament to defend the proposal. The presidency, free of such inhibition (but perhaps having some of its own), may be able to suggest a position to which all can agree. It may also have the technical help of the Commission to get there. If the compromise means changing the Commission's proposal, it will need unanimity. If the Commission is prepared to amend its proposal along the lines of a presidency compromise which is gaining acceptance ('flying'), a qualified majority may be obtained.

The presidency represents the Council on a number of occasions. It speaks for the Council in the European Parliament. Twice a year the President of the European Council addresses this body. In certain international negotiations the presidency speaks on some points on which the member states have taken a common position, while the Commission speaks on matters within Community competence. The presidency also receives, on behalf of the Council, personalities and delegations from third countries visiting Brussels and Strasbourg.

Finally, the presidency takes responsibility, as the Council's memory (via the Council Secretariat) and conscience, for ensuring co-ordination between Councils meeting in different formations, especially where their work converges or overlaps. This helps to give colour to the legal fiction that 'there is only one Council', meaning that it can never be in contradiction with itself. This fiction does not correspond to some public perceptions, notably the charge that the agriculture ministers combine to best the finance ministers, irrespective of who won the domestic argument about the scale of agricultural support.

In exercising the same responsibility of ensuring singleness of purpose, the presidency is expected to co-ordinate work proceeding within the Community and related extramural activities (for example, in Political Co-operation or in the framework of the meetings of ministers responsible for immigration).

INTRA-GOVERNMENTAL CO-ORDINATION AND PRESIDENCY SECRETARIATS

In order to react to Commission proposals and to the reactions of others, each member state has equipped itself with a European secretariat in some form, a meeting point at which the different advocacies of ministries (and ministers) can be reconciled and a co-ordinated position upheld. The ministries of external affairs and of agriculture and the economic ministries are core members. These inter-ministerial forums prepare or commission the telexes which are sent to the countries' Brussels representatives, or taken (as briefs) by visiting delegates. The return telexes, reporting the discussion and possibly making proposals for the line to take at the next stage, flow back to capitals and the traffic continues for the next meeting. Permanent representation staff, especially at the top levels, travel regularly to their capitals for the inter-ministerial meetings which discuss Community affairs. When ministers come to Brussels and Luxembourg the permanent representative and his or her staff become their local advisers. In a minister's absence the permanent representative stands in for him or her.

The person who is chairing a meeting, at ministerial or official level, usually calls for a preparatory briefing session with his or her own people and with the Council secretariat (both of whom will have provided written briefs) and sometimes also with the Commission. Three bureaucracies are consequently involved in Community work. The Commission 'services' participate in all meetings at official level and support their Commissioner at Council meetings. The Council secretariat is at the service of delegations and particularly the presidency. The national bureaucracy instructs its representative and prepares (and usually accompanies) its minister.

5 The European Parliament and the European Court of Justice

Besides the Commission and Council two other major institutions play a key role in Community decision-making and development. This chapter examines the nature, function and powers of the European Parliament and then the European Court of Justice.

THE EUROPEAN PARLIAMENT

The European Parliament, which has been elected by direct universal free suffrage since 1979, was, according to the treaties, advisory and supervisory. Elections take place every five years. The treaties did not envisage that the Parliament should be a legislature; that was the preserve of the Council.

Both before and after the direct elections, Parliament has sought to acquire, or to exercise, greater power.

In the treaty revisions of 1970 and 1975 Parliament became one half of the budgetary authority. The directly elected Parliament celebrated its advent by rejecting the draft budget of 1980 and requiring the Commission and Council to produce a new one. The budgetary role and power of the Parliament are discussed fully on pp. 90–1 and 100–8.

Parliament strengthened its advisory role in the isoglucose case in 1979. In the interval between the last meeting of the outgoing Parliament and the arrival of its successor, the Council adopted a regulation, within the common organization of the sugar market, imposing a levy on isoglucose. It did so without having had an

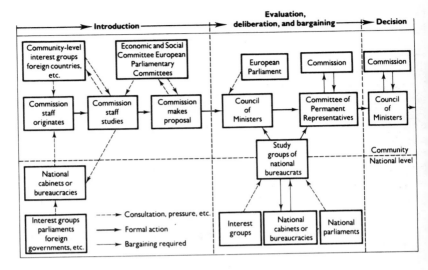

Figure 5.1 *The legislative process in the European Community*

opinion from the European Parliament, which had been statutorily consulted. The regulation, challenged in the European Court of Justice, was annulled: the Council had not 'exhausted the possibilities' of obtaining the missing opinion.[1] Parliament gained further ground in 1983 when it took the Council to the Court, with some success, for its failure to produce a common transport policy.[2]

The European Parliament made up a large part of the pressure exercised on the European Council before, at and after its Milan meeting in June 1985, leading to the major reforms incorporated in the Single European Act. The Act fell far short of Parliament's objectives but it did introduce:

- The 'co-operation procedure', which allows Parliament two interventions into the legislative process, where it applies.[3]
- An assent procedure for the entry of new member states into the Community (article 237) and for association agreements (article 238). In either case a positive vote of more than half the members of Parliament is required. In 1988 such a majority could not be found for new developments in the Association Agreement with Israel, either on a first attempt or on a second, which had to be deferred; it was found at the third try (October 1988).

The Inter-Institutional Agreement of June 1988 on budgetary procedures and objectives marked another reinforcement of Parliament's influence. The medium-term spending plan which it incorporated cannot be modified without Parliament's agreement.

Responding to continuing parliamentary complaint about the 'democratic deficit', the Treaty on European Union, article 189b, institutes a strengthened parliamentary control over legislation adopted by virtue of specified treaty articles. It provides that in case of disagreement between the Council and the Parliament the latter may seek and the former may convene a Conciliation Committee composed of members of the two institutions, sitting with representatives of the Commission. If conciliation is not successful, the Council may adopt a decision, but the Parliament may negate it. Legislation that is adopted by agreement between the Council and the Parliament is promulgated in their joint names, making the Parliament a joint legislative authority.

The consultation procedures – 'simple consultation', co-operation procedure, '189b procedure' (co-decision) – are shown diagrammatically in Figure 5.2.

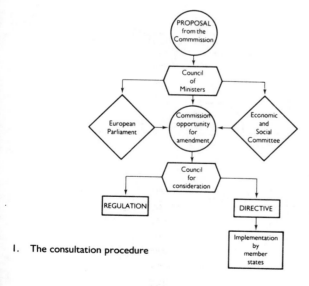

I.   The consultation procedure

Figure 5.2 *The consultative procedures*

Figure 5.2 *continued*

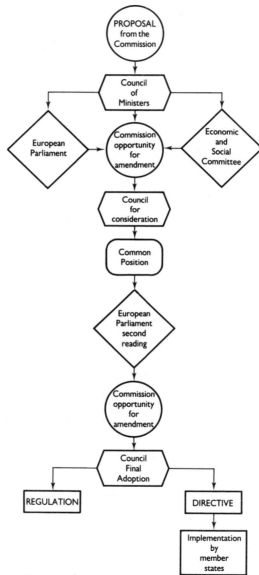

2. The co-operation procedure

Figure 5.2 *continued*

3. The co-decision procedure (article 189b of the Treaty on European Union)

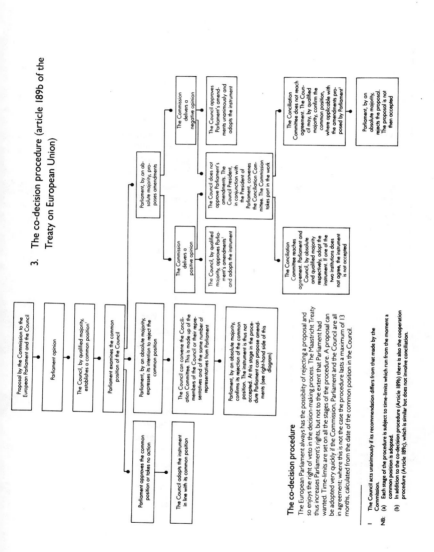

The co-decision procedure

The European Parliament always has the possibility of rejecting a proposal and so enjoys the right of veto in the decision-making process. The Maastricht Treaty thus increases Parliament's rights, but not to the extent that Parliament had wanted. Time-limits are set on all the stages of the procedure. A proposal can be adopted very quickly if the Commission, Parliament and the Council are all in agreement; where this is not the case the procedure lasts a maximum of 13 months, calculated from the date of the common position in the Council.

[1] The Council acts unanimously if its recommendation differs from that made by the Commission.

NB: (a) Each stage of the procedure is subject to time-limits which run from the moment a common position is adopted.

(b) In addition to the co-decision procedure (Article 189b) there is also the cooperation procedure (Article 189c), which is similar but does not involve conciliation.

Exhibit 5.1 *The EC Treaty articles and the procedures that apply to them after the Treaty on European Union*

Source: Committee on Institutional Affairs of the European Parliament (PE 155.427/fin) 7, February 1992.

Treaty articles in order	Applicable procedure
6	Co-operation
8a	Assent
8b	Consultation
8e	Consulation
43(2, 3)	Consultation
49	Co-decision**
54(2)	Co-decision**
56(2) first sentence	Consultation
56(2) second sentence	Co-decision**
57(1)	Co-decision**
57(2) second sentence	Consultation
57(2) third sentence	Co-decision**
73g(2)	Information
75(1)	Co-operation*
75(3)	Consultation
87	Consultation
94	Consultation
99	Consultation
100	Consultation
100a	Co-decision**
100b	Co-decision**
100c	Consultation
103(2)	Information
103(4)	Information
103(5)	Co-operation***
103a(2)	Information
104a	Co-operation***
104b(2)	Co-operation***
104c(11)	Information
104c(14)	Consultation
105(6)	Assent
105a(2)	Co-operation***
106(5)	Assent
106(6)	Consultation
109(1) first sentence	Consultation
109(1) third sentence	Information
109a(2b)	Consultation
109b(3)	Information
109c(3)	Information

Treaty articles in order	Applicable procedure
109f(1)	Consultation
109f(6)	Consultation
109f(7)	Consultation
109j(2)	Consultation
109j(4)	Consultationq
109k(2)	Consultation
118a(2)	Co-operation
125	Co-operation*
126	Co-decision***
127	Co-operation***
128	Co-decision***UN
129	Co-decision***
129a	Co-decision***
129d first paragraph	Co-decision***
129d third paragraph	Co-operation***
130(3)	Consultation
130b	Consultation
130d first paragraph	Assent
130d second paragraph	Assent
130e	Co-operation
130i(1)	Co-decision*/***UN
130i(4)	Consultation
130o first paragraph	Consultation
130o second paragraph	Co-operation
130s(1) and (3) second paragraph	Co-operation*
130s(2) and (3) second paragraph	Consultation
130s(3) first paragraph	Co-decision*
130w	Co-operation***
138(3)	Assent
201	Consultation
206	Budget
209	Consultation
228(3) first paragraph	Consultation
228(3) second paragraph	Assent
J(7) first sentence	Consultation
J(7) second sentence	Information
K(6) first paragraph	Information
K(6) second paragraph	Consultation
2(2) Agreement Social Policy	Co-operation***
2(3) Agreement Social Policy	Consultation

* currently subject to the Consultation Procedure
** currently subject to the Co-operation Procedure
*** a new EC competence

The elections of 1989, like those of 1984 and 1979, were contested on the basis of national political groupings, with some co-ordination at the level of the transnational political families. Mainland Britain was the only state that did not practise proportionality: apart from one successful Scottish National Party candidate, only Labour and Conservative members 'passed the post'. The proportional representation system in Northern Ireland was maintained.

The European elections that took place in June 1989 caused major changes in the political composition of the Parliament when it met at the end of July. The Socialist Group remained the largest single faction and within it the British Labour component, which had previously ranked equal with the German Socialists, became the largest national subgroup. The traditional Centre-Right majority was replaced by a Left majority of 265 (out of 518) (if everything not Centre, Right or Independent is counted as Left). The Rainbow Group, which had included German and Belgian Greens, lost them to a new 'Greens' group, which included the influx of French Greens. The former Communist Group disappeared. Two new groups to the left of the Socialist Group emerged: the European United Left (mainly Italian and Spanish), and the Coalition of the Left (of which French members made up half).

The European Democratic Group lost thirteen seats to Labour candidates and also lost its Spanish members to the European People's Party. Its strength fell from 66 to 34, making it the fourth largest group instead of third. The European Democratic Alliance (French, Irish and one Greek) lost ten seats. Its Scottish National member transferred to the Rainbow Group.

Table 5.1 *Composition of the European Parliament, January 1993 by state and party*

	B	DK	D	GR	ESP	F	IRL	I	L	NL	P	UK	EUR
Soc	8	3	31	8	27	22	1	34	2	8	8	46	198
EPP	7	4	32	10	17	12	4	27	3	10	3	33	162
LDR	4	3	5	–	5	10	2	3	1	4	9	–	46
Greens	3	1	6	–	1	8	–	7	–	2	–	–	28
EDA	–	–	–	1	2	11	6	–	–	–	–	–	20
RBW	1	4	1	–	3	1	1	3	–	–	1	1	16
ER	1	–	3	–	–	10	–	–	–	–	–	–	14
LU	–	–	–	3	–	7	–	–	–	–	3	–	13
Ind	–	1	3	2	5	–	1	7	–	1	–	1	21
	24	16	81	24	60	81	15	81	6	25	24	81	518

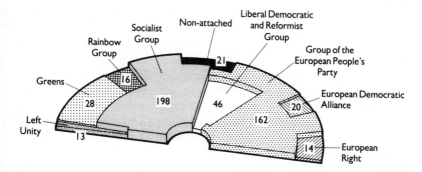

Figure 5.3 *Composition of the European Parliament, January 1993 by political group*
Source: European Parliament January 1993

Some 250 members did not return, either because they did not stand again or because they were not elected. The latter group included the last two Conservative members from Scottish constituencies. Among the British members two are members of the House of Lords, and two (from Northern Ireland) are members of the House of Commons. Table 5.1 and Figure 5.3 show the composition

Table 5.2 *Composition of the European Parliament post-1994 elections by state*

	Post-1994	Change from 1989
Belgium	25	+1
Denmark	16	0
Germany	99	+18
Greece	25	+1
Spain	64	+4
France	87	+6
Ireland	15	0
Italy	87	+6
Luxembourg	6	0
Netherlands	31	+6
Portugal	25	+1
United Kingdom	87	+6
Total	567	+49

Notes:
1. The new parliamentary majority is 284.
2. The new numbers are based on a report from the European Parliament.
3. The increase in British MEPs will require an increase in constituencies and is expected to affect mainly the south of England.

of the European Parliament in January 1993 by state and political grouping size.

In May 1992 the members of the European Democratic Group, predominantly British Conservatives, joined the European People's Party, despite their different ideological origins. The two had generally voted together. The Edinburgh European Council agreed to enlarge Parliament's size from 1994.

The European Parliament works by means of committees which report to plenary sessions and submit draft resolutions. There are currently nineteen committees (see Exhibit 5.2 for the committees in 1992). The system is generally the same whether the committee is

Exhibit 5.2 *The European Parliament: the committees*

Parliament's work is prepared in nineteen *committees*. Each member belongs to one or more specialist committee, as follows:

- Foreign Affairs and Security
- Agriculture, Fisheries and Rural Development
- Budgets
- Economic and Monetary Affairs and Industrial Policy
- Energy, Research and Technology
- External Economic Relations
- Legal Affairs and Citizens' Rights
- Social Affairs, Employment and the Working Environment
- Regional Policy, Regional Planning and Relations with Regional and Local Authorities
- Transport and Tourism
- Environment, Public Health and Consumer Protection
- Youth, Culture, Education and the Media
- Development and Co-operation
- Civil Liberties and Internal Affairs
- Budgetary Control
- Institutional Affairs
- Rules of Procedure, the Verification of Credentials and Immunities
- Women's Rights
- Petitions

In addition to these nineteen *standing committees*, Parliament can also set up *subcommittees, temporary committees* or *committees of inquiry*, which examine more specific problems within the EC, such as drugs, racism and agricultural surpluses.

working on exogenous material, such as Commission proposals or Council common positions, or on internally generated ideas, known as 'own initiative' reports. There are also a number of inter-parliamentary delegations for joint meetings with parliamentarians in other states.

Outside the formal committee structure there are a number of inter-party groups, such as Kangaroo, which covers the internal market, and Animal Welfare. When required, Parliament has also appointed Committees of Enquiry, for example, into drug trafficking, alleged irregularities at a nuclear power station and trade in cattle illegally dosed with hormones.[4]

Members join committees according to their interests. The committee chair is the general custodian of the committee. Chairs have an informal group among themselves to prepare forward work programmes, which should avoid conflict among them for parliamentary time. For each subject handled the committee appoints a *rapporteur*, who writes the report and draft resolution. When approved by the committee (by simple majority vote, and amended by the same) they are sent forward to the plenary for inclusion in an agenda, debate and vote on the resolution. In some committees the *rapporteur* works with 'co-ordinators', who are the representatives in the committee of their group interests.

Administrative questions are discussed and decided by the Bureau. This consists of the President, the fourteen Vice-Presidents and the five Quaestors (administrative managers). The Enlarged Bureau consists of the Bureau plus the nine group leaders, and, attending by invitation, the doyen of the committee chairs. The Commission and Council are represented at Enlarged Bureau meetings for selected items, especially the drawing-up of future sessional agendas. The other duty of Vice-Presidents, along with the President, is to preside at sittings of the House, at the monthly week-long (Monday evening to Friday lunch-time) part-sessions.

The Parliament has a General Secretariat including interpreters, translators and technical services. Under a secretary-general this consists of a Legal Service and seven Directorates General. There is at present little inter-institutional recruitment, but there is some co-operation between the Parliament and the Commission. Each political group also has a secretariat. Although graded and remunerated on the Community model, the members of group secretariats are personal appointees of the group – although they may also be seconded from the General Secretariat. They number some 500. Many members also employ personal assistants; these are also personal appointees.

Each political group caucuses before and during a part-session to decide on how its members will vote on draft resolutions and amendments. Group leaders, co-ordinators and group secretariats negotiate with each other to find compromises and composite resolutions. Group secretariats prepare voting lists which guide members during voting periods.

Except when voting for the office bearers of the House, members vote by show of hands, or if that is visually inconclusive or if enough members wish insistently enough, electronically. The scoreboards show total votes cast for and against, and abstentions. This is particularly important when the majority is narrow or when a certain minimum participation is required, as in budget votes and the co-operation and assent procedures. With electronic voting and shows of hands the House can despatch very large numbers of votes in a relatively short stretch. In a budget debate there can be 500 votes in the course of an afternoon sitting. The quorum is one-third of the members, but this becomes material only if at least thirteen members join forces in a quorum call, or if the President announces that there are fewer than thirteen members in place. Proceedings abound with points of order. Agendas are dropped and changed at short notice.

Parliament's relations with the Council are conflictual but it wishes to engage in dialogue and concertation, and various provisions have been made for exchanges between the two institutions. At every session the Council answers oral questions for 1 hour (and the same minister answers for Political Co-operation for 30 minutes). The President of the European Council attends a parliamentary session after the meeting over which he presided in order to give an account of it. This often coincides with the appearance of his colleague, the Foreign Minister, the president of the Foreign Affairs Council, who gives a report on his country's presidency (and who, at the beginning of his term also appeared to talk about his presidency's programme). Council ministerial representatives also take part in debates in plenary sessions, either at their own request, or to answer questions which have been put down to the Council. At least once and often twice, during each presidency, the president of every Council attends the specialized committees meeting which shadows the Council and talks about the Council's programme. This can run to thirty or more such appearances in a year.

In 1975, when the Parliament increased its budgetary responsibilities, it was agreed that for certain matters having budgetary implications there should be conciliation (in French, *concertation*) between Parliament and Council before the latter took a decision if it was likely to diverge from Parliament's opinion (Joint Declaration of 4 March 1975). The stated objective of conciliation is to reach agreement. By about 1980 the conciliation procedure had become discredited, especially in Parliament's eyes, because it considered that the Council had already exhausted its flexibility in its internal negotiations.

In the budgetary field there is dialogue between the Council and a parliamentary delegation prior to the meetings at which the Council reads the draft budget for the first and second times. This is not conciliation: it is not stated that the object of the dialogue is to reach agreement. Without any formal or informal understanding, a custom has developed for the Council to gather in Strasbourg in December for negotiations (usually conducted for the Council by its president) towards an agreement before Parliament takes its final (second reading) budgetary vote.

Out of the budgetary dialogue emerged, in 1981, the Trilogue. This brings together the President of the Budget Council, the President of the Commission usually with the Commissioner responsible for the budget, and the President of Parliament usually with the President of the Committee on Budgets. The Trilogue scored a notable success in the summer of 1988 when it negotiated the Inter-Institutional Budgetary Agreement which was subsequently approved by the three institutions. The Trilogue has so far only once been used outside the budgetary field as a way of resolving disputes among the institutions.

The Commission and Parliament, which both stand for the supranational aspect of the Community, are in some sense natural allies *vis-à-vis* the Council. The President of the Commission presents an annual programme to the Parliament. The vote which Parliament takes after the ensuing debate is regarded as a mark of confidence in the Commission. The Commission President and Commissioners attend plenary sessions – the Commission then holds its weekly meeting in Strasbourg – participate in debates, answer oral questions and give a monthly account of the action they have or have not taken on parliamentary resolutions.

The Parliament has sought to strengthen its influence with the Commission – and thereby to obtain a foothold in the legislative process – by being ready not to give opinions. This thereby blocks the process unless the Commission accepts Parliament's amendments, and undertakes to amend its original proposal accordingly and subsequently to defend the amended proposal in the Council discussion at which the Commission is present.[5]

In February 1990, Parliament accepted a Commission offer of a 'code of conduct' in which it undertook to have regard to Parliament's right to consultation and re-consultation, and to remind the Council of them; to explain why whenever it was not ready to accept amendments proposed by Parliament to draft legislation; to keep the Parliament informed of the lines of Council discussions; and to take account of Parliament's interest in and powers affecting international agreements, especially in the determination of the legal basis for them. (If the basis is article 238 EEC, Parliament has an assent/veto power.) Article 138b, paragraph 2 of the Treaty on European Union provides that the Parliament, by a majority of its members, can ask the Commission to make a proposal. The Council already possessed this power (article 152). According to Council doctrine, the Commission may not then refuse, but it may produce a proposal which the Council does not like.

The Commission and the Parliament also agree on an annual legislative programme. The Council does not formally participate, but a co-ordination group of officials from the three institutions (Neunreiter Group) tries to avoid major conflict. Since 1987 incoming Council presidencies have circulated preliminary versions of the agendas which they expect Councils to have before them during the six months.

The Treaty on European Union, article 158, gives the Parliament new powers regarding the appointment of the members of the Commission, as from the Commission due to take office, if the treaty is in force, on 7 January 1995. The governments of the member states appoint the person they intend to be President of the Commission, after consulting the Parliament. (This already happens, but the Parliament regards itself as being presented with a *fait accompli*.) The nominated President and the other nominated members of the Commission are subject 'as a body' to a vote of approval by the Parliament. (Simple majority of members present, unless Parliament adopts a stricter rule.)

The Treaty on European Union also requires the Parliament to appoint an Ombudsman to receive complaints concerning mal-administration in Community institutions or bodies (article 138e).

In 1991 Parliament held twelve sessions (none in August, two in October), all in Strasbourg. It passed 308 resolutions giving opinions on consultations and 312 other resolutions, including 271 on own initiative reports, which were therefore almost as significant quantitatively as the opinions. Members tabled 3,313 written questions (2,905 to the Commission, 257 to the Council and 151 to Political Co-operation) and 1,303 oral questions (838 to the Commission, 238 to the Council and 227 to Political Co-operation).

THE EUROPEAN COURT OF JUSTICE

The European Communities have created a new and distinctive legal order. Their judicial organs are the Court of Justice, situated in Luxembourg, and national courts. To national courts, Community law is not foreign law, but part of the law which they apply. In its publication *The ABC of Community Law*, the Commission shows the sources of Community law (see Figure 5.4).

In the Community of Twelve, there are thirteen judges in the European Court of Justice (an odd number avoids tied judgments; dissenting judgments are not delivered). Judges are appointed for six years, renewable, and six or seven appointments expire every three years. The judges select their own president. For each case the president appoints a judge-rapporteur, who takes the lead in the deliberations. The Court may work in plenary or in chambers. There are four chambers of three judges and two chambers of six judges. The chambers do not specialize in particular legal questions or in particular subjects. The full Court must consider cases brought by a member state or by a Community institution. The staff of the Court is headed by the registrar, who is appointed by the Court.

In addition to the judges, the Court is served by a number of Advocates General. They have no analogue in the United Kingdom. An advocate general makes a reasoned presentation of the case before the Court, usually giving a summary of the submissions of the parties, observations on matters raised in the oral hearings and on the relevant Community statute law and previous cases and an opinion on the decision which the Court might take. The Advocate

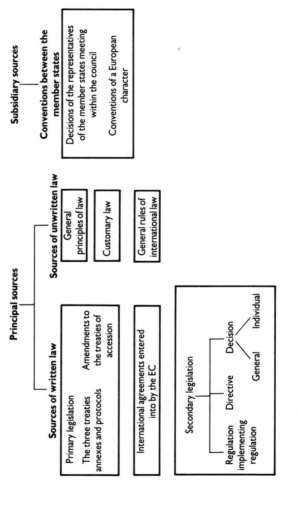

Figure 5.4 *Sources of Community law*

General's opinion, which is published, is not binding on the Court, but is frequently accepted.

In 1991, 340 cases were brought before the Court. It gave 227 judgments. The types of action which come before the Court are:

- Action for annulment, aimed at obtaining the cancellation of binding legal acts. These actions can be brought by the Council, the Commission or a member state. They can be brought by individual citizens if the act complained of is addressed to them or, if addressed to another individual, is of direct and individual concern to them. Individual citizens cannot seek the annulment of regulations and directives.
- Action for failure to act. These actions can be brought by Community institutions or member states. Individual citizens may bring actions to demand that a decision should be addressed to them, but cannot demand the adoption of directives or regulations, or of opinions and recommendations, which have no legal force.
- Actions for infringement of the EEC and Euratom Treaties. These actions can be brought by the Commission or by member states (for example, against each other). In the ECSC the Commission determines whether a member state has infringed the ECSC Treaty and the member state can appeal to the Court. In the new article 33 of the Treaty on European Union, actions may be brought by a member state or by the Council to have decisions or recommendations of the Commission declared void on grounds of lack of competence, infringement of an essential procedural requirement, infringement of the Treaty or of any rule of law relating to its application, or misuse of powers.
- Preliminary rulings. A national court may make a reference to the Court of Justice for a ruling on a point of Community law at issue in proceedings before the national court. The national court decides for itself whether to seek a preliminary ruling. The parties in the case cannot compel it to do so. A national tribunal must also refer to the European Court of Justice if the tribunal considers that an act adopted by a Community institution is invalid.[6] In Euratom and the EEC the request for a ruling may concern the validity of an act and how the treaties should be interpreted. In the ECSC only the validity of acts can be questioned. The preliminary ruling of the Court is binding on the national court in the case concerned.

There are differing views on whether it has wider application but generally speaking this is a legal nicety.

- Action for damages resulting (by a clear causal link) from illegal actions or, in principle but rarely successfully in practice, from damages caused by (properly adopted) legislative measures.
- Actions brought by members or prospective members of staff seeking application of the Staff Regulations. This can include such matters as allegations that a staff report is biased or that the day fixed for an examination is a holiday in the religion practised by the examinee.

The Council, the Commission or a member state may ask the Court for an Opinion on whether an international agreement that the Community is minded to conclude is compatible with the EEC Treaty, or whether agreements negotiated by member states or private persons in the nuclear field are compatible with the Euratom Treaty. If the Court gives an unfavourable Opinion, the agreement or draft agreement concerned must be revised to have effect.

In view of the increase in the Court's workload, the member states agreed to provide in the Single European Act (new article 168A of the EEC Treaty) for a Court of First Instance to decide on points of law in certain fields, excluding actions brought by a Community institution or by a member state. The subjects which have been assigned to the Court of First Instance are ECSC matters, competition cases and actions brought by staff (Council decision 88/591/ECSC, EEC, Euratom of 24 October 1988). At any one time, however, the European Court of Justice still has roughly two years' work in cases already filed with it.

There are differences of nomenclature as between the legal instruments which are adopted under the different treaties. The vocabulary and equivalence is as follows:[7]

ECSC (article 14)	EEC (article 189)		Euratom (article 161)	
decision (general)	=	regulation	=	regulation
recommendations	=	directive	=	directive
decision (individual)	=	recommendation	=	recommendation
opinion	=	opinion	=	opinion

In the EEC/Euratom system, a *regulation* is binding in its entirety and directly applicable in all member states. A *directive* is binding as to the results to be achieved, but leaves the choice of form and method to the member states' authorities. Recommendations and opinions are not binding.

Written constitutions might be expected to contain an affirmation of the fundamental rights of the persons who have accepted the particular form of government. There is no such enumeration in the constituent treaties.[8] The draftsmen seem to have taken the view that the three treaties were such that they could not violate fundamental rights. From 1969 onwards, however, the Court was led towards recognizing that fundamental rights, even if not exhaustively enumerated, are part of the bedrock of the Communities' legal order. It did so in such pronouncements as 'the protection of such rights, whilst inspired by the constitutional traditions common to the Member States, must be ensured within the framework of the structure and objectives of the Community' (Case 11/70, *Internationale Handelsgesellschaft*). Later, the Court concluded that the European Convention for the Protection of Human Rights and Fundamental Freedoms, 1950, which all member states had ratified by 1976, gives guidelines which must be followed in Community law.

In 1977 the Parliament, Council and Commission adopted a Joint Declaration on the protection of human rights and fundamental freedoms, and declared that in the exercise of their powers and in pursuance of the aims of the European Communities they respect and will continue to respect these rights. It remains the case, however, that definitions of human rights must be looked for elsewhere than in the treaties. It has been suggested – by the Commission and by the European Parliament – that the European Convention should be incorporated directly and *en bloc* into Community law. Under article F 2 of the Treaty on European Union, the Union must respect fundamental rights as guaranteed by the European Convention signed in Rome on 4 November 1950 and as they result from the constitutional traditions common to the member states, as general principles of Community law.

National and Community law are complementary. There can be no conflict between them because Community law has primacy. It is in part directly applicable, it does not require for its validity to be passed into national law by a national law-making body. The rights and obligations accrue directly to the citizens. This effect may or may not have been foreseen by the authors of the treaties, but it has been successfully upheld by the Court and is no longer under legal challenge.

Most regulations are directly applicable, but the test is not what the instrument is called but what it does. If it is complete in itself, so that its implementation and validity do not require any intervention by the Commission or by the member states, then it is directly applicable. On this principle, some provisions of the EEC Treaty itself have been judged to be directly applicable – for example, article 48 conferring freedom of circulation on workers.

Whereas it was held that directives being addressed to member states (and not to their citizens) were not directly applicable, the Court has held otherwise in a series of cases since 1970. Direct applicability is one of the distinguishing factors of the European Communities. It turns freedoms into rights which citizens can demand to be vouchsafed to them and it brings the transactions between governments down to the citizens without any further say or choice for the government.

If ultimately there is a conflict between a piece of national law and a piece of Community law, something has to give – and it is national law. The Court uttered this principle in the landmark judgment it gave on 15 July 1964 in *Costa* v. *ENEL* ([1964] CMLR 425) (in which a Milanese shareholder in an electricity enterprise which had been nationalized refused to pay the full amount of his electricity bill because he considered that wrong had been done to him). The Court said (Case 6/64):

> The integration into the laws of each Member State of provisions which derive from the Community, and more generally the terms and the spirit of the Treaty, make it impossible for the States, as a corollary, to accord precedence to a unilateral and subsequent measure over a legal system accepted by them on a basis of reciprocity. Such a measure cannot therefore be inconsistent with that legal system. The executive force of Community law cannot vary from one State to another in deference to subsequent domestic laws, without jeopardizing the attainment of the objectives of the Treaty set out in Article 5(2) and giving rise to the discrimination prohibited by Article 7.
>
> The obligations undertaken under the Treaty establishing the Community would not be unconditional, but merely contingent, if they could be called in question by subsequent legislative acts of the signatories . . .
>
> The precedence of Community law is confirmed by Article 189. . . .

This provision, which is subject to no reservation, would be quite meaningless if a State could unilaterally nullify its effects by means of a legislative measure which could prevail over Community law.

It follows from all these observations that the law stemming from the Treaty, an independent source of law, could not, because of its special and original nature, be overridden by domestic legal provisions, however framed, without being deprived of its character as Community law and without the legal basis of the Community itself being called into question.

The Court upheld this principle in a further series of cases, such as in the seminal *Van Gend en Loos* and *Simmenthal* judgments. Along with direct applicability, the primacy of Community law is a distinctive and distinguishing feature of Community law. Lord Denning, the former Master of the Rolls, said in 1974, 'The Treaty [of Rome] is like an incoming tide. It flows into the estuaries and up the rivers. It cannot be held back.'

Mr Justice Graham expressed the point less poetically in *Aero Zipp Fasteners* v. *YKK Fasteners (UK) Ltd* ([1973] CMLR 819): 'This [European Communities] Act to put it very shortly enacted that relevant Common Market Law should be applied in this country and should, where there is a conflict, override English Law.' The principle is a legal and political milestone and is at the heart of the continuing political controversy over the status of the United Kingdom parliament, which in the nineteenth century, but not consistently earlier, was held to be 'sovereign' in the sense that its powers were unlimited and incapable of being curbed.[9]

The primacy of Community law was illustrated in the case concerning Spanish fishermen who had registered vessels in the United Kingdom and were fishing in UK waters. The British parliament passed an Act to prevent them doing so, but the Court ruled in 1990 that the Act was invalid.

6   The Budget Interaction, 'Lesser Institutions' and Other Interested Parties

The four major institutions discussed in Chapters Four and Five are central to Community decision-making and development, but they do not operate in a vacuum. For Commission, Council and Parliament this is most clear in the budgetary process, but in other areas an examination of Community decision-making is incomplete without examining the impact and role of both so-called 'lesser institutions' – the Court of Auditors, the Economic and Social Committee, and the new Committee of the Regions – and the role of what might be termed 'other interested parties'.

THE BUDGETARY INTERACTIONS

According to a pop song of the 1960s, money is the root of all evil, a Biblical misquotation for 'the love of money is the root of all evil'. The song continued 'won't contaminate myself with it'. The General Budget of the European Communities is the root of much trouble, and it has contaminated inter-institutional relations for many years.

The root of the trouble is an uneasy partnership between the Council and the Parliament, which are joint budgetary authorities. Originally, the Council was the budgetary authority, but Parliament was given powers in the 1970 treaty revision, when the Community was endowed with its 'own resources'. These are the funds which belong legally to the Community. They are paid in by the member states, which collect them, but they do not transit member states' budgets, because they are not their property. This means that there

Exhibit 6.1 *The Community budget*

> The Community's general budget for 1991 was around ecu 58.5 billion (in commitment appropriations),[1] or approximately 1.2 per cent of the gross national product of the Twelve.
>
> The budget is financed by the Community's own resources:
>
> - customs duties and agricultural levies on imports from the rest of the world;
> - a proportion of the VAT collected in the member states, calculated according to a uniform assessment base;
> - a new resource created in 1988 and based on the gross national product of the member states.
>
> As percentages of total commitment appropriations, expenditure under the main headings of the 1991 budget broke down as follows:
>
> - Support for farm prices (including reduction of stocks and the monetary reserve) – 57.2 per cent. It should be borne in mind that in agriculture more than any other area, Community finance has replaced expenditure by the member states. Over the last few years, the Community has taken a number of measures to curb such expenditure.
> - Structural policies and other regional or social measures – 26.6 per cent.
> - Joint action in research, energy, industry, the environment and transport – 4.7 per cent.
> - Co-operation with Third World countries – 3.6 per cent (plus non-budgetary expenditure from the European Development Fund financed by national contributions, which doubles the sums available).
> - Co-operation with the countries of Central and Eastern Europe – 1.4 per cent.
> - Administrative expenditure – 4.5 per cent, which covers the salaries of 21,800 officials and other employees of all the various Community institutions as well as the cost of buildings, administration, etc.
>
> [1] 1 ecu = about UK £0.70, July 1991.

is no national parliamentary control. Joint responsibility was bound to be uncomfortable. Generally speaking, the majority of the member states do not want Community expenditure to increase by much, and especially in sectors which give them no net national benefit. They are obliged to finance a common agricultural policy,

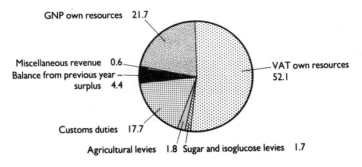

Proportion of the EC's total budget for 1992
accounted for by the different own resources (in %)

GNP own resources 21.7

Miscellaneous revenue 0.6
Balance from previous year – surplus 4.4

VAT own resources 52.1

Customs duties 17.7

Agricultural levies 1.8   Sugar and isoglucose levies 1.7

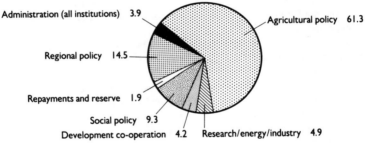

Proportion of the EC's total budget for 1992
accounted for by the various categories of expenditure (in %)

Administration (all institutions) 3.9

Agricultural policy 61.3

Regional policy 14.5

Repayments and reserve 1.9

Social policy 9.3

Development co-operation 4.2   Research/energy/industry 4.9

Figure 6.1 *The Community budget*

which despite all efforts to contain it, continues to consume the lion's share of the available resources. They are reluctant to see more spent on other purposes. Speaking equally generally, the parliamentary majority is in favour of increased expenditure by the Community, replacing national expenditure and obtaining synergy effects. The same majority complains that agriculture costs too much, criticizes as weak the attempts to reduce it, and wants budgetary funds for desirable objects like regional development, research and development, aid to the suffering Third World and aid to the new democracies in the East.

Relatively speaking, the amounts in contention are not over-whelming. The Community Budget is less than 1.2 per cent of Community GNP. National budgets can be as much as 50 per cent of GNP. The Community budget is less than 4 per cent of the combined total of member states' public spending.

The Community budget is also of little significance in economic management. It plays no part in money supply, in credit creation or in anti-inflation strategy, except in the general sense that most member states are opposed to increased spending.

The amount of revenue is pre-fixed by primary Community law: 'own resources' decisions are subject to national ratifications as if they were treaties. The resources consist of:

Own resources	1990 yield (m. ecus)
Customs duties on imports	11,341.2
Levies on imports of CAP products	2,493.1
Max. 1.4 percentage points of VAT	34,232.4
An amount based on a GDP key – the 'fourth resource'	14,280.8

There are no Community taxes. The Community has no power to levy taxation. The Parliament has no revenue raising power. Thus the budget is a spending plan, using up to the amount of money available, without regard to what, if any, additional spending might be 'necessary'. As in legislation generally, a separation-of-powers principle rules in the budgetary field:

Commission: presents a preliminary draft budget (PDB).
Council: adopts, by qualified majority a draft budget (DB), and sends it to Parliament.
Parliament: proposes amendments and sends it back to the Council.
Council: accepts, rejects or modifies amendments; back to Parliament.
Parliament: decides whether to maintain its amendments and whether to adopt the budget.

This is the so-called 'shuttle', in operation between June and December and often ending in a very long night in Strasbourg when the Council and the Parliament, with the help of the Commission, try to come to terms. If they succeed, there is a budget. If not, the cycle has to begin again. Spending does not come to a halt. An emergency spending provision is used, but it is cumbersome and divisive, intended to put pressure on all concerned to reach an agreement.

The amount of revenue puts one constraint on expenditure. There are several others. Agricultural spending must remain within the discipline of a guideline: it may not rise by more than 74 per cent of the estimated percentage increase in GNP for the coming year. Much of the non-agricultural part of the budget is technically described as 'non-compulsory expenditure' and it is subject to another discipline, called the 'maximum rate of increase', an amount calculated by the Commission from objective GDP data. The great budgetary battles of the 1980s lined up the Parliament, which was determined to go through this ceiling, and the Council, where there was often a blocking minority, if not a majority against exceeding the 'maximum rate'.

Some of the other, less public, battles were within the Council itself. The Community three times ran out of money. Commitments had been accepted which could not be financed from the available revenue. After exhausting the charms of creative accountancy – which purports to balance the budget by creating phantom expenditure – the member states had to bite the bullet and make up the difference from national budgets through 'inter-governmental agreements', which had to be approved by national parliaments. This was a painful process for most, especially when the same national parliaments were being told that austerity at home was the order of the day.

Similar agonies were felt when the Council had to accept the argument for increases in own resources, for example in 1988, when the Commission had produced a package under the title 'Making the Single European Act Succeed', popularly known as 'Delors I'. The proposal combined increases in expenditure with strengthened discipline and put forward a new control instrument. This was the 'Financial Perspectives', eventually agreed between the Council and the Parliament. The financial perspectives are a five-year spending plan broken down by main categories within fixed ceilings. The plan was annexed to an inter-institutional agreement on how the system would work. The financial perspectives, which could be modified by agreement, replaced the other devices which had been found wanting. Aside from argument about amending the provisions to take account of such unforeseen expenditures as the needs of the countries of Eastern and Central Europe, the Financial Perspectives proved their worth in the first five year period, which expired in 1992.

By the time the Financial Perspectives came to be renewed for a further period, the Community's programmes had changed, following the signature of the Treaty on European Union. Whereas the first Financial Perspectives had been proposed and adopted with the Community out of funds to pay for the expenditure which had accumulated, the additional resources which had been provided at that time were enough to keep it going for part of the second period. In that sense there was no resources crisis as the 1993 budget was under preparation. There was, however, political trouble.

Early in 1992 the Commission produced proposals for the next five years' spending, known as 'Delors II'. In this package the Commission proposed increases partly to take account of the Treaty on European Union, which pointed to additional Community Research and Development and established a 'Cohesion Fund' to benefit those member states whose GDP is less than 90 per cent of the Community average – Greece, Ireland, Portugal and Spain.

The Commission's proposals drew fire from the member states who would be called on to find the money for the cohesion transfers. No agreement could be reached on Delors II by the time the Council had to adopt the 1993 draft budget for transmission to the Parliament in the 'shuttle'. For the first time since 1988 there were no agreed Financial Perspectives to set the budgetary frameworks. The four countries that are to benefit from cohesion transfers are two votes short of a blocking minority and were unable to prevent the Council from sending to the Parliament a draft budget which provided no money for a cohesion fund, while reaffirming that it will be established. The financing of the Community budget for seven years ahead – which meant stretching Delors II by two years – was agreed at Edinburgh in December 1992. The new Financial Perspectives which it drew up are shown in Table 6.1.

The other historical battle, and battle honours, of the budget was fought and won from 1980 to 1984. This was the insistence of the British government, under Mrs (now Baroness) Thatcher that Britain should be relieved of what she regarded as its excessive 'net contribution' – the difference between the amount it paid in and what

Table 6.1 *Financial perspective agreed by Edinburgh European Council for 1993–9*

Appropriations for commitments (million ecu – 1992 prices)

	1993	1994	1995	1996	1997	1998	1999
1. Agricultural guideline	35,230	35,095	35,722	36,364	37,023	37,697	38,389
2. Structural actions	21,277	21,885	23,480	24,990	26,526	28,240	30,000
– Cohesion Fund	1,500	1,750	2,000	2,250	2,500	2,550	2,600
– Structural Funds and other operations	19,777	20,135	21,480	22,740	24,026	25,690	27,400
3. Internal policies	3,940	4,084	4,323	4,520	4,710	4,910	5,100
4. External action	3,950	4,000	4,280	4,560	4,830	5,180	5,600
5. Adminstrative expenditure	3,280	3,380	3,580	3,690	3,800	3,850	3,900
6. Reserves	1,500	1,500	1,100	1,100	1,100	1,100	1,100
– Monetary Reserve	1,000	1,000	500	500	500	500	500
– External Action							
= emergency aid	200	200	300	300	300	300	300
= loan guarantees	300	300	300	300	300	300	300
Total appropriations for commitments	69,177	69,944	72,485	75,224	77,989	80,977	84,089
Appropriations for payments required	65,908	67,036	69,150	71,290	74,491	77,249	80,114
Appropriations for payments (% GNP)	1.20	1.19	1.20	1.21	1.23	1.25	1.26
Margin for unforeseen expenditure (% GNP)		0.01	0.01	0.01	0.01	0.01	0.01
Own resources ceiling (% GNP)	1.20	1.20	1.21	1.22	1.24	1.26	1.27

	1993	1994	1995	1996	1997	1998	1999
Total external expenditure	4,450	4,500	4,880	5,160	5,430	5,780	6,200

The inflation rate applicable for the budget is 4.3 per cent.

it received back. This was an ideological heresy, since the amounts paid in were by law the property of the Community, and the amount received back was not considered to be any barometer of the benefits to a country of Community membership. Orthodoxy was upheld, notably by countries which were net beneficiaries. Given the weight of agricultural spending in the budget, the net positions bore no relationship to any measure of a country's capacity to pay.

Figures are hard to come by, if only because the Commission declines to publish net positions. It disowned the following analysis which appeared in the British press early in 1992, although the UK Foreign and Commonwealth Office told the House of Commons Committee on European Legislation that the orders of magnitude were right.

1992 budget: net positions	bn ecu
Belgium	1.7
Denmark	0.5
Greece	3.9
Spain	3.2
France	−0.9
Germany	−8.5
Ireland	2.4
Italy	1.1
Luxembourg	0.7
Netherlands	0
Portugal	1.2
United Kingdom	−5.0

After acrimonious argument through a run of European Councils from 1980 on, the British government received a budgetary rebate, originally in the form of additional payments ostensibly linked to the execution of schemes of infrastructure improvement in the United Kingdom and later, when this became a fiction and occasioned a clash with the European Parliament, which insisted on having its say on the expenditure, in the form of a reduction in the amounts paid in. The rebate was worth about 2 billion ecus in 1992. The Delors II package provoked re-examination of the existing financial arrangements and in particular prompted some member states to call in question the justification for the British budgetary rebate, which had preceded Spanish and Portuguese membership.

The decision which instituted it could be changed only by unanimity and there was no possibility that the United Kingdom would agree to forgo it.

THE COURT OF AUDITORS

The Court of Auditors, with its seat in Luxembourg, is the Community institution responsible for controlling the Communities' financial regularity. It consists of twelve members, appointed by the Council after consultation of the Parliament. The members choose their president. The Court's staff audit the accounts of the Community institutions and the Court publishes a general report and special reports. The general report is discussed by the ECOFIN Council and in Parliament is debated in the framework of the discharge which Parliament gives to the Commission's accounts. The special reports examine particular branches or problems of expenditure. In the early 1980s the Court gave early warning of the developing financial crisis and exposed the measures of creative accountancy which were being used to put off the evil day. In 1989 it revealed cases of large-scale fraud in several member states and documented the cases.

THE ECONOMIC AND SOCIAL COMMITTEE

The Economic and Social Committee, which sometimes calls itself a consultative assembly, is representative of three groups: employers, workpeople and independents. It consists of 189 members, evenly divided among the three groups, and divided among the member states as follows: Belgium 12, Denmark 9, Germany 24, Greece 12, Spain 21, France 24, Ireland 9, Italy 24, Luxembourg 6, Netherlands 12, Portugal 12, United Kingdom 24. The members are appointed by the Council on the basis of member states' nominations. The four-year term is renewable. The chair rotates between groups and nationalities and, with two posts of vice-chair, is decided by the members.

The Committee is organized in sections (that is, committees). Under article 197 of the EEC Treaty there must be sections for Agriculture and Transport. There are, in addition, sections for

Economic Affairs, Social Affairs, Environment, Industry, Regional Development, Energy and External Relations. The sections appoint for each referral a *rapporteur*, whose report and draft opinion are debated and voted upon by the Committee at its monthly meetings. Numerous treaty articles require the Committee to be consulted by the Council and the latter also consults the Committee optionally. Opinions are not binding on the Council and it can, if it considers it necessary, impose a time-limit beyond which the absence of an opinion does not prevent the Council from proceeding (in practice the Council virtually never finds a time-limit necessary). The Committee also undertakes reports on its own initiative. Unlike the other bodies of the Community, the Economic and Social Committee field is confined to the EEC and Euratom Treaties. An Advisory Committee under article 18 of the ECSC Treaty has similar functions *vis-à-vis* the High Authority (Commission). Its members, not more than 96 and not less than 72 in number, are equally divided among producers, workpeople and consumers, and dealers. They are appointed by the Council. The ECSC Consultative Committee meets about six times a year. It is serviced by the Commission.

THE COMMITTEE OF THE REGIONS

Under article 198a of the Treaty on European Union, the Community establishes a 'Committee of the Regions' consisting of representatives of regional and local bodies, appointed by the Council on nominations from the member states. The Committee is to have advisory functions and must be consulted where treaty articles so provide. The Committee is to be served by the staff of the Economic and Social Committee. Regions and localities are not defined: they are a matter for national governments.

The national composition of the Committee is the same as for the Economic and Social Committee (see above, p. 108).

THE INTERACTIONS

The ways of the Communities are often regarded as Byzantine. In Britain the derogatory word 'legalistic' is often directed at the Communities, independently of the actual and often controversial content of the policies which they adopt. However, the basic constitutional rule, which continues to evolve, is straightforward. The Commission proposes, and generally speaking has the monopoly of the power to propose. It also executes agreed policies, and in doing so collaborates with national agencies (although, for example, there is a single customs tariff, the customs officers are national civil servants). It enforces obligations as 'guardian of the treaties'. Between 1953 and 1985 it brought actions against the ten member states as follows: Belgium 71, Denmark 11, Germany 33, Greece 16, France 76, Ireland 22, Italy 140, Luxembourg 20, Netherlands 20, United Kingdom 21 (total 430).

The Council decides, and in doing so uses a variety of tools. The Council also adopts resolutions and makes recommendations (usually to the member states) but these do not have legal force. The members of the General Affairs Council are also the ministers who meet in Political Co-operation.

The Parliament advises but has some decision-making power over Community budgets and has the power to assent (or to refuse to assent) to the entry of new member states into the Community or to the conclusion of new association agreements. A key interaction involving the insitutions is the budget.

INFORMATION

The amount of published information about the activities of the Communities is torrential. Economic interests have made their arrangements to establish contact points. Lobbying, especially for dealings with the Commission and Parliament, has become a major industry. Since virtually all Commission proposals are published, and are regarded more as White Papers than as Bills, and since Parliament debates in public both in plenary and in committee, the system is transparent, with one major qualification. Under article 18 of its Rules of Procedure, the Council's deliberations are secret. The world knows what goes into a Council discussion – the published Commission proposal – and the world learns what comes out – the published decision – but it does not know what is happening in the Council's working groups, in the Committee of Permanent Representatives, and around the Council table. The Council does not have to account to the European Parliament for its decision, although individual Council members are accountable to their democratically elected national parliaments. There has been a move towards openness. When it sends its draft budget to Parliament the Council annexes an Explanatory Memorandum in which it explains why it departed from the Commission's proposals. Under the co-operation procedure the Council sends to the Parliament, along with its 'common position', a statement of the reasons which have led it to adopt the common position.[1] But for many parliamentarians, especially British Conservatives, this amount of *glasnost* is far from enough and there is constant attack on the Communities' 'democratic deficit'.

In a declaration annexed to the Treaty on European Union, the inter-governmental conference which approved it considers that the transparency of the decision-making process strengthens the democratic nature of the institutions and the public's confidence in the administration. This statement may strike some readers as unconsciously ironic, coming after 228 pages of largely incomprehensible treaty language and unconsolidated text. The Conference asked the Commission to prepare a report on measures to improve public access to information held by the institutions. At Edinburgh in December 1992 the European Council agreed that certain Council debates would be televised live to the press room in the Council building.

THE OUTSIDE OBSERVERS

A group of extramural participants play an important role in the functioning of the Communities. The media are strongly represented internationally in Brussels. The quality press and radio have resident correspondents and the agencies are also present. There are several Commission press conferences each week, and after each Council meeting the president gives a press conference. The European Parliament gives out press releases, as do its political groups. Apart from the general press there are specialized publications, with a reputation for hard inside information. The daily *Agence Europe* published by Emanuele Gazzo, a doughty federalist and tireless leader writer, is almost essential morning reading and is usually impeccably informed. There are numerous other newsletters, in many languages. The proceedings of the plenary meetings of the

European Parliament are televised. UK stations do not take the feed regularly.

The media thus make available a large flow of information about what is being discussed, and scoops about what the Commission is likely to propose shortly. Unfortunately, sub-editors freely confuse 'Commission' and 'Community' and sometimes present a proposal as a *fait accompli*. Many Brussels journalists are long-serving and experienced commentators whose factual (and slanted) reporting is a significant input into the process. The Commission (and the European Parliament) maintain information offices in all member states and in some third countries, providing publicity material in the national media, and seeking to influence opinion-makers.

Another group of Euro-watchers consists of the Brussels offices of organizations which wish to be closely informed and to have a relationship which enables them to intervene. Some major companies have 'EEC affairs' offices under different names. Some major national trade associations, such as the Milk Marketing Board or the Confederation of British Industry have Brussels representatives who keep their ears close to the ground. Some sectors of commerce and industry have set up international trade associations with premises and staff in Brussels: UNICE representing the national employer organizations, COPA representing farmers' unions, and countless others. Normally such organizations seek to become accredited with the Commission, which gives them standing to pursue their search for pertinent information and to feed into the Commission, and to the members of the European Parliament, material about developments which their organizations favour or oppose.[2]

LOBBYING

In British English usage 'lobbying' is regarded as something ungentlemanly. It is not so in American English, and private intervention in public affairs is an accepted fact in most European countries. The Commissioners, their staff and members of the European Parliament expect to be lobbied. It is almost impossible to lobby the Council collectively because it is corporate only during its meetings, and it is then not available to outsiders. Council members are, however, lobbied by their national interest groups at home.

A profession of lobbyists exists in Brussels. It may run to a dozen or more partners or associates covering the necessary disciplines, especially law and economics, who may be more report writers than gladhanders. There are also freelance consultants with particular expertise and access, usually looking after the affairs of several clients. They are part of the network of information exchanges, forecasting and intervention which is essential to making the machine work. There are proposals to establish a register of lobbyists and their clients.

Distinct from the lobbyists are the law firms established in Brussels, advising clients and general lawyers on Community law and pleading in the Court of Justice in Luxembourg for interests in member states or in third countries.

By the standards of Whitehall, Brussels is an open information arena, where what British traditions would regard as indiscretions abound. But a particular skill is needed for Euro-watchers to find their way through the system in order to obtain hard information, to identify in the timetables the crucial moment for intervention, and to build up the contacts which they and their clients need.

Part Two: Further Reading

Brown, L. N., *The Court of Justice of the European Communities*, 3rd edn., London, Sweet and Maxwell, 1989.

Bulmer, S. and Wessels, W., *The European Council*, Basingstoke, Macmillan, 1987.

Cassese, S., ed., *The European Administration*, Paris, Institut International des Sciences Publiques, 1988.

de Bassompierre, G., *Changing the Guard in Brussels: an insider's view of the EC Presidency*, New York, Praeger, 1988.

Hartley, T. C., *The Foundations of European Community Law*, 2nd edn., Oxford, Clarendon Press, 1989.

Hay, R., *The European Commission and the Administration of the Community*, Luxembourg, OOP, 1989.

Hohscheit, J. M. and Wessels, W., eds., *The European Council 1974–1986: Evaluation and Prospects*, Maastricht, European Institute of Public Administration, 1988.

Jacobs, F., ed., *The European Parliament*, Harlow, Longman, 1992.

Jacobs, F. and Corbett, R., *The European Parliament*, Harlow, Longman, 1990.

Keohane, R. O. and Hoffman, S., eds., *The New European Community: decision-making and institutional change*, Boulder, Col., Westview, 1991.

Kirchner, E. J., *Decision-making in the European Community: the Council presidency and European integration*, Manchester, Manchester University Press, 1992.

Lasok, D., and Bridge, J. W., *Law and Institutions of the European Communities*, 4th edn., Sevenoaks, Butterworth, 1987.

Mazey, S. and Richardson, J., eds., *Lobbying in the European Community*, Oxford, Oxford University Press, 1993.

Sbragai, A. M., ed., *Euro-Politics: institutions and policymaking in the 'new' European Community*, Washington DC, The Brookings Institution, 1991.

Shackleton, M., *Financing the European Community*, London, Pinter, 1990.

Wessels, W. and Engels, C., eds., *The Institutions After the Single European Act*, Bonn, Europa Union Verlag, 1991.

The Policies of the Community

7 The Common Policies

In the EEC Treaty, three policies are described as 'common':

- the common commercial policy (article 113);
- 'a common agricultural policy' (article 43);
- 'a common transport policy' (article 74).

Article 130(b) talks about the 'common policies' without specification. Article 130(f) refers to common policies, especially in competition and trade. Part Three of the treaty is entitled 'Policy of the Community' and sets out a number of policy areas, some added by the Single European Act and others by the Treaty on European Union. It would be difficult to establish a hard-and-fast distinction between something called a 'common policy' and another called a 'Community policy'.

COMMON COMMERCIAL POLICY (CCP)

Competence

The Common Commercial Policy assigns exclusive competence to the Community.[1] The member states may not negotiate commercial agreements with third countries even if such agreements do no damage to the common customs tariff or to Community legislation concerning imports and exports. Only the Community can act, and article 113 says how. The Commission makes recommendations to the Council, which issues a 'directive' adopted by qualified majority.

The Commission then negotiates and reports back to the Council. The text which the negotiations have produced is initialled by the negotiators on both sides and is thus fixed. The Council concludes the negotiations, deciding by qualified majority, and signs on behalf of the community. The member states keep a close watch on the negotiations (they are present, silently observing, during the sessions). Parliament is informed by the Council of the opening of the negotiations, by the Commission of the way the negotiations are moving, and by the Council prior to signature (Westerterp procedure). These commercial agreements may be multinational, the Community being one participant among many, or they may be bilateral. They may be non-preferential, where they essentially provide a rendezvous for the two sides to meet at intervals, or they may be preferential, heading towards or creating a free trade agreement, consistent with the pertinent rules of the General Agreement on Tariffs and Trade (GATT).

Association

From the beginning the Community held out the possibility of association under article 238. Associate status takes different forms. The earliest, the Greek and Turkish Association Agreements, were explicitly a preparation for possible membership of the Community.

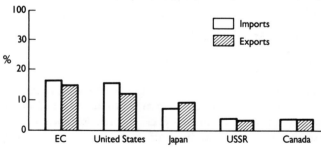

The European Community, world's leading trading power

The share of world trade[1] held by the principal trading nations in 1989 (in %):

[1] Excluding trade between Community countries.

Figure 7.1 *Europe, world partner*

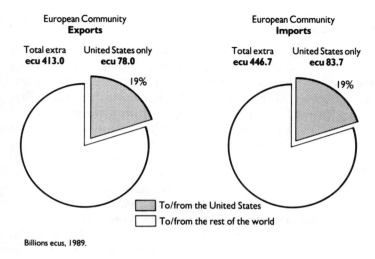

European Community
Exports

Total extra   United States only
ecu 413.0   ecu 78.0

European Community
Imports

Total extra   United States only
ecu 446.7   ecu 83.7

To/from the United States
To/from the rest of the world

Billions ecus, 1989.

Figure 7.2 *Trade statistics*

The Yaoundé conventions (1963 and 1969), with the former African colonies of the Six, were not a prelude to membership and they involved some reciprocity. In return for preferential access to the Community market, the African countries made tariff and quota concessions to the Community, although they could also withhold them to further their own economic development. The Lomé Convention (currently Lomé IV, which runs from 1990 to 2000, never described as an association agreement although concluded under article 238) made away with reciprocity. Other association agreements do not envisage Community membership and are preferential. In addition to trade provisions, they usually contain financial protocols under which the Community pledges itself to grant aid for development. The Parliament is informed of the opening and progress of association negotiations. The results are initialled (Commission) and signed (Council), but before the agreements can be concluded Parliament must, by virtue of the Single European Act, give its assent (*avis conforme*) expressed by the vote of the majority of its members – not of members present and voting. If the majority is not attained, the Council cannot conclude the agreement.

Eastern and Central Europe

When communism collapsed in the former Soviet Union and in Eastern and Central Europe, the Community moved to normalize its trade and economic relations with the states of the former Warsaw Pact and their successors, who had cold-shouldered the Community. It concluded a series of 'first-generation' agreements with several of the new democracies, falling under article 113, and confined to recognition that the two sides accorded each other most favoured nation treatment. *De facto*, the Community already gave all its trading partners most favoured nation (mfn) status, since unlike the United States, where mfn rights are a politico-economic issue, the Common Customs Tariff has only one column.

But the Community wanted to go further. As well as initiating aid programmes on a noncontractual basis, it sought to find a special relationship with as many of the new democracies as could be considered to be possible future members of the Community. This relationship took the form of 'European Agreements' negotiated under article 238 EEC. They cover trade, economic co-operation, aid and political dialogue. They recognize, without binding commitment on the Community side, that the partner countries have declared their intention to become members of the Community. 'European agreements' were concluded with Poland, Hungary and (former) Czechoslovakia in December 1991. The Community has offered similar agreements to Bulgaria and Romania, usually seen as further away from membership than the first three; Bulgaria was the Soviet bloc country most closely integrated into the Soviet economy, and Romania has had a troubled political situation after the horror of the Ceaucescu period.

The European Agreements are criticized within the Community and outside it for being insufficiently liberal in their trade provisions. Among the products which the Eastern states have for sale are steel, textiles and food. The Community has a glut of them all and maintained limitations on the amounts which it would authorize for importation from the other side.

On behalf of the twenty-four states of the OECD which support the PHARE programme of economic assistance to Eastern and Central Europe, the Commission of the EC acts as co-ordinator, as well as managing the Community's own contribution.

Relations with North America

There is continuous Community participation in discussions and negotiations in the General Agreement on Tariffs and Trade (GATT), in the UN Conference on Trade and Development (UNCTAD) and in the Organization for Economic Cooperation and Development (OECD), as well as in international commodity agreements.

The Community has no full-scale trade agreements with the United States or Japan. Trade relations are conducted within the GATT and in frequent bilateral consultations. These often concern crises in the Community's relations, especially with the United States: the 'chicken war' over the Community's treatment of chicken pieces imported from the United States; the steel battles over the limitation of exports to the United States and the alleged dumping of steel on the US market; controversy over the supply by member states of equipment for the Soviet gas pipeline; the 'pasta war', in which the United States retaliated against allegedly objectionable practices by cutting its pasta imports; the textile problem, under which the Community intervened to limit certain imports from the United States; the airbus wrangle, a question of whether member state governments were subsidizing the sale of Airbus planes to US users; and the ban on the use of hormones in livestock, which threatens US exports. The general background is of sustained US criticism of the Common Agricultural Policy because of its allegedly damaging effects on US exports and on the stability of world agricultural trade, and of Community attacks on successive Trade Bills which pass through the US Congress and are protectionist.

The two sides decided, in response to a proposal by the US Secretary of State James Baker in December 1989, that they needed to improve the quality of their dialogue and adopted a Declaration on US–EC relations in November 1990. The declaration sets out the framework for consultations:

- twice-yearly summit meetings between the Presidents of the United States, the Commission and the European Council;
- twice-yearly consultations between EC foreign ministers, the Commission and the US Secretary of State;
- ongoing consultations between the Council presidency/troika and the US Secretary of State;

- twice-yearly consultations between the Commission and the US cabinet officers;
- briefings to US government representatives on meetings of the European Political Co-operation at ministerial level.

The EC and Canada made a similar Declaration in November 1990, building on the consultation arrangements established in the EC Canada Economic Agreement.

Sanctions

Trade policy and the member states' external policies interact, especially at times of international crises. In 1980 the bulk of world opinion condemned Iran for taking and holding American hostages. While adopting political sanctions, the Community did not take trade measures. In January 1980, following the Soviet invasion of Afghanistan, the Council adopted two economic measures: cancellation of the food aid programme for Afghanistan, but provision of emergency aid for Afghan refugees; and a decision that exports to the Soviet Union should not replace US exports, which had been embargoed. In April 1982, following the Argentine invasion of the Falkland Islands, the Council imposed an embargo on imports from the Argentine. The use of a commercial policy instrument (article 113) as a political weapon was controversial and insecure, and the foreign policy aspect itself created internal difficulties in some member states.

When in 1990 and 1991 respectively the UN imposed sanctions on Iraq, following its invasion of Kuwait and on the warring factions in the states of the former Yugoslavia, the Community gave effect to the action by using its commercial policy powers, and no doctrinal questions were asked.

China

The People's Republic of China, making its own distinctive foreign policy, had no inhibitions about the Community from the 1970s and even expressed the hope that the United Kingdom would remain a member. Negotiations for a trade agreement opened in 1977 and it came into force on 1 June 1978. Among its provisions is the setting up of a joint committee. Its meetings in Beijing and in Brussels have provided a basis for visits of substantial delegations, including on the Community side exporters and on the Chinese side representatives of the foreign trade organisations and exhibitions of Chinese products.

Dumping

The Community has exclusive responsibility for anti-dumping action. Dumping occurs when the export price of a product is lower than its fair or normal value. This latter serves as a benchmark against which the extent of any dumping is assessed. On a complaint by a Community producer the Commission investigates, and if dumping is established, it either obtains assurances from the exporters that true prices will be used or proposes that the Council decide to impose anti-dumping duties. The Commission acts within the GATT Anti-Dumping Code. Foreign suppliers often contest the Council's decisions in the European Court of Justice; they rarely succeed.

Developing states

Alongside the trade concessions which the Community grants to developing states in its agreements with them, it also gives autonomous benefits in its Generalized Preference Scheme. This scheme, under which developed countries give tariff preferences to products (and some produce) exported from developing countries, grew out of the GATT discussions in the 1960s. The Community reviews its preferential list and list of beneficiaries annually.

Early Community relations with the African, Caribbean and Pacific (ACP) countries have been discussed in Chapter 2. The Lomé Convention of 1975 was replaced by Lomé II in 1981 and by Lomé III in May 1986. The negotiation of Lomé IV began late in 1988. Lomé Conventions provide non-reciprocated tariff concessions, development aid (under the European Development Fund), stabilized export earnings ('Stabex'), and mining co-operation ('Sysmin'). Stabex and Sysmin compensate for losses of export earnings by reference to a fixed base. The institutions of the Lomé Convention are the Committee of Ambassadors, the Council of Ministers and the ACP–EEC Joint (Consultative) Assembly.

There are arrangements similar to Lomé for twenty-five overseas

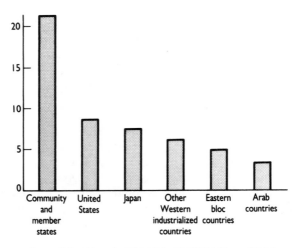

Figure 7.3 *Aid to the Third World ($US billions, 1987)*

countries and territories, dependencies of Britain, France, the Netherlands and (since Greenland left the Communities) Denmark. Under
the 'overall Mediterranean approach', the Community has had 'co-
operation agreements' under article 238 with Cyprus, Malta, Turkey,
Algeria, Egypt, Israel, Jordan, Lebanon, Morocco, Syria, Tunisia and
Yugoslavia. It also has co-operation agreements with the Yemen and
with the Gulf Co-operation Council under articles 235 and 113.

COMMON AGRICULTURAL POLICY (CAP)

The Background

An agricultural policy in which countries with agricultural populations protect their farmers against price competition from outside
suppliers has a social dimension. A shift of population from a
low-income or otherwise unattractive farming sector towards the
urban and industrial sector can be regarded as changing a natural
national character which society may wish to preserve. It may also
involve unwelcome economic and ecological cost where land ceases
to be tended and reverts to wilderness and where pressure develops
for the provision of social facilities in towns and for building roads,
factories and houses in areas regarded as a national heritage of beauty.

Table 7.1 *Structural data on European agriculture in 1986*

	Farm size (ha)	Area per agricultural work unit	Share of agriculture in gross domestic product (%)	Share of agriculture in working population (%)
Belgium	14.1	13.7	2.5	2.9
Denmark	30.7	15.9	5.0	6.8
FR of Germany*	16.0	8.9	1.8	5.3
Greece	4.3	5.6	16.6	28.5
Spain	12.9	15.6	6.1	16.1
France	27.0	20.5	3.7	7.3
Ireland	22.7	33.8	10.2	15.8
Italy	5.6	7.8	5.0	10.9
Luxembourg	28.6	19.7	2.6	4.0
The Netherlands	14.9	8.2	4.2	4.8
Portugal	4.3	5.1	23.1	21.9
United Kingdom	65.1	30.1	1.8	2.6
EUR 12	8.9	12.8	3.5	8.3

* Pre-unification.

Agriculture also has weight in national politics. Partly because of the tradition of government interests in them, farmers are usually well organized in coherent lobbies and pressure groups, have representatives in legislatures and are able to exercise a 'farm vote', often considered crucial to a party's electoral success.

In developed areas such as Europe, total demand for food is largely inelastic and is satisfied. Elsewhere in the world, despite the 'green revolution' of the 1960s, vast populations which are dependent on water that never comes as rain or that floods and ruins the crops live in famine. Food then enters the arena of international politics, becoming a form of aid to the Third World and giving support to the idea that areas such as Europe with a capacity to expand agricultural output beyond their own needs could become, commercially or charitably, suppliers to the world.

Guaranteed price

The hallmark of the Community agricultural support system is the guaranteed price. In principle, the price should be at a level which calls for production sufficient to meet at least the major part of demand and to ensure that relative income on the land does not fall behind income in other sectors. Independently of price, farming output is characterized by a secular productivity gain, based on applied research which makes better use of inputs and cuts costs, and is in the grip of weather conditions. These factors make forward planning inexact. If imports are not regarded as a buffer, one way of evening out year-to-year surplus and deficit is storage. Private or state stores take unsaleable produce off the market and release it when the market is running short.

World market prices are pretty well notional. At most times the quantities in international trade are surpluses, sold for what they will fetch (costs having been covered on the domestic market) and often subsidized. Because of geography Community farming is more intensive than much farming elsewhere, and for historical reasons the average unit size of holding is smaller than elsewhere, resulting in relative diseconomies of scale. This means that the cost of Community farming feeds into prices which are higher than they would be in a theoretical free market or in one where supplies could be obtained from outside opportunistically.

Principles

In the Communities' beginnings a common market without agriculture was unthinkable. It would have cut out of the operation of the common market a large slice of output and it would have distorted competition among the food-processing industries and, through divergent food prices, in unit wage cost in industry. Agriculture had to be in.[2] The guidelines were mapped out at a conference held in Stresa in July 1958 bringing together the representatives of the Six governments, the Commission and national farmers' organizations in the Six. It was accepted that the family character of the farm unit should not be undermined. Agricultural prices were to be brought to a common level, and for this purpose agricultural markets would have to be managed. Prices would normally be above the world market price; thus unless there was some support, Community agriculture would not compete. Self-sufficiency was not a declared aim but security of supplies was already a treaty objective. These analyses crystallized in the three principles of the CAP, which the Council adopted in June 1960:

1. The single market (free movement of agricultural goods).

2. Community preference (protectionism).
3. Joint financial responsibility (Community funding for the disposal of produce which could not be sold on the market).

Mechanisms

After the principles came the mechanisms. They differ importantly from one agricultural product to another and in their details are matters for the practitioner and specialist (for whom they are amply documented). But in general terms the operation is as follows. An annual price is fixed around April–May. It may be called a target price. It is the price which the farmer should realize in the market. If the farmer obtains the price, the system is in balance. The market is not a true one because consumers cannot make choices and are probably paying more than a true market would charge them. If, however, the market price is less than the fixed price because consumers have enough, and if the price disparity goes beyond a certain point, the farmer can withdraw his offer from the market and sell it to a CAP agency at an intervention price.

Intervention agencies of different kinds exist in all member states. Contrary to prevailing belief, they are financed not by the Community but by national governments: or, perhaps better put, they were so financed when they began. From the General Budget the Community pays part of the cost of storage (rent, heating or cooling, transport, insurance, wages, maintenance, etc.), some depreciation (taking account of natural deterioration and of the inflated book-value of purchases to intervention), and the difference between what the agency paid and what it collects when it sells the produce. Sales are for export (in the hands of exporting firms, who are accordingly remunerated partly by their clients and partly by the Community budget) or to the Community itself as food aid for developing countries in food deficit, for sale at reduced prices to needy social groups in member states ('Christmas butter'), or, more rarely, for 'denaturing' – destruction.

Imports are not allowed to perturb Community production which can sell at the fixed price, or to bid the market price down, thereby provoking higher sales to intervention. A threshold price is set consisting of the world market price, the cost of transport to the Community frontier, the cost of distribution to an inland consuming centre and the margin to make up the intervention price. The difference between the threshold price and the (lowest) import offer is charged on the imports concerned as a levy. The agricultural levies accrue to the Community budget. Conversely, where a farmer (or dealer) exports Community produce, he obtains as 'restitution', drawn from the agricultural section of the Community budget, the difference between the world price (or the rock-bottom sale price) and the Community price. Figure 7.4 shows the make-up of prices.

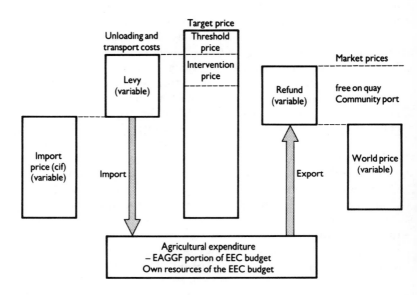

Figure 7.4 *Levy and refund system for wheat*

There are market organizations (under Community regulation) for the following products:

Cereals	The intervention system just described.
Sugar	A system of production quotas, partly price guaranteed, partly subject to a levy on production and partly for export without support.

Certain fruit and vegetables	Intervention, known as withdrawal, partly operated by the producers' organizations. Imports must respect reference prices.
Olive oil and vegetable fats	Intervention and direct aids to producers (based on a tree count) and to consumers – in this case the processors of the raw material.
Wine	Protection against imports accompanied by a price grid. A minimum price can be brought in below which wine may not be sold. Other prices can trigger intervention. There is financial aid for private storage and for distillation. To reduce production, grubbing-up premiums can be paid.
Dairy products	Intervention. To reduce output, milk production is subject to quota. There are also measures to promote better consumption. A tax on margarine, proposed more than once by the Commission, has not been accepted.
Pig meat	Private storage aided in preference to intervention.
Beef	Guide pricing and intervention, plus various premiums (for e.g. suckler cows, extensified breeding practices).
Sheepmeat	A system of premiums to make up the difference between a reference price and the forecast market price.
Certain oilseeds	Direct aids paid to producers, partly to compensate for a lower level of import protection, itself derived from wider commercial policy considerations.
Flax and hemp, hops, silkworms, seeds	Production subsidies.

The day-to-day management of the agricultural markets is a Commission responsibility. The Commission works in collaboration with a series of management committees, consisting of representatives of member states' agriculture ministries. The committees give opinions, if necessary by vote, on the execution measures which the Commission proposes. This is one of the smoothest-running parts of Community work: over the years the member state representatives and the Commission have developed a high level of co-operation and mutual understanding.

The financial aspect

In the financial negotiations of 1987/8 one of the objectives pursued was to limit the Community's commitment to support farm prices by limiting the guaranteed quantities. There had been similar endeavours in the past, by agreements – difficult to sustain – to reduce guaranteed prices in order to discourage production (for example, of cereals) and by the imposition of quotas or co-responsibility levies which made producers pay towards the cost of surpluses. Alongside the tighter budgetary controls applied in 1988, 'stabilizers' were introduced by wholesale amendment of the regulations for market organization. In general terms, and varying in their form from one product to another, stabilizers fix upper limits to guaranteed quantities. At the same time, additional income aids were introduced together with a scheme for payments to 'set aside' land and leave it out of production. (For the budgetary side, see pp. 100–8.)

The policy aim was to reduce price support and discourage production. Between 1987 and 1988 support prices were cut by 3.2 per cent in real terms. The results obtained from the reform package were initially encouraging – especially a sharp decline in stocks and in the extravagant cost of holding them, from 10.5 billion ecu in 1987 to 4.6 billion ecu in 1988 – but they did not last. By 1991, stocks of cereals had doubled to 20 million tonnes, and were rising. There were 1 million tonnes of dairy products in stock, a fourfold increase and 750,000 tonnes of beef, rising at the rate of 15,000–20,000 tonnes a week. It was a reminder of the secular trend: between 1973 and 1988 agricultural production in the EC rose by 2 per cent per annum whereas internal consumption rose by 0.5 per cent per annum. The Community was increasing its subsidized exports to help clear its stocks and also increasing tension with its competitors. Meanwhile agriculture was the blocking item in the stalled GATT negotiations for reductions in trade protection (Uruguay Round), and EC export subsidies were regarded as the leading culprit.

Reform

These internal and external pressures combined to produce a new wave of CAP reform, negotiated between June 1991 and May 1992, and progressively applied from July 1992. The guidelines were:

- a substantial reduction in the price of agricultural products;
- compensation for the consequent reduction in farm income through amounts or premiums not released to production.

The forms of compensation include 'set-aside', in which, in return for the withdrawal from production of up to 15 per cent of 'reference areas', cultivators of cereals, oilseeds or protein plants receive payments, all calculated at a compensation rate for cereals. Set-aside land can be used commercially, provided the crop is not for human or animal consumption. Correspondingly, the target prices for cereals are cut cumulatively over three years. For oilseeds, there are no price guarantees, but fixed aid per hectare. (The rate was attacked by the United States, which proposed retaliatory measures.) The Community reduced overall the quotas for milk, i.e. the volumes of production for which farmers can obtain price support. It decided to reduce the intervention price for beef by 15 per cent over three years, and to limit the premiums paid for sheepmeat. No changes were made in the arrangements for supporting pigmeat, poultry and eggs. These products are often described as conversions of the cost of cereals.

The 'accompanying measures' include encouragement to farmers to take early retirement at 55, and payments for the conversion of agricultural land into woodland. Farmers can also benefit from environmental improvement grants, if they undertake to adopt practices which reduce pollution, including 'extensification', involving the reduced use of chemical and energy inputs.

It was on the basis of these reforms, involving reductions in subsidized production, that the EC revised its offer in the Uruguay Round. Hopes of a settlement, in which the other participants sought to draw more from the Community, were shaken when in August

1992 the United States announced as a defensive measure a new drive for export markets for cereals, backed by a large subsidy scheme. However, a deal was finally arrived at between the United States and the EC after many anxious moments and much drama in November 1992. This deal did not suit all the member states and the French were particularly upset, threatening early in 1993 to attempt to veto the entire package. The US–EC agreement required to be consolidated into the overall settlement of the Uruguay Round in 1993.

Common prices?

One of the guiding principles of the CAP is common pricing. Prices are expressed in the Community's monetary unit, the ecu, and are translated into national currencies. If the national currency is revalued, the price of a product at the new ecu exchange rate will fall and farmers will lose income. To avoid the opposition that this could provoke, states can hold their local prices unchanged, using 'green rates'. At these green rates the selling price is now higher in all other currencies than the ruling ecu price yields in these currencies; and if the produce were exported to another member state, it would cost more in the local currency than the local produce. This phenomenon, which would split the common agricultural market, brought about the system of Monetary Compensation Amounts (MCAs) under which levies (taxes) are charged on imports into a member state that is using a green rate for the products concerned, while its exports benefit from a premium (subsidy). Over time the system of MCAs has undergone much tinkering and refinement to become vastly complex, far from neutral in its effects on trade, intensely controversial in price-fixing negotiations among the members states and between them and the Commission. (In the most cynical manifestation a state could hold out for a politically popular low Community ecu price but hold up its national prices by devaluing its green rate.) The more positive rationale of green rate changes is that a devaluation is the only way in which a state with relatively high inflation can maintain the real – and presumably intended – effect of an agreed increase in a common agricultural price. MCAs are regarded as a temporary, necessary evil in an unstable financial world and all policy decisions are supposed, by agreement, to be aimed at eliminating them. They will disappear finally with, if not before, European Monetary Union (EMU).

CAP's impact

The results obtained from thirty-odd years of the CAP, possibly the part of the European Communities which has provoked most debate and acrimony, point in several directions. The interpretation of them depends largely on the observer's particular desiderata. Self-sufficiency – or more – exists for common wheat, barley, wine, meat, vegetables, milk-powder and butter. The single market has encouraged specialization: trade in agricultural products between the member states increased fourfold between 1973 and 1985.

Farm incomes, which according to the treaty are to be safeguarded, have fluctuated from year to year and from member state to member state: overall in the mid-1980s they were in real terms at about the level of the early 1970s. Of course, nobody can say whether, taking account of the economic recession, they would have been better or worse if there had been a different CAP or none at all. In the latter case it is a safe bet that there would have been national uncommon agricultural policies.

Food prices have increased less rapidly than consumer prices as a whole and this is often held up as an example of the virtue of the CAP. No doubt if food prices had been higher, national price indices would have deteriorated, but this kind of statement gives no guide to whether Community food prices are reasonable. Input costs and productivity improvements or deteriorations are specific to sectors and it may not be a virtue in sector A or a vice in sector B if A prices rise more slowly than B prices.

Farming employment has perhaps been sustained generally. This would have counted as a negative effect in the 1960s: one of the aims of the Mansholt plan which the Commission put out in 1968 was to facilitate movement off the land. With the mass unemployment levels of the 1970s and 1980s and allowing always for the subtleties of the labour market, farming employment at least provided a pool of jobs.

The CAP is often criticized for its unsettling effect on the agricultural trade of the rest of the world. Some effects there must be, but the Community's share of world agricultural exports has fluctuated around a stable figure; and Community imports of farm products and foodstuffs doubled in value between 1973 and 1987 (See Tables 7.2 and 7.3; Figure 7.5.)

Inside the Community, the most vocal criticism of the CAP concerns its resource cost. A much-quoted study, *The Political*

Table 7.2 **Degree of self-sufficiency in main agricultural products**

(%)

	Total cereals	Wheat	Sugar	Fresh fruit	Butter	Cheese	Beef	Sheepmeat & goatmeat
1968/9 (EUR 9)	86	94	82	80	92	99	95	56
1973/4 (EUR 10)	91	104	100	82	98	103	96	66
1984/5	118	129	101	83	134	107	108	76
1985/6 (EUR 12)	119	120	126	88	130	106	106	80
1986/7	111	119	127	85	105	106	108	80

Table 7.3 **Level of public stocks in the Community**

(1,000 t at end of year)

	1979 EUR 9	1983 EUR 10	1986 EUR 10	1987 EUR 12	1988 EUR 12
Cereals	2,677	9,542	14,717	8,147	8,312
Olive oil	53	121	283	299	346
Skimmed-milk powder	215	957	847	600	11
Butter	293	686	1,297	860	120
Beef					
— carcasses equivalent	310	410	576	776	425
Alcohol (1,000 hl)	–	–	4,026	9,000	10,556

Economy of International Agricultural Policy Reform (Australian Department of Primary Industry, 1980) suggested that the additional cost of higher food prices together with the higher levels of taxation needed to finance the CAP was up to £550 a year for a non-farming family of four. Ten years later a study by the Consumer Council in Britain concluded that the cost of the CAP to the average British family, in high prices and EC budget costs, was more than £700 a year, comparable to the incidence of the detested and contested 'poll tax' which the Conservative government had introduced. The cost to the Community budget is disproportionate: 60 per cent of the budget is for agriculture, 34 billion ecus out of 63 billion in the draft 1993 budget. Half the budgetary cost goes in storing and disposing of surplus food. In 1987 those stocks reached a book-value of 11 billion ecus against a possible realizable value of some 4–5 billion ecus,

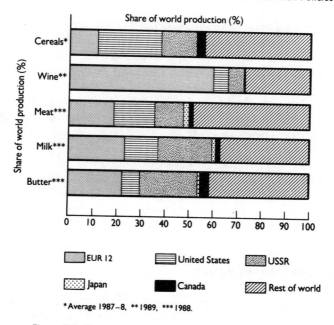

Figure 7.5 *European agriculture in the world: a major force*

representing a resource loss of up to 7 billion ecus, comparable to the annual spend on regional and social policy.[3]

In addition to EAGGF Guarantee there is EAGGF Guidance, spending some 1.5 billion ecus a year on a number of schemes to improve the structure of agricultural production.

COMMON FISHERIES POLICY (CFP)

The CFP is a relatively recent arrival, not reaching its fully articulated form until 1983.[4] During the late 1970s it was bitterly fought over and much delayed between conception and implementation. The problem was simple: too many fishermen, too few fish.

The Common Fisheries Policy has an important chapter for the conservation of stocks to prevent overfishing. Member states may not take national conservation measures. Overfishing is prevented by the comprehensive allocation to interested member states of quotas within Total Allowable Catches (TACs) and by regulating fishing areas and fishing equipment such as mesh sizes. Local dependent communities receive special consideration. Because of the depletion of stocks, conservation measures tend to be tightened including a limit on 'days at sea'.

The market organization places emphasis on the management role of fishermen's organizations, and gives them certain powers over non-members. There are guide and withdrawal prices, and quality standards.

Some traditional fishing grounds of Community fishermen are in waters under the jurisdiction of third countries, and vice versa. The Community negotiates fisheries agreements for, in some cases, reciprocal access to defined quantities and species, and in other cases, the payment of a fee for fishing rights.

COMMON TRANSPORT POLICY

Transport was one of the headings picked up in the Messina communiqué of 1955 as needing joint effort. The EEC Treaty (article 84(1)) applies its transport title only to rail, road and inland transport, and until 1973, it was argued that air and sea transport were outside the treaty. The Court judgment in Case 167/73 stipulated that the general rules of the EEC Treaty applied also to air and sea, and the Council proceeded – by the unanimity required by article 84(2) – to take a number of decisions affecting sea and air transport. Because the article does not say how it was to be implemented, this was one of the rare cases where the Council could act without first receiving a Commission proposal. This peculiarity was dropped in the Single European Act (article 16(6)).

One important reason for slow progress was trouble with the railways. By the beginning of the 1980s 85 per cent of domestic goods transport was going by road and only 7.5 per cent by rail. But the railways trailed clouds of glory from their past (the Prussian Railway had been a unit in the army and senior railway employees wore sabres), served social as well as purely economic purposes (carrying commuters and people living in outlying communities), and were state subsidized (about 20 billion ecus a year in the early 1980s about the same as the then budgetary cost of the CAP). The Commission concluded:

In most European countries the railways are indispensable. . . . However, with their extensive organization and extraordinary appetite for subsidies, the railways are also one of the Council's main problem areas. Both these factors suggest that the common transport policy hinges on finding a solution to the problems of the railways.[5]

In September 1982 the European Parliament broke new ground by taking the Council to Court for its failure to lay down the foundations of a common policy. The Court (Case 13/83, judgment given on 22 May 1985) held that the Council was in breach of the treaty. On the other hand, the Court found that the treaty did not define the common policy sufficiently precisely to enable the Court to say, as Parliament wished, exactly what was missing. It recommended the Council to work towards a common transport policy.

Road

The Council responded in the area of road transport. In December 1984 it tackled a dossier which had long lain on its desk: the maximum weights and dimensions of goods vehicles. Different rules in different countries block traffic flows. The Council was able to agree on common standards, except for the maximum weight on the driving axle, completing the task – with temporary derogations for the United Kingdom and Ireland, where road architecture would not admit the largest sizes – in July 1986 (*Official Journal*, L217, 5 August 1986; L221, 7 August 1986). The study of balancing fiscal charges on road transport, which had previously been a precondition of harmonization, was to continue and remains a major blockage in EC transport policy. On 30 July 1986 the Council crossed another bridge. Road transport among the member states was governed by quotas, which protected national carriers and possibly also held down the density of traffic on some of the main axes which are a charge on national and local authority budgets. The Council now decided that quotas should be increased, to reach a free market situation by the end of 1992, the 'single market' achievement year (Council Regulation No. EC 1841/88, *Official Journal*, L163, 30 June 1988). There remained a highly protected sector – cabotage, which is the ability of a non-resident carrier to trade in another member state: a Dutch lorry to carry goods from Milan to Rome. In June 1992 the Council agreed on a regulation to liberalize most cabotage. Regular service frontier zone services were liberalized on 1 January 1993. Other regular services are for the time being still excluded. Some non-regular services were also liberalized from 1 January 1993 and the whole range of non-regular services will be from 1 January 1996.

Rail

For the railways, there is not a lot the Community can do, except encourage co-operation and realistic tariff structures. In June 1991, the Council agreed that state-owned railway management must be independent. It was also agreed that the transport of passengers and the management of the railway networks should be handled separately, at least from an accounting point of view. Where there are several users, the body managing the network will charge them non-discriminatory fees. In a separate regulation, railways' obligation as a public service were redefined and replaced by contracts between companies and the state. Their public service obligations were to be carried out independently of their commercial activities.

Air

Air transport within the Community has been high cost and high tariff as compared with route costs elsewhere in the world. Many states see a national airline as part of the national identity, carrying the name and the flag abroad.

In 1987 the Council took the first step towards a regulated common air transport policy. On air fares it decided that a carrier should no longer be obliged to align its fares on the competition. Governments' powers to reject reduced fares outside peak periods, or for particular classes of customer, were curtailed. There had been a long-standing rule that carriers authorized to operate routes between two states should divide the traffic equally. This was changed to authorizing share-outs within the scales of 60/40 per cent, which could make deals more attractive. Market access was enhanced by providing that member states could allow several companies to fly bilateral links (instead of one only) and that carriers could establish links between regional airports in one country and principal airports in another. Finally in this liberalization package, Fifth Freedom rights were awarded – the right of an aircraft carrier to undertake to transport passengers, freight and mail between two states other than the state in which it is licensed. A British airline could pick up passengers in Paris and take them to Rome.

Within the first air transport package, regulations were passed to apply competition rules to air transport, to prevent abusive agreements among airlines and the abuse of dominant market positions. A second transitional package was adopted in September 1989. It went further in price flexibility by establishing the general rule that prices should be fixed by the operators rather than by agreement between the two member states concerned. It took further the flexibility in the share-out of seat capacity by easing the 60/40 ratio. Originally these arrangements were confined to passenger traffic, but in December 1990 they were extended, where applicable, to freight.

The third and complementary package was approved in June 1992:

- A licensing regulation sets out requirements for obtaining operating licences; any carrier holding a licence is to be granted traffic rights between any Community airports. Route licences cease to be the control instrument.
- The regulation on air fares provides that a fare or rate is considered approved if no member state or the Commission has opposed it within 14 days of notification.
- On market access carriers will have access to all routes between airports on Community territory, apart from transitional limitations on cabotage.

Together the three packages represent the comprehensive dismantlement of fragmented national regulations and their replacement by a single liberalized system, with essential safeguards for passenger safety and the interests of consumers.

The extension of Community regulation of European air travel did not always seem to produce a consumer benefit in terms of more aggressive price competition. Fares remained high in international comparisons. The Commission began to alarm the air travel authorities by contending that the policies had been Europeanized to the point that member states' governments were no longer competent to negotiate route facilities with third states. They did not enjoy the prospect of seeing their markets bartered for the benefit of airlines in other member states. For its part, the Commission was sometimes criticized for taking no clear view on the mergers and acquisitions which began to intervene in 1991.

Sea

Despite the decline in member states' fleets since the 1980s in the face of low-cost competition, registration under other flags and shipping protectionism, a third of intra-Community trade and 90 per cent of external trade was carried by sea between 1980 and 1990.

In December 1986 the Council adopted four comprehensive regulations on sea transport. Regulation 4055/86 EEC provides for a free market in the provision of shipping services:

- by ships flying member state flags and plying between member states (by 31 December 1989);
- by ships flying member state flags and plying between member states and third countries (by 31 December 1991);
- by other ships between member states and between them and third countries (by 1992).

Regulation 4056/86 EEC determines the application of the competition rules in articles 85 and 86 of the EEC Treaty to sea transport. Regulation 4057/86 EEC introduces a kind of 'anti-dumping' tax on unfair tariffs by third country shipowners to the detriment of Community shipowners. Regulation 4058/86 EEC provides for the member states to take co-ordinated action against a third country or its operators if they limit or threaten to limit free access of Community ships to certain traffics.

In June 1992 the Council agreed on a regulation on the freedom to provide maritime cabotage – the provision of shipping services within the waters of a member state other than that in which the vessel is registered, effective on 1 January 1993. Different manning rules apply to mainland cabotage and to island cabotage. In its proposals, the Commission had made a link between cabotage and the creation of a Community flag 'Euros', to coexist with national registers. The Council kept this proposal under study.

Road safety

Road safety is an important part of the policy. 1986 was named

European Road Safety Year. On 14 November 1985 the Council overhauled the social legislation which governs drivers' working hours. The earlier versions of this legislation introduced the tachograph, which measures lapsed time, speed and distance and was originally resisted in Britain as being the 'spy in the cab', until a court case went against Britain. In 1989 the Commission proposed a batch of road safety measures, including a standard maximum alcohol level in blood. The European Parliament, in giving its opinion on such measures, asked that courts should have the right to disqualify drivers whose licences were issued by other member states.

8 Key Economic Policies

At the heart of the Community enterprise have been debates about how truly to achieve the original wider aspirations than just a 'common market' and a few 'common policies' in the economic area. This chapter looks at progress on three key economic questions: the single internal market, competition policy, and economic and monetary policy.

THE SINGLE INTERNAL MARKET

The most widely publicized programme which the Community has ever undertaken goes by the name of '1992', the creation by 1993 of a Single Market within the EC, with free movement of capital, goods, services and people. Trade across an EC internal border will be conducted as if it were trade within a border.

Such a market is the clearly stated aim of the EEC Treaty of 1957. It succeeded, in a shorter time than was planned, in creating the Customs Union. As years passed it also adopted a large number of harmonization or approximation measures, which dismantled some of the barriers to cross-border trading. But the process was laborious, requiring unanimity and not marked by a sense of priorities. Moreover, much faster than existing barriers were dismantled, new 'non-tariff' barriers went up, as governments pursued regulatory policies as part of consumer protection, company law, competition, public health, environmental control, transport protectionism (and if truth be told, the protection of national production and employment). By the late 1970s, there was much debate about the cost of 'non-Europe' and demands from European business leaders for an end to market fragmentation by regulation. But political leadership in the Community had other things on its mind – the search for monetary stability, the long drawn-out negotiations for the entry of Spain and Portugal, and the British demand for budgetary relief.

The turning point came with the appointment of the first Delors Commission in 1985. The new British Commissioner for Industry, Lord Cockfield, with the strong support of M. Delors, presented a White Paper to the Council and Parliament in June 1985 on the completion of the Internal Market. This was a list of some 300 measures needed to unify the market. Each measure was described and annotated and brought within a coherent timetable, culminating in the Single Market by the end of 1992, whence the programme took its name. The European Council gave its blessing to the programme without underwriting every single proposal, and Lord Cockfield bent his formidable energies to bringing out the precise proposals and piloting them through.

The negotiators of the Single European Act adjusted the legislative procedures to the needs of the 1992 programme. A new article 100a replaced unanimity by qualified majority voting for internal market legislation, except in so far as it concerned fiscal matters, the free circulation of people and the rights and interests of salaried employees.

The economic case for the Single Market was brilliantly expounded in the report 'The European Challenge', prepared under the leadership of a recently retired Commission official, Paolo Cecchini and published in April 1988. With it were thirteen reports on sectors and case studies to buttress the conclusions.

At first the Council moved slowly, and the Commission reproached it for lack of zeal. But under the guiding hand of Lord Cockfield and, from 1989 his successor, Mr Martin Bangemann, a former German Economic Minister, the Council and the Parliament worked through the proposals and the problems, tackling such long-standing difficulties as the recognition of professional qualifications, national rules on the construction and use of vehicles, the control of insurance and the state monopolies in telecommunications. The two principles were, for goods, the definition of essential requirements and mutual recognition and, for providers of services, home

Table 8.1 *Macroeconomic consequences of EC market integration for the Community in the medium term*

This table shows the positive or negative effects on GDP, consumer prices, etc. of a number of measures connected with the single market: abolition of customs formalities, open public procurement, liberalization of financial services and supply-side-effects.

	Abolition of customs formalities	Open public procurement	Liberalization of financial services	Supply-side[1] effects	Total
GDP (%)	0.4	0.5	1.5	2.1	4.5
Consumer prices (%)	−1.0	−1.4	−1.4	−2.3	−6.1
Employment (thousands)	200	350	400	850	1,800
Budgetary balance (% of GDP)	0.2	0.3	1.1	0.6	2.2
External balance (% of GDP)	0.2	0.1	0.3	0.4	1.0

[1] Economies of scale, increased competition, etc.

Source: 'The Economics of 1992', in *European Economy*, No 35, March 1988 (Cecchini Report).

authority control, leading to the single passport for operators. At its December 1992 meeting the European Council was able to note that since 1985 over 500 internal market measures had been agreed and that the White Paper programme would in all essential respects be completed by 31 December 1992. The event was marked by the lighting of beacons across Europe as the year ended. There was one

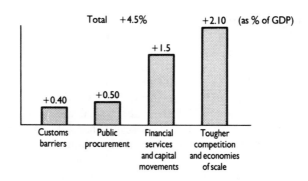

Figure 8.1 *Additional growth likely to be generated through achievement of the 1992 objectives*

Exhibit 8.1 *Implementation of Single Market measures*

> Nearly 95 per cent of the measures set out in the White Paper on the completion of the Single European Market had been agreed by 5 February 1993. Of a total of 282 measures, 261 had been definitively adopted and 3, adopted by EC ministers, had yet to come before the European Parliament before being definitively adopted, making a total of 264. Among these measures and 'European laws', 257 are already in force in principle, while 213 of them require to be transposed into the national laws of the Twelve. Of course only 95 of these 'laws' have been transposed in all twelve EC countries without exception; but 80 per cent of national transposition measures have already been taken – a substantial advance over 1992. Denmark continues to lead its EC partners when it comes to transposing EC legislation with 92 per cent; it is ahead of Italy (87 per cent), the United Kingdom (86 per cent) and Belgium (85 per cent). Greece is the laggard with 72 per cent, while the other countries range between 74 and 82 per cent. As for the four freedoms of movement promised by the Single Market, three are almost complete: they are the freedom of movement of goods, services and capital. The fourth, freedom of movement of people, is still awaited. Such is the balance sheet the European Commission presented to EC ministers on 8 February 1993.

incomplete matter – the free movement of persons, in accordance with article 8a of the Treaty of Rome, was not secured. One major difficulty was the possible danger for public security of illegal immigration.

COMPETITION POLICY

Competition policy is a field where:

- Competence is shared between the Community and member states' authorities;
- The Commission, not (generally speaking) the Council, takes the Community decisions, subject to reference to the Court of Justice.

Competition policy is principally concerned with three things:

1. *State aids*: subsidies, grants and relief to enterprises, whether publicly or privately owned. State aids which distort competition are banned but on application to the Commission can be authorized, possibly subject to conditions, if there is justification for them. Justification can include the demands of regional policy, conformity with a planned programme of structural adjustment (for example, shipbuilding), support for the launch of a venture with promise to improve competitiveness, etc.
2. *Trusts, cartels, abuse of dominant market positions*: the classic anti-trust fields, involving on the one hand, agreements among enterprises to rig markets to the detriment of consumers, and on the other, predatory behaviour based on market or financial strength. They come into play when trade between member states is affected or when there is abuse of a dominant position within the common market or in a substantial part of it. Exemptions can be and have been given to agreements among enterprises which satisfy the tests set out in article 85(3), such as exclusive dealership arrangements.
3. *Mergers*: In the 1970s, the Commission proposed that the Community should exercise control over mergers. Such control existed in some member states, but without common criteria, and in others not at all.

For many years, most member states took the view that the issues raised by some mergers were too important in their domestic political situations to be allowed into the less sensitive hands of outsiders – matters such as employment or the loss of it, location of new investment, defence production, industrial champions, power of the media. But at the end of the 1980s with two Commissioners in a row who invested much effort in obtaining the policy, Mr Peter Sutherland and Sir Leon Brittan and with the selfless support of the French presidency the Council reached agreement after what may have been the longest gestation period ever and adopted Regulation no. 4064 EEC of 21 December 1989 on the control of concentrations between undertakings. When it came to apply the regulation the Commission (which is responsible for the examination of proposed mergers and decides independently of the Council) usually found no reasons to intervene. But there was one celebrated case in which it blocked the takeover by a Franco-Italian consortium of a Canadian aircraft builder (De Haviland) because it would have created an excessive concentration of market power.

In applying the provisions of competition law the Commission has extensive powers to require the production of information and to carry out on-the-spot investigations with or without prior notice ('dawn raids') to those concerned. Until 1978 the Commission conducted surprise investigations in only a few cases. The situation has changed somewhat ... the Commission now likes to gather the maximum amount of evidence of suspected infringements.'[1]

Community competition law can apply to enterprises outside the Community, having no branches or subsidiaries inside the Community but selling to customers within the Community. This principle of extra territorial application was confirmed by the European Court of Justice in the Woodpulp cartel case (September 1988).

In 1991 the Commission concluded an agreement with the US Justice Department to co-operate and exchange information on anti-trust matters.

ECONOMIC AND MONETARY POLICY

The EEC Treaty is about creating a customs union, known familiarly as the Common Market. The Single European Act catches up with ongoing activities to give them a treaty basis and it completes the common market by attacking the non-tariff barriers which outlasted the abolition of customs duties and import quotas within the union.

According to some, enough is enough, or enough for the time being. According to others, the common or Single Market is not enough for an economic community. The argument is that, while a single market will enable the factors of production to move freely, it does little to affect the extent to which and the ways in which governments intervene to manage the economy of their countries. Their actions affect growth rates, employment levels and investment decisions in time and space. Moreover, since the opening of markets makes the separate economies more interdependent, the results of the economic management in one may spill over into the others, for good or for ill. Rather than leave these effects simply to the laws of the market to absorb, it is argued that the member states should, as a minimum, pursue compatible 'conjunctural' policies in the short term and, in time, should reach economic union. Economic union means the taking, by the responsible authority, of decisions which directly affect the citizen's welfare, and therefore implies sensitivity and a certain consensus regarding the aims to be pursued.

This leads some to the conclusion that economic union is not easily dissociable from the creation of a some kind of political union, in which the necessary consensus can be obtained. In turn, this view leads others to reject anything more than economic co-ordination, without superior authority, precisely because they see a path leading irreversibly to a centralized political entity, to which the former nation states would be subsidiary.

The nature of the debate

The twenty-year debate about economic integration has tended to be marked by two discussions. The first is oversimplified, but conveniently so, by being represented as one between 'economists', who believe that the way forward is to adopt policies which will reduce regional disparities in growth, inflation, employment and investment, and 'monetarists' who believe that the use of instruments which promote stability among the different currencies in use in the constituent parts of the union will, as a first stage, create the conditions for closer integration. When a sufficient point has been reached, a common currency and a banking apparatus for managing it internally and externally will be possible. Most 'monetarists' would accept that the price of exchange rate stability may be damage to some local economies as part of the process of adjustment.

This is the starting point of a second debate: what concurrent measures need to be taken to enable all to participate in the prototype of economic and monetary union? To some extent this debate mirrors another which is strictly independent of the monetary issue. It is a debate which arises with every enlargement. Geographically, the six new members are peripheral, and economically five of them (not Denmark) were below Community average performance. Part of the negotiations before or after enlargements has been about directing help towards them. In the UK and Irish cases the recognizable outcome was the Regional Development Fund. In the Greek case it was the Integrated Mediterranean Programmes. In the Iberian case it is the doctrine of 'cohesion', along with the strengthening of the (redistributive) structural funds and some measures which recognize the special vulnerability of Portugal.

The guidance given in the EEC Treaty on this complex of questions is thin. At the time, economies were growing, although not without problems, and governments preferred to keep their hands free – elections are partly won on parties' economic performances and promises. Member states are enjoined to regard short-term economic policies as a matter of common concern (article 103); to run their economies in pursuit of the three virtues of equilibrium in the balance of payments, full employment and low inflation (article 104); to co-ordinate their economic policies (article 105); to use their best endeavours to free capital movements (article 106); and to treat exchange rate policy as another matter of common concern (article 107).

The Commission initiative, 1969

In 1969 the Commission brought out the first substantial plan for concerted action, named after the Commissioner responsible, Raymond Barre (of France). The Barre plan called for the joint definition, by consultation, of medium-term strategies and for mutual financial help when a member state gets into trouble which might oblige it to jeopardize the continuing functioning of the common market. The Werner Report (whose author was the Luxembourg Prime Minister) of October 1970 was more monetarist than the Barre plan. It looked forward to fixed and unchangeable parities among national currencies, at which stage a single currency could (not must) be introduced. In this circumstance there would need to be a single decision-making centre for economic management and central banks acting in accordance with Community policy.

By the end of the 1960s there were signs of a phase change in world economic conditions. Cyclical crises were leaving behind them a rising level of built-in unemployment. Inflation was moving beyond 3 per cent, which had been regarded as a sign and stimulant of growth. Monetary instability hit the EEC countries with the devaluation of the French franc in August 1969 and the revaluation of the Deutschmark in October.[2] In the days of fixed positions against the US dollar, devaluations and revaluations, and the wave of rumour preceding them, were truly awesome events. At their meeting in The Hague in 1969 the six heads of state or government decided that 'a plan by stages should be drawn up with a view to the creation of an economic and monetary union'.[3]

The case for a stabilization plan was reinforced in the summer of 1971 when the convertibility of the dollar was formally suspended.

With the eclipse of the post-war Bretton Woods agreement, which had fixed durable parities, a new arrangement was concluded in Washington at the Smithsonian Institute to fix central rates with allowable margins of fluctuation ('the tunnel'). The Council of the European Communities asked central banks to remain within narrower bands ('the snake'). The pound sterling and the Scandinavian crowns also joined, but by 1977 only the countries of the so-called DM zone had held on – the mark, the Dutch guilder, the Belgo-Luxembourg franc and the Danish krone. The others could not hold a fixed rate under the pressure of inflation at different rates, speculation against them and the presumed benefit of floating freely, which on at least one theory is itself a corrective.

The launching of EMS

At the beginning of 1977 Roy Jenkins, himself a former finance minister, became president of the Commission. In May 1977 the Committee which the previous Commission had appointed under Sir Donald MacDougall published its report, *The Role of Public Finance in European Integration*. The report was not a formula for monetary union, but it examined the role of public finance in a state, in a community and in a federation. After careful preparation and on the 300th day of his office, 27 October 1977, Jenkins, speaking at the European University Institute of Florence, called for economic and monetary union to be put back at the top of the Community agenda.

The result was not entirely the one which he had sought. The German Chancellor, Helmut Schmidt, and the French President, Valéry Giscard d'Estaing, both former finance ministers and on close terms with each other, set out to devise a system for monetary stability. The technical work was entrusted to a German, a French and a British Treasury official, but the United Kingdom was unable to make the necessary pre-commitments and the work became Franco-German. A first public showing occurred at the European Council meeting in Copenhagen in April 1978, more substance was given at the meeting in Bremen on 7 July 1978, and the system was established at Brussels on 5 December 1978 with a starting date of 1 January 1979. This date could not be kept because of tense negotiations on agricultural prices – kept going by France into the New Year – which would be reduced in national currencies if the new accounting basis of the European Monetary System (EMS), the ecu, were to be applied directly to them – but on 13 March 1979 the EMS began. In the preparatory discussions attention had been given to the 'concurrent measures' necessary to cushion the less prosperous countries against possible adverse effects. The three countries that contended that they needed this facility were the United Kingdom, Ireland and Italy. But Britain decided that it would not participate, and Ireland and Italy received compensatory finance in the form of soft loans and other inducements.

The nature of EMS and ERM

The EMS exchange rate mechanism is a hybrid – not entirely Community, not entirely outside it. It was created by a resolution of the European Council followed by a decision of the Council and an agreement between the participating central banks. It consists only of those member states that elect to join it. (All but Greece did: the United Kingdom joined late, and with Italy withdrew in September 1992.) But all member states have the option to join; non-member states, including those who were in the 'snake', that is, the narrower band of exchange rate fluctuation allowed within the wider allowable margins of fluctuation (the tunnel) agreed in the early 1970s, do not. The EMS itself is not based on treaty articles. Although Jenkins broke the ice, the system was not the one formally proposed by the Commission under article 235 of the EEC Treaty.

The EMS exchange rate mechanism is in two parts. One is a parity grid in which each currency has a parity with every other. This parity may fluctuate by 2.25 per cent (or for some 6 per cent). If it goes further, members must intervene. In a bilateral system two countries will exhaust their margins at the same time. The intervention obligation falls on both – the one going strong (which should sell its currency) and the one going weak (which should buy its currency). The second mechanism is a divergence indicator. It uses the ecu, which is composed of a basket of currencies of all member states weighted for their economic importance. When a currency deviates from the ecu by 75 per cent of the spread of divergence (that is, its relationship to the ecu is no longer what its current weighting would make it, and the change in their relationship is greater than 75 per cent of the currency's possible fluctuation under the bilateral parity grid) the country is required to take appropriate steps. These can, if necessary, include fixing a new parity grid and a new weighting of the ecu.[4] To help countries intervene in the exchange markets there is a very short-term credit facility, a short-term support facility and medium-term financial assistance.

Between its inauguration in 1980 and 1987 the ERM worked as flexibly as had been intended. There were frequent changes in the parity grid as divergent economic performance among the member states came out as the inability to hold the going rate. After 1987, the new upbeat era of the third enlargement, the drive for the Single Market and the new sense of purpose encapsulated in the Single European Act, there were no parity changes and the ERM took on the appearance of a fixed parity grid. Italy moved from the wide fluctuation band to the narrow band (2.25 per cent) and Spain joined the ERM in 1989.

Two states belonged to the EMS without belonging to the ERM – Greece and the United Kingdom.[5] The United Kingdom preferred its own monetary policy, which did not use the exchange rate as a control. This was the official and declared position. It has emerged from the political memoirs that followed the 1990 crisis that, from 1985, influential ministers in the British government were in favour of sterling joining the ERM.[6] At the June 1989 meeting of the European Council in Madrid, the British Prime Minister, allegedly under threats of resignations, confirmed that Britain would join the ERM when specific conditions were satisfied: capital movements had been liberalized and the Single Market had been completed and could be seen to be working. These conditions were rarely referred to subsequently.[7]

In October 1990, on the eve of the Conservative Party conference, the British government announced that sterling would enter the ERM at a parity of DM 2.95. Although the rates are officially expressed in ecus, the Deutschmark had in practice become the anchor of the mechanism. Portugal joined in April 1992, like Spain, during its period as Council Presidency.

Economic and Monetary Union?

In the Single European Act there is glancing reference to Economic and Monetary Union along with a reminder that if it needed new institutions, they could only be created through treaty amendment after an inter-governmental conference (Title II, chapter 1).

At its meeting in Hanover in June 1988, the European Council:

- recalled that in the Single European Act the member states had confirmed the objectives of the progressive realizations of economic and monetary union;
- entrusted to a committee, chaired by the President of the Commission, the task of studying and proposing concrete stages leading towards this union;
- decided to examine the means of achieving this union at its meeting in Madrid in June 1989.

For an understanding of the debate which these decisions opened it is important to have in mind that the European Council was not asking Jacques Delors and his colleagues on the Committee, who included the governors of the central banks, what they thought about economic and monetary union and whether it was realizable. They were unambiguously asked to propose 'concrete stages leading towards Union'.

The Committee reported in April 1989. It notes that arrangements already exist, in the form of ongoing Council–Commission activity, to secure greater economic co-ordination and convergence. This chapter does not therefore require new institutions, but does need a considerable strengthening of rules – for example, guidance and later legally binding requirements relating to the size of annual national budget deficits and their financing.

On the monetary side the *Report on Economic and Monetary Union* is concerned both with policy formulation and with institutional reform. It stresses that a greater convergence of economic performance is needed and that there must be parallel advancement in economic and in monetary integration, in order to avoid imbalances which could cause economic strains and loss of political support for developing the Community further. While acknowledging that economic and monetary union implies more than the Single Market programme, it also notes that the full liberalization of capital movements – an essential ingredient of that programme – and the integration of financial markets create a situation in which the co-ordination of monetary policy would have to be strengthened in any case.

Much of the report is devoted to the steps to be taken to create and operate a proposed 'European System of Central Banks' (ESCB). In this new Community body, centralized and collective decisions would be taken on the supply of money and credit as well as on other

Exhibit 8.2 *Stages on the way to economic and monetary union*

1969:   The Community Summit in The Hague commissions a report on the possibilities of developing the Community into an economic and monetary union.

1971:   The Community concludes a phased plan for the creation of an economic and monetary union within ten years. The project fails mainly because of the collapse of the dollar-based world monetary system, which results in several member states allowing the exchange rates of their currencies to float.

1972:   The setting-up of the 'currency snake'; a first attempt to make the exchange rates of participating countries stable in relation to one another and flexible in relation to the dollar. The number of member states that participate and then withdraw varies over time.

March 1979:   The European Monetary System (EMS), on which agreement was reached in late 1978, comes into force; the participating member states, eight at first, are required to maintain their exchange rates within certain fluctuation margins. Creation of the ecu.

July 1987:   The Single European Act, which reforms the EEC Treaty, comes into force. Its objective is the completion of the frontier-free internal market by the end of 1992.

June 1988:   The Hanover European Council appoints a committee of experts (chaired by Jacques Delors) to examine ways and means of completing economic and monetary union.

June 1989:   The Madrid European Council approves the Delors Report. The heads of state or government decide to begin the first stage of EMU on 1 July 1990 and to prepare for an inter-governmental conference on economic and monetary union.

June 1989:   The peseta enters the European Monetary System.

July 1990:   First stage of economic and monetary union involving the removal of most of the remaining restrictions on capital movements, increased co-ordination of individual economic policies and more intensive co-operation between central banks.

October 1990:   Sterling enters the European Monetary System.

December 1991:   The European Council agrees the Treaty on European Union in Maastricht: completion of economic and monetary union and introduction of the single European currency, the ecu, by 1999 at the latest.

April 1992:   The escudo enters the European Monetary System.

Exhibit 8.3 *Economic conditions for participation in the final stage of economic and monetary union (convergence criteria)*

Price stability: A member state must be able to demonstrate sustainable price stability. The average rate of inflation, observed over a period of one year before the examination for the final stage (not until 1996), must not exceed by more than 1½ percentage points that of the three best performing member states in terms of price stability.

Public Finances: At the time of the examination the Council should not detect any excessive deficit on the part of the member state. The deficit is deemed to be excessive if the budget deficit is more than 3 per cent of gross domestic product or if total government debt exceeds 60 per cent of gross domestic product.

Exchange rates: A member state must have respected the normal fluctuation margins (currently 2.25 per cent) provided for by the exchange rate mechanism of the European Monetary System (EMS) without severe tensions for at least two years before the examination. During that same period the member state must not have devalued its currency against any other member's currency.

Interest rates: Observed over a period of one year before the examination the average nominal long-term interest rate may not exceed by more than 2 percentage points that of the three member states that have the best results in terms of price stability.

instruments of monetary policy, including exchange rates. These decisions would be consistent with and would articulate in the monetary sphere the economic policy of Community authorities. On top of the convertibility of Community currencies which already exists, and the capital liberalization which is to come in the single market, there would be in the monetary union the elimination of margins of fluctuation among member states' currencies and the irrevocable locking of exchange rate parities. The ESCB should, according to the report, be independent of instructions from national governments and Community authorities (including the European Council). It would submit an annual report to the European Council and European Parliament. Although the report does not say so, it is to be assumed that the controlling authorities of the ESCB would seek to have and hold the support and confidence of these two bodies and would listen to what they might have to say to them.

The British government, while upholding co-operation in economic and monetary policy (part of the title of article 102(a) of the EEC Treaty, as amended by the Single European Act – the rest of the title placed in brackets, is 'Economic and Monetary Union'), regarded the Delors Report as unrealistic. The Conservative Party manifesto for the 1989 European elections said:

> We support practical steps of this kind to promote closer economic and monetary co-operation. On the other hand, as the recent report of the Delors Committee makes clear, full economic and monetary union would involve a fundamental transfer of sovereignty. It would require new European institutions to administer a common currency and decide interest rates, and a considerable degree of central control over budgetary policy. The report, if taken as a whole, implies nothing less than the creation of a federal Europe. Such ideas go way beyond what is realistic or desirable in the foreseeable future. Indeed to think in these terms is not only unrealistic but damaging, for it distracts political attention and energy from the Community's central task – completing the single market by 1992.[8]

In the run-up to the Madrid meeting of the European Council it appeared that a large majority of the member states were in favour of following the Delors Report and that some insisted on what was known as 'automaticity': all stages in the Delors Report hang together and the decision to begin implementation implied and required a continuous process and progress to the end result. The discussion of EMU effectively monopolized the Madrid meeting. The outcome was a compromise, such that all could consider that they had secured their aims. It was agreed that the 'first stage' should begin on 1 July 1990, and that preparatory work should be carried out for an inter-governmental conference to lay down the subsequent stages. This is the Inter-governmental Conferences envisaged by article 236 of the EEC Treaty to amend the treaty. A decision to convene an inter-governmental conference can be taken by simple majority (seven member states voting for), but the agreement of all member states is necessary for the conference to have a successful outcome.

Preparatory work began under the French presidency – strong advocates of economic and monetary union – in July 1989 and their Italian successors, notably at a meeting of the European Council in Rome in October 1990, which drew up a comprehensive annotated agenda for the conference. Emerging from the conference room, the British Prime Minister announced that her colleagues were living in cloud cuckoo land. Her inveterate and mounting opposition to any moves towards monetary union contributed to her fall a few weeks later.

The Treaty on European Union, signed at Maastricht on 7 February 1992, creates an economic and monetary union. The United Kingdom exempted itself from any commitment to participate in the final stage. A decision on whether to participate would be taken by the United Kingdom parliament.

The crises of 1992

Among the clouds which began to gather over the Treaty on European Union after the negative result of the Danish referendum on 2 June 1992 was the inability of the ERM to stand up to the strain which was put on it in September. Several of the currencies began to lose their exchange value against the DM and currency dealers throughout the world began to believe that devaluations were in the air, and to deal accordingly by getting out of the losing currencies (including the dollar, weakened by the vagaries of the presidential election campaign and poor economic statistics) and into the stronger, especially the DM. Events moved very fast in the fortnight preceding the French referendum on 20 September 1992. On 5 September, the Economic and Finance Council (ECO/FIN) meeting informally in Bath issued a formal statement that there would be no realignment. On 13 September, the lira was devalued. It was also announced that German interest rates, which were boosting the DM, would be reduced, but the announcement on 14 September was of the smallest possible cut, of 0.25 per cent. On 16 September, 'Black Wednesday', the British interest rate was briefly pushed up to 15 per cent, but this failed to halt the slide of sterling and in the evening Britain and Italy withdrew from the ERM. The peseta was also devalued, but stayed in. The United Kingdom, as presidency, proposed the total suspension of the ERM, but this was not accepted. With the sterling rate no longer being defended by the Bank of England or by the Bundesbank in Frankfurt, the pound continued to fall. After the narrow vote in favour of the Treaty in the French referendum the franc came under selling pressure, but with heavy intervention and help from the Bundesbank, held out. Thus eight months from the signing of the Treaty, monetary co-operation within the EC was in disarray, further troubled by a quarrel which broke out between the United Kingdom and Germany over responsibility for the situation. The British Prime Minister, Mr John Major, said that there would be no early return of sterling to the ERM and that it would have to be a different ERM that it returned to, free of the 'fault-lines' which he had detected in it.

Rumours began to circulate and to be denied that the states whose currencies were already tied to the DM, the Dutch guilder, the Belgo-Lux franc and possibly the French franc perhaps to be joined by the Swiss franc and the Austrian schilling, would come together in a monetary union independently of the timetable and institutional structure of the EMU in the Treaty on European Union.

Two sets of doubts enshrouded the EC Economic and Monetary Union. The first was whether the treaty which gives birth to it would be ratified, and when. The second was the recognition that its timetable for EMU and the single currency by the end of the decade was over-ambitious. The events in the summer of 1993 confirmed these second apprehensions.

9 Other Policies

It is arguable that most aspects of the policies discussed in Chapters Seven and Eight have been crucial to the success and failure of the economic dimension of the Community overall, but equally there are a number of other policies that bear on those already discussed, and some of which are particularly important in terms of their impact on the Community's population. This chapter focuses on the most significant of those policies.

THE EUROPEAN INVESTMENT BANK

The European Investment Bank (EIB) is not in law an institution of the Community, but is one of its arms. The 1957 EEC Treaty set up the EIB and charged it with the task of contributing to the balanced development of the Community. This task took on added significance with the adoption in the Single European Act 1987 of the principle of economic and social cohesion, which consolidated the concept of resources flowing towards the regions of the Community which lack indigenous wealth. Regional development has been the EIB's prime concern but not its only one. Between 1987 and 1991 it lent 31.8 billion ecus for regional development, but also to other areas as shown:

1987–91: EIB lending other than regional development (billion ecus)	
Community infrastructure	12.0
Industrial competitiveness	13.9
Environment	8.3
Energy	9.7

A second task of the EIB is to contribute to the financing of capital development projects in the ACP states (signatories of the Lomé Conventions), Mediterranean countries and in Eastern and Central Europe.

1991: EIB financing provided outside the Community (million ecus)	
Central and Eastern Europe	285.0
Mediterranean	241.5
Africa	315.6
Caribbean	62.1
Pacific	11.4

The EIB is non-profit-making and its AAA rating (i.e., the highest possible credit worthiness rating) enables it to borrow on capital markets on terms which will be favourable to its own borrowers. From 1989 to 1991 it borrowed 33.6 billion ecus, mainly in public bond issues.

The EIB's headquarters are in Luxembourg, which is the seat of Community bodies concerned with finance and with the law. Its members are the member states of the EC. Its Board of Governors consists of one minister from each member state. Its Board of Directors consists of 22 directors and 12 alternates, senior officials from member states' economic and finance ministries and from the Commission. Its management Committee consists of the President (from 1993 a Briton) and six Vice-Presidents, appointed by the member states.

THE EUROPEAN BANK FOR RECONSTRUCTION AND DEVELOPMENT

The European Bank for Reconstruction and Development (EBRD) was proposed by President Mitterrand when France held the presidency of the Council in 1989. The negotiations for its establishment were concluded in April 1990. London was selected as the Bank's seat.

The purpose of the EBRD is to foster the transition towards open market-oriented economies and to promote private entrepreneurial initiative in the Central and Eastern European states committed to and practising the principles of multi-party democracy, pluralism and market economies (article 1 of the agreement establishing the EBRD). Although it was the brainchild of the EC, and its first chairman was French, membership goes much wider. It includes the prospective beneficiaries (including the newly independent states of the former Soviet Union, which still existed when the Bank opened its doors), other European countries, among which is numbered Israel, not normally regarded as being in Europe, and several non-European countries, including Japan and the Republic of Korea, as well as the United States. Its members are its shareholders, who subscribed capital amounting initially to 10 billion ecus. The EBRD's operations complement aid programmes instituted by the countries of the EC and of the OECD in favour of the new democracies. In early 1993 the EBRD ran into difficulties with complaints that it had spent too much on its London headquarters and not enough on fulfilling its mandate.

INDUSTRY

The Community does not proclaim an industrial policy. If any part of it did so, a number of member states might declare that they do not believe in such things. However, the Common Commercial Policy, the rules of competition, the research and technological development programmes, the free circulation of goods in the single market, the energy objectives, the co-ordination of economic policy, the social policy, the operation of the European Investment Bank – all have a bearing on conditions in Community industry.

Until the Research and Development Programme took off, Community concern with industry tended to be with those where the workforce and/or production were in decline, such as shipbuilding, steel and textiles. In such industries there was planning for contraction, on the basis of equality of misery, and arrangements for state aid to be authorized, if member states wanted to give it, under defined conditions and as part of the phasing-out operation. In the case of steel, the Community operated a crisis plan with price fixing (to prevent undercutting), production quotas and agreements with third counties under which they restricted their exports to the Community. The price fixing and quotas were phased out by 1988.

Outside the 'sunset' industries, Community enterprises are helped by the widening of their home market, by harmonized technical standards which afford longer production runs, by the encouragement and part-financing of research including pre-competitive co-operative , research, and by the opening up of public purchasing – where typically 90 per cent of purchases are from national suppliers. Industrial enterprise is encouraged by deregulation. Special attention is given to small and medium-sized firms. Commission proposals are accompanied by a 'fiche', which assesses the impact that the proposal may have on them. Some Community industries have benefited from anti-dumping duties imposed on damaging imports, especially of electronic consumer goods from Japan and Korea. Textile and clothing firms in the Community, as elsewhere, are protected from disruptive competition from low-cost producers by quota restrictions maintained under the Multi-Fibre Agreement, which is a world-wide managed market, but up for review in the GATT Uruguay Round.

RESEARCH AND TECHNOLOGICAL DEVELOPMENT

The Euratom Treaty has eight articles devoted to research. The ECSC Treaty contains one reference to research. The original version of the EEC Treaty is silent on research but the 'catch-all' article 235 was used to get some programmes going. The Single European Act in 1987 added a Title on research and development (VI, article 130 (f)–(q)) and budgetary effect was given to it. This underpins the drive towards the single market (by harmonizing product standards and test methods), encourages information exchange and industrial co-operation, flags priorities and reduces overlap.

Under Euratom the Community set up a Joint Research Centre (JRC) at Ispra on Lake Maggiore in Italy. By the early 1970s the member states concluded that this kind of collective research – apart from work on reactor safety – was no longer required and the JRC diversified its activities. Meanwhile, on Commission proposals, the Council began to agree to research programmes, especially in information technology. The European Strategic Programme for Research and Development in Information Technology (ESPRIT) was an early result in 1984. ESPRIT is a series of projects for which the Community gives funding provided there are participants from at least two member states. ESPRIT became a model for the administration of programmes in other fields. Fusion research, on which Britain had been engaged since the 1950s, became a Community concern in 1977 when the Joint European Torus (JET) project was inaugurated at Culham (currently the only Community body physically situated in the United Kingdom).

Encouraged by the success of the ESPRIT, including the response given to it by the information technology industry, the Commission, which for some ten years had been calling for a Community R & D policy and budget, urged on the Council a new approach. It noted that total R & D spending in the member states was comparable to levels in the United States and Japan, that the member states were rich in Nobel Prize laureates, but that the Community was falling behind in the production of high technology goods, whereas Japan (particularly) was at the forefront and was capturing markets – including those in the member states. It proposed a major increase in the resources to be put into R & D at Community level, the actual work to be done 'out-house' by supporting projects put up by combinations of firms and research laboratories in which more than one member state would be represented. The driving force was the phenomenally active Industry Commissioner of the day, Viscount Davignon, from Belgium. He discussed and reshaped his ideas in a series of discussions with the 'Round Table', captains of industry who might have opposed an interventionist industry strategy, but welcomed enhanced support for research. Their support was relayed back to their home governments and helped to break down the resistance of those responsible for national scientific policy to the transfer of spending to the Community.[1]

The necessary legislative base for the Community to act was set out in the Single European Act, and the Community adopted the first 'framework programme' in 1987.

The procedure was laid down in article 130 Q of the Single European Act. It involved simple consultation of the European Parliament and unanimity in the Council. Such unanimity is unusual for on-going work and does not correspond to the budgetary rules – qualified majority voting – which would be necessary to authorize R & D spending. The specific programmes, on the other hand, were to be adopted by qualified majority, and using the co-operation procedure, with two readings in the Council and in the Parliament. Agreement was facilitated by making specific provision for R & D in the first 'Financial Perspectives' (see pp. 104–5 above).

Within a few years the co-operation between the Council and the Parliament began to wear thin. The Parliament wanted steady growth; the Council noted that some parts of the programme were being underspent and it took this as evidence that industrial support for them was weak. It would therefore have preferred to cancel some of the funding and save the money. The Parliament wanted the amounts maintained. At times the Parliament considered that the Commission was not robust enough in the face of Council opposition to some of its demands.

The Treaty on European Union addresses these inter-institutional difficulties. It changes (article 130 i 1) the procedure for the adoption of the framework programme by subjecting it to the co-decision procedure, giving Parliament a final veto power (see pp. 81–5 above). But it makes a twist in the procedure: the Council must act unanimously throughout (as it did under Single European Act provisions – but in all other cases of the co-decision procedure the Council acts by qualified majority).

The change made in the rules for specific programmes is even more sweeping. Under the Single European Act, they were adopted under the two-readings co-operation procedure. Under the Treaty on European Union (article 130 i 4) the Council adopts them by qualified majority after consulting the European Parliament – no co-operation, no co-decision. This is an unusual – by Treaty on European Union standards – retrocession of power to the Council.

A separate development which now complements the Community's R & D programme also pre-dates it. When President Reagan announced that the US government had launched the Strategic Defence Initiative (SDI), which would push military communications and space technology into new limits of performance, it was realized, especially in France, that SDI could have spin-offs for American industry. The European response was Eureka, which began in 1985. Eureka is not the property of the EC. Other Western European countries belong to it. It has no funds apart from what it needs to run itself. The Commission provides a secretariat. Eureka projects arise from the coming together of firms and research bodies, which work out their ideas with Eureka assistance. The projects are financed either by the firms themselves, or by national governments. Since enterprises in the member states are predominant in Eureka, the Community often refers to the arrangements as belonging generically to it.

ENERGY

Although the ECSC Treaty and the Euratom Treaty have a direct concern with two major energy sources, energy policy as a subject is not mentioned in the EEC Treaty or in the Single Act. The Council's annual reviews of its activities refer modestly to the 'Development of a Community Energy Policy'. The quadrupling of oil prices in 1973 and the subsequent tripling in 1979 certainly concentrated the Community's mind, and mention is made of energy problems regularly in the published conclusions of European Councils. But these preoccupations do not seem to have inspired the Community to equip itself with a full-dress energy policy.

Generally speaking, meetings of the Council (Energy) have received communications, rather than legislative proposals, from the Commission. Members have exchanged views and agreed on objectives, the latest of which run to 1995. They are (Council resolution of 16 September 1986; *Official Journal*, C24, 25 September 1986):

- the development of Community energy resources in satisfactory economic conditions;
- the diversification of the Community's outside sources of energy supply;
- flexibility for energy systems;
- effective crisis management measures, especially for crude oil;
- a vigorous policy of energy conservation and rational use;
- diversification among the different forms of energy.

Among the reasons for the adoption of relatively open positions and of aims rather than measures is the different degree of dependence on energy imports in the member states, another reason may be the need for flexibility in the face of the fluctuation of the energy market, where shortages are succeeded by surpluses and where prices gyrate. A third reason may be the wish of member states to keep the management of their own energy policies, including the external relations aspects, in their own hands. (One example of this in 1975 was the insistence of the United Kingdom in participating in its own name at the International Energy Conference, although the Community was also to be represented as such.)

In 1985 the Council adopted a regulation (EEC No. 3640/85;

Official Journal, L350, 27 December 1985) on the provision of financial support for demonstration projects – 'a mainstay of the Community's energy strategy'.[2] These covered the development of alternative energy sources, energy saving and the liquefaction and gasification of solid fuels. The experiences gained from these projects are analyzed and disseminated through the Community's 'information market' (an entity which used to be the title of one of the Commission's Directorates General and has a budget of 36 million ecus over two years).

The Dutch presidency of 1991 launched the idea of a 'European Energy Charter' by virtue of which the technological capabilities of the West could be harnessed to the hydrocarbon resources of the former Soviet Union and Eastern Europe. The West would gain a new source of supply; the other side would earn hard currency. The Charter itself, concluded at the end of 1991 – and the first document to be signed by the newly independent states of the former Soviet Union – was seen as paving the way for more specific commitments, for which work continued in a conference presided over by a former Dutch permanent representive to the EC and directed by an official of the Energy Directorate of the Commission. Despite its title, the United States and Japan are signatories and participate in the follow-up.

SOCIAL POLICY

In its original text the EEC Treaty is cautious about anything resembling a common or Community social policy. In the negotiation phase there had been alarm and counter-alarm: alarm that prospective members whose labour costs included relatively low social security contributions might have a competitive edge, and counter-alarm that they might have to harmonize their labour costs upwards to the detriment of their competitiveness.

The original Title III 'Social Policy' bears the hallmark of compromises. A social policy is said to exist, but it is squarely in the hands of the member states. The Council is mentioned only once (article 121) and then only on procedure. Article 117, the scene-setting provision, presupposed that social objectives would ensue directly from the dynamism of the common market, as well as from an in-built market force favouring harmonization (that is, labour would move to where it would be best off).

Equal pay, demanded by article 119, became a Community canon despite hesitation and backsliding. Migrant workers (from other member states) were covered by social security provisions. The Social Fund, named in the treaty, was set up; successive revisions of its objectives took it beyond 'rendering the employment of workers easier and increasing their geographical and occupational mobility' and into measures acting against the rising tide of unemployment and for the benefit of particular groups such as young people, the handicapped, the long-term unemployed and women. Safety and health at the workplace – which is both a kind of human right and a factor affecting competition – also commanded attention and gave rise to directives concerning exposure to or working with harmful substances or energy sources.

A more controversial part of a social development programme concerns intervention in support of workers' rights, which became the rebalancing of power between workers and employers and the rethinking of state (or Community) responsibilities. Those who have reservations about the value or justification of this type of intervention dismiss it as 'social engineering'. One of the more notable endeavours of the late 1970s was the Vredeling draft directive, a Commission proposal which aimed at giving workpeople explicit and defined rights to be consulted in the affairs of complex companies,[3] typically multinationals with irons in fires in several member states. These proposals, and others (like the draft fifth company law directive) concerning employee representation on boards, were opposed particularly but not exclusively by Britain, which contended that such matters were not appropriate for top-down legislation but belonged to negotiations within industries or firms.

The Single European Act was greeted as adding a caring, social dimension to the purely entrepreneurial aspects of the single market. The argument was that 'ordinary people' needed to be given a stake in the Single Market and that the adaptations which it would force on firms could damage employment in some areas while favouring growth and welfare generally. While the 'social dimension' became a major concern of some member states, others viewed it as the condemned 'social engineering'. The Commission's first collected body of suggestions (Marin Memorandum, September 1988) were cautious – excessively so for some but nevertheless 'the writing on the wall' for others. The Commission, in *The Social Policy: Looking*

Ahead to 1992 (OOP, 1988), argued that 'Contractual policy must remain the basis of the European social model'.

In December 1989 three member states having socialist governments had held the presidency of the Council for 18 months. In that month, at the conclusion of the French presidency, the majority of member states adopted the Social Charter, the United Kingdom opposing and Denmark reportedly lukewarm.

In these two states relations between employers and their workplace were a matter for negotiation between them. Health and safety at work were everywhere for government regulation, but there was disagreement among the member states as to priorities and as to how far the Community should be involved. The European Parliament was a strong partisan, through its majority, of 'Social Europe', presented as a balance to the 'Business Europe' which was the theme of much other work, including the Single Market programme (see above pp. 144–7). The Commissioner responsible for social policy, Mrs Papandreou, who had been President of the Social Affairs Council when she was a minister in the Pasok government in Greece, described her philosophy as 'Higher standards, whether they have to do with training, health and safety,

Exhibit 9.1 *The Social Charter*

The Charter of the fundamental social rights of workers, adopted in December 1989, sets out twelve basic principles:

1. The right to work in the EC country of one's choice.
2. The right to a fair wage.
3. The right to improved living and working conditions.
4. The right to social protection under prevailing national systems.
5. The right to freedom of association and collective bargaining.
6. The right to vocational training.
7. The right of men and women to equal treatment.
8. The right of workers to information, consultation and participation.
9. The right to health protection and safety at work.
10. The protection of children and adolescents.
11. The guarantee of minimum living standards for the elderly.
12. Improved social and professional integration for the disabled.

working conditions or workers' rights, pay off. It is not only a question of solidarity and social justice. It is also a question of common sense from an economic point of view.' The Conservative government of Mrs Thatcher saw the proposals as socialist reconstruction, which they prided themselves on having reined back at home. The party and its leadership had been upset by a speech which M. Delors had delivered at a TUC conference in 1988 in which he forecast that 80 per cent of social and economic legislation in the member states would be made in Brussels.

In the negotiations leading to the Treaty on European Union in 1991 there was strong support for the amplification of social policy. When the United Kingdom continued to dissent, an innovative solution was found, attributed to the then President of the European Council, Mr Lubbers of the Netherlands. This took the form of an agreement among eleven member states, excluding the United Kingdom, picking up the language and aims of the Social Charter, renamed for the purpose 'Social Chapter' and converting them into treaty terms. The agreement foresees decision-making procedures which are those of the Community, and speaks of what the institutions of the Community will do. But the decisions will not be those of the Council and they will not apply in the United Kingdom. These differences of view between the United Kingdom and its partners continued into early 1993, when the United Kingdom stood out against the proposed Working Time Directive, which sought to introduce in some work environments a maximum 48 hours working week. The United Kingdom objected on several grounds, including the argument that it would cripple Europe's competitiveness.

Social affairs created their own organs. They are discussed in a specialized council, which meets two or three times a year. A Standing Committee on Employment brings together employees' and employers' representatives, representatives of publicly owned enterprises, ministers of employment (not meeting as the Council) and the Commission. They discuss measures to stimulate investment and employment, the impact on the labour force of new technologies, training schemes, etc. The Commission, acting on article 118 (b), has promoted discussions between the two sides of industry (in the language of Brussels 'the social partners') in a series of meetings which it has convened known as the 'Val Duchesse dialogue'.

REGIONAL POLICY

The Communities' regional policy shows concern for those of its regions that are economically backward, especially the peripheral areas, and for those that are in industrial decline. With the aim of avoiding competitive subsidization it defines the intensity of regional aid which national governments can offer, and it provides grant aid under the Regional Development Fund to help to correct regional disparities. Regional Fund aid may be for financing productive enterprises (including tourist assets) or it may be for infrastructure such as road-building. Projects are put forward by their sponsors with support from the competent national authority and are selected by the Commission according to need.

Exhibit 9.2 *Objectives 1 and 5b (1989–93)*

- **Objective 1** – the promotion of structural adjustment in regions whose development is lagging behind. Expenditure under this heading is concentrated on particular member states or regions identified on the basis of socio-economic criteria; the areas comprise the whole of Portugal, Greece, Ireland, much of Spain, southern Italy, Corsica and the French overseas departments and Northern Ireland. Many of these regions, which cover 38 per cent of Community territory and 21.2 per cent of the population, are primarily rural in character. At the end of 1989, the Community agreed development plans with financial commitments, so-called Community support frameworks, for Objective 1 regions. The funding total amounts to ecu 36.2 billion for the period 1989–93.
- **Objective 5b** – promoting the development of rural areas. These areas tend to be smaller in size and have been selected according to specific criteria relating to the share of agricultural employment and income in regional output, low level of income, levels of population density, the degree of remoteness, environmental pressures, etc. In order to concentrate resources on the areas most in need, a total of 57 regions covering a further 17.3 per cent of the Community's area and 5.1 per cent of its population have been selected for support under this heading. Funding agreed in 1990, to cover the period 1989–93, amounts to a total of ecu 2.6 billion.

Table 9.1 *Structural Funds, 1992*

Indicative budgetary provisions by objective, million ecu	
Objective no. 1	10,693
Objective no. 2	1,718
Objective nos 3 and 4	1,887
Objective no. 5a	846
Objective no. 5b	1,071
Transitional measures	347
Five new *Länder*	1,246
Miscellaneous	201
Total	18,009

Source: Commission

In 1988 it was agreed to double over five years the money available for regional assistance and to concentrate the bulk of the funds on 'Objective 1' regions, where regional GDP is less than 75 per cent of the Community average. Apart from increasing the budget, the effectiveness of the assistance was enhanced by co-ordinating the use of the Structural Funds – European Regional Development Fund, European Social Fund and the Guidance section of the European Agricultural Guarantee and Guidance Fund (usually known by the French acronym, FEOGA). Northern Ireland until 1993 was the only Objective 1 region in the United Kingdom, but in 1993 that status was also granted to Merseyside and Highlands and Islands.[4]

ENVIRONMENT POLICY

It has been said that the environment was discovered and the environmentalist born about 1965.[5] The EEC Treaty does not say a word about the environment or about a policy for it. When, however, concern about the damage being done to the environment became a political preoccupation in Europe as elsewhere, and since environmental problems straddle frontiers, the EEC became involved. In 1973 it adopted the first Action Programme on the Environment, followed by programmes in 1977, 1983 and 1987, running up to 1992.[6] These programmes took the form of Council resolutions, which are not legally binding and are regarded as indicative rather than as implying that everything mentioned in them will actually happen.

The constitutional difficulty about the environment policy is that the member states and the Community continue to exercise competence concurrently. One side-effect of this – the main effect was protracted argument about who can do what – was that ultimate agreements on environmental measures were minimal standards which individual member sates could surpass, thereby damaging the intended unity of the policy and of the singleness of the market. A practical difficulty is the different perception of the weight to be given to environmental protection and improvement as opposed to other factors such as cost, industrial investment, job creation, economic growth, and central and local government spending.

The first series of Community environmental measures concerned the purity of water intended for different uses – drinking, bathing, supporting fish-life, etc.

Atmospheric pollution was not taken up until much later, from 1980. There was growing public concern in northern Europe over the destruction of forests and the damage inflicted on the environment and on wildlife by acid rain. There were also public health anxieties – for example, from lead in petrol – although mention of public health tended to excite additional controversy over the division of competence between the Community and its member states, some of which insisted that there was no Community competence. Measures discussed or adopted included the limitation of (especially sulphurous) emissions from large power stations and heat-raising plants; car exhausts; and the inert gases (CFCs) used in aerosols and other applications and found to be attacking the ozone layer. Concern began to be felt about the 'global climate' change and interconnections between phenomena like rising temperature and increased concentrations of carbon dioxide in the atmosphere ('greenhouse effect').

Other environmental measures concerned noise levels – of aircraft and motor vehicles. (Separately, and not strictly part of the environment programme, there were proposals and decisions concerning noise at the workplace and the protection of workers against hearing loss.) Another noise source with which the Community concerned itself was the noise of lawnmowers. This – like the mythical Euro-sausage of *Yes Minister*-fame – is often held up as showing the ridiculous side of European integration. Why bother with such trivia? In fact, the work was initiated by British industrial interests, which feared that they would be shut out of markets if national governments adopted excessively tight standards.[7]

The environmental action programmes also took up the dumping of waste and especially of dangerous waste. The discovery in 1983 that forty-one barrels of highly contaminated soil from the explosion of a chemical plant at Seveso in Italy were somewhere adrift without anyone seeming to know where or what was to happen to them came as a shock and give impetus to Community action.

The programmes also concerned themselves with wildlife. In 1976 the Commission broke new ground by proposing a directive on the protection of wild birds. The Council adopted it on 2 April 1979 (*Official Journal*, 103, 2 April 1979), although no member state respects it. The massacre of baby seals for their pelts provoked public outcry in 1982. In a rare reversal of roles, however, it was not the Commission but the European Parliament which took the initiative and virtually induced the Commission to propose a draft regulation banning imports of the skins of baby seals and objects made therefrom. The Council, which was worried about relations with Norway and Canada, adopted a directive in March 1983.

In the field of the prevention of pollution, rather than in repairing damage already done, the Community opened up relatively small budgetary provisions, largely for research, but it also held fast to its central principle: the polluter pays. It discussed for five years, and finally adopted in 1985, a directive instituting a Community system of Environment Impact Assessments (*Official Journal*, L175, 5 July 1985). This measure requires public authorities responsible for licensing certain kinds of development project to consider, in relation to a set of criteria, the impact which the project would make on the environment. The directive also provides for information to be made available to the public. This directive was regarded as a landmark in the Community approach to the conservation of the environment.

The absence of mention of the environment from the EEC Treaty meant that the measures adopted had as their legal basis the 'catchall' article 235. The Single European Act provides in the three articles (130(r)–(t) of Title VII) a new treaty basis for decisions about the environment. The principles are set out in article 130(r), para. 2:

> preventive action should be taken, that environmental damage should as a priority be rectified at source and that the polluter should pay.

Article 130(s) is the operational legal basis. It provides for the Council to take decisions unanimously after consulting the Parliament and the Economic and Social Committee. This is the classic consultation procedure, not involving the two phases of the new co-operation procedure. Article 130(s) also provides, however, that the Council can decide unanimously that there are some matters in which it can decide by qualified majority. Finally, article 130(t) harks back to the principle of environment measures being minima: it allows for member states to go beyond them, and it refrains from laying down any procedure which they must follow if they decide to do so. In addition to the new Title VII which is dedicated to the environment, the Single European Act offers, in article 100(a), another instrument for the protection of the environment.

But there is a reminder of the 'minimum standards' doctrine in article 100(a), para. 4. A member state, which presumably was outvoted when it argued that the proposed Community measure was not rigorous enough, can apply additional national provisions 'on grounds . . . relating to the protection of the environment' if:

- it notifies the Commission;
- the Commission confirms that the provisions are not a means of arbitrary discrimination or a disguised restriction on trade (for example, they do not protect a national producer against import competition).

No use has been made of article 100(a), para. 4.

IMMIGRATION CONTROL

The policies previously examined in this chapter are decided and executed in the Community mode. Immigration control, on the other hand, belongs to the competence of the member states. Common policies and actions are conducted in the framework of inter-governmental co-operation. It is due to become one of the pillars of European Union, consecrated by treaty, but still narrowly controlled by the member states, acting by consensus or not at all.

Immigration refers here not to the movement of a national of one member state to another, but to the arrival at the Community's external frontiers of a national of a third country. There was a period in which some of the member states positively encouraged immigrant workers to meet the needs of their labour markets, but by the mid-1970s several of them had begun to operate a restrictive immigration policy for precisely the opposite reason – to protect their own workpeople at a time of rising unemployment.

Immigrants can fall into five categories: (1) would-be workers, now generally not wanted unless they have special skills; (2) close family members, joining a resident immigrant, and subject to different requirements in the different member states; (3) students, welcomed if genuine; (4) asylum-seekers; (5) clandestines.

Asylum-seekers are those who claim to have a well-founded fear of persecution in their country of origin. Numerous ethnic conflicts around the world have swollen the numbers who seek asylum, in fear of their lives or livelihoods. But with restrictions imposed on traditional immigration, there are among the applicants for asylum many who are not political refugees but economic refugees. Faced with economic misery at home, they try to escape abroad, sometimes encouraged by the stories they hear of the well-being of relatives and compatriots who reached the European countries earlier. To improve their chances of acceptance, asylum-seekers, genuine and spurious, often apply simultaneously in several countries, which clogs an already over-stretched adjudication system, and become 'asylum-seekers in orbit' as their cases are examined. Examination can be complicated by applicants having no papers, either because in the conditions of departure they could not obtain them, or because they took the precaution of destroying them.

Clandestine immigrants seek to evade immigration controls and to disappear into the population of the host country, often among relatives and friends legally established there. Since they are on the wrong side of the law, they may be drawn into crime, for example, by being recruited as drugs couriers.

The main instruments used in national immigration control are visas, the exchange of information and agreed procedures for handling applications, for asylum, so that, if possible, one member state can examine the case and its decision holds for all. This is an ideal; in practice national law, although partly inspired by international convention, differs from one member state to another, and the harmonization of criteria and objectives is the next matter for the member states to address.

Similarly, member states have taken their own view of which foreigners should require visas, corresponding to their assessment of the threat from terrorism, drug traffickers and population pressure, combined with their political assessment of their historical, economic, cultural and linguistic links with the countries concerned. The visa question takes on a new dimension when passport checks are abolished at internal frontiers in the Community. In their informal co-operation the member states worked on a common visa list. In article 100c of the Treaty on European Union visa policy is transferred to the 'Community' mode of decision – proposal by the Commission, consultation of the European Parliament, decision by the Council, unanimously until 1995, by qualified majority from 1996.

Meanwhile, the member states continue to work on a convention on the controls to be maintained at external frontiers, which is a confidence-building measure looking to the time when member states will have abolished controls at their internal frontiers.

Five member states – France, Germany and the Benelux states – decided to act outside the Community framework to create a single control-free travel area, which they saw as a prototype for the Community at large. This is the Schengen Agreement, to which most of the other member states, but not the United Kingdom, Denmark and Ireland, now want to belong. Due to come into force in 1993, the Schengen Agreement's implementation has been postponed by France's new right-wing government, in a move reflecting the heightened sensitivity over freedom of movement at a time when concern over immigration was rife.

Immigration control belongs to the co-operation between Ministers of Justice and the Interior, which also extends to the fight against terrorism (in the so-called 'Trevi' Group) and drugs. A Declaration in the Treaty on European Union records agreement on the setting up of Europol, which is to exchange information and experience, in the first instance about drug traffic, but without police powers of its own (which is why the earlier name 'European FBI' was inappropriate.) The Europol drug unit began work in Strasbourg in 1992, its creation being independent of the ratification of the Treaty on European Union.

Exhibit 9.3 *Schengen: the beginnings of a frontier-free area*

Key dates

June 1984:   the Fontainebleau European Council agrees in principle to abolish customs and police formalities at the Community's internal borders.

July 1984:   the Saarbrücken Agreement between France and Germany marks a first step towards attaining this objective.

14 June 1985:   Belgium, France, Germany, Luxembourg and the Netherlands sign the Schengen Agreement, committing themselves to the gradual abolition of checks at shared borders and free passage for everyone crossing these borders, whether they are nationals of a signatory country, another Community country or a non-member country.

19 June 1990:   the same five states – Belgium, France, Germany, Luxembourg and the Netherlands – sign a further agreement spelling out conditions and guarantees for implementation of the free-movement arrangements. This Agreement, comprising 142 articles, amends national laws and is subject to ratification by national parliaments.

27 November 1990:   Italy joins the first five states.

18 November 1991:   Spain and Portugal join too.

The Schengen area

Free movement
Free movement applies to all, regardless of nationality.

   For Community nationals, the principle has largely been put into practice in the area covered by the Schengen Agreement.

   Arrangements for tourists, asylum-seekers and legal immigrants from non-member countries are included in the Agreement, the main aim of which is to standardize procedures throughout the Schengen area.

Law and order and security
Police will continue to operate on their own national territory, in ports and airports, but they will adopt a different approach. Closer co-operation will make controls at external borders more effective.

   There are common rules on measures to combat terrorism, smuggling and organized crime. The Agreement also makes provision for co-operation between courts, police forces and government departments. Once this new form of co-operation has been tried and tested in the Schengen area, it should be possible to move gradually to the complete abolition of internal borders.

Part Three: Further Reading

Alexandratos, N., *European Agriculture: policy issues and options to 2000*, London, Belhaven, 1990.

Aydalor, P. and Keeble, K. R., *High Technology Industry and Innovative Environments: the European experience*, London, Routledge, 1991.

Cecchini, P., *The European Challenge, 1992*, Aldershot, Gower, 1988.

Collinson, S., *Europe and International Migration*, London, Pinter, 1993.

Dawson, A. H., *A Geography of European Integration*, London, Belhaven, 1993.

Dermine, J., ed., *European Banking in the 1990's*, 2nd edn., Oxford, Blackwell, 1993.

Erdmenger, J., *Vers une politique de transport pour l'Europe*, Brussels, Editions Labor, 1984.

Fennell, R., *The Common Agricultural Policy of the Community*, 2nd edn., London, Granada, 1988.

Freeman, C., Sharp, M. and Walker, W., *Technology and the Future of Europe: global competition and the environment in the 1990s*, London, Pinter, 1991.

Grilli, E. R., *The European Community and the Developing Countries*, Cambridge, Cambridge University Press, 1993.

Gros, D. and Thygesen, N., *European Monetary Integration*, Harlow, Longman, 1992.

Hannequart, A. and Vandamme, J., eds., *Economic and Social Cohesion in Europe*, London, Routledge, 1992.

Harrop, J., *The Political Economy of Integration in the European Community*, 2nd edn., Aldershot, Edward Elgar, 1992.

Hine, R. C., *The Political Economy of European Trade: an introduction to the trade policies of the EEC*, Brighton, Wheatsheaf, 1989.

Hitiris, T., *European Community Economics*, 2nd edn., Hemel Hempstead, Harvester-Wheatsheaf, 1991.

Leigh, M., *European Integration and the Common Fisheries Policy*, London, Croom Helm, 1983.

Leifferink, J. D., ed., *European Integration and Environmental Policy*, London, Belhaven, 1993.

Locksley, G., ed., *The Single European Market and the Information and Communication Technologies*, London, Belhaven, 1990.

Maresceau, M., ed., *The European Community's Commercial Policy after 1992*, Dordrecht, Martinus Nijhoff, 1993.

Mayes, D., ed., *The European Challenge: industry's response to the 1992 programme*, Hemel Hempstead, Harvester-Wheatsheaf, 1991.

Molle, W. and Cappellin, R., eds., *Regional Impact of Community Policies in Europe*, Aldershot, Avebury, 1988.

Moyer, H. W. and Josling, T. E., *Agricultural Policy Reform*, Hemel Hempstead, Harvester-Wheatsheaf, 1990.

Padoa-Schioppa, T. et al., *Europe in the 1990s: efficiency, stability and equity; a strategy for the evolution of the economic system of the European Community*, Oxford, Oxford University Press, 1987.

Pinder, D., *Regional Economic Development and Policy: theory and practice in the European Community*, London, Allen and Unwin, 1983.

Robson, P., *The Economics of International Integration*, 3rd edn., London, Allen and Unwin, 1987.

Shapp, M. and Shearman, C., *European Technological Collaboration*, London, Royal Institute of International Affairs, 1987.

Springer, B., *The Social Dimension of 1992*, London, Adamantine, 1992.

Tracy, M., *Government and Agriculture in Western Europe 1880–1988*, Hemel Hempstead, Harvester-Wheatsheaf, 1989.

Vickerman, R. W., *The Single European Market: prospects for economic integration*, New York, Harvester-Wheatsheaf, 1992.

Wise, M. and Gibb, R., *The European Community in the 1990s: Single Market to social Europe*, Harlow, Longman, 1993.

The European Integration Debate

10   From EPC to CFSP:
an inter-governmental model

ORIGINS OF AN ALTERNATIVE DECISION-MAKING SYSTEM

The earlier chapters have traced the evolution and nature of the Community method *per se*. This framework, however, has been challenged by a number of variants over the years. Perhaps the strongest challenge to the Community system of decision-making has come from the evolution and nature of European Political Co-operation, which has been founded deliberately on an inter-governmental basis, that basis continuing post-Maastricht with the further evolution to a Common Foreign and Security Policy (CFSP).

Chapters One to Three traced the gradual laying and evolution of the Treaty of Rome objective of creating 'an ever closer Union among the peoples of Europe', an objective reiterated at Maastricht.[1] While the original Rome Treaty identified certain policies, mechanisms and principles for achieving that union, it did not encompass defence, security or foreign policy. None the less, the member states have had to grapple with these issues ever since. This is partly because the Community was never to be properly seen as confined to the formal application of the treaties, but rather belonged to a wider political environment, especially the aspiration to achieve political integration, and the articulation of common foreign and defence policies.

Inherent in the original integration ideal espoused in the late 1940s and early 1950s, for example, was the notion that Europe, or the Europe that came to be embodied in the EC and its constituent member states, would act as a single unit in world affairs. One important mainspring of the European momentum had been the realization that in 'a world dominated by political and economic units of continental dimensions, the European nations cannot hope to survive on a basis of political or economic independence'.[2] By the time of the Messina conference in 1955, the path of unity was regarded as 'indispensable if Europe is to maintain her position in the world, regain her influence and prestige'.[3] The new Europe was to become an actor on the world stage in its own right. This basic aspiration has surfaced on several occasions, for example, in the ill-fated attempt in 1972–3 to define 'the European identity' at least partially on the basis of Europe's position and responsibilities with regard to the rest of the world. In the autumn of 1973 the foreign ministers of the then Nine stressed that the Nine intended to 'play an active role in world affairs', to 'progressively define common positions in the sphere of foreign policy' and to seek to act 'as a single entity', bringing out the 'distinctive character' of that entity. In sum, in their external relations the ministers agreed 'progressively to undertake the definition of their identity in relation to other countries or groups of countries . . . [for] in so doing they will strengthen their own cohesion and contribute to the framing of a genuinely European foreign policy.'[4]

There were several false starts in trying to put these into operation and similar aspirations, most notably the abortive Fouchet talks of 1961–2 on a treaty of European political union.[5] The Hague summit in 1969, however, led to what became European Political Co-operation (EPC), a system involving an organizational order outside the formal treaty framework, and based on inter-governmental co-operation. The Hague summit, as was seen in Chapter Two, agreed among other things to pave the way for the enlargement of the Community, to instruct foreign ministers to report on 'the best way of achieving progress in the matter of political unification, within the context of enlargement' and to pave 'the way for a united Europe capable of assuming its responsibilities in the world of tomorrow and of making a contribution commensurate with its traditions and its mission'.[6] The subsequent foreign ministers' report made clear that such progress was most likely to be achieved by a decision 'to co-operate in the field of foreign policy'. They acknowledged that they were heavily influenced in this by their belief that:

- conformity with the preambles of the founding treaties required that 'tangible form should be given to the will for a political union';

- the evolution of common policies 'requires corresponding developments in the specifically political sphere'; and
- 'Europe must prepare itself to discharge the imperative world duties entailed by its greater cohesion and increasing role.'

Current developments within the Community were regarded as making it necessary to step up 'political co-operation' and as an initial step 'to provide . . . ways and means of harmonizing their views in the field of international politics'. Bringing all these considerations together, the foreign ministers 'felt that foreign policy concertation should be the object of the first practical endeavours to demonstrate to all that Europe has a political vocation'. This co-operation was to have two objectives: first, to engender 'greater mutual understanding' on international issues 'by exchanging information and consultation regularly' and second, to 'increase their solidarity by working for a harmonization of view, concertation of attitudes and joint action when it appears feasible and desirable'. The scope of the consultation was to be 'all major questions of foreign policy' and states could propose any topic for discussion.[7] The mechanism for carrying out this task became known as European Political Co-operation (EPC).

THE EPC SYSTEM

The initial basic system comprised the following elements:

> a meeting of foreign ministers at least twice a year; prepared by a Political Committee, comprising the heads of the political departments of the member states' foreign ministries. It would meet at least four times a year; and could set up working parties for special tasks and panels of experts; in each state an official would act as 'correspondent' with his or her counterparts in other states.

This system was to operate separately from the Community system and was outside any treaty framework. The Commission had no integral role, merely being 'consulted if the activities of the European Communities are affected by the work of the Ministers'. There was no question of voting – every decision was to be through consensus. The EPC was to be chaired by the state occupying the Presidency of the Council of the European Communities, that state also hosting the meetings and being responsible for providing 'secretarial service and . . . the practical organization of the meetings'.[8]

This EPC system was avowedly inter-governmental and was to run in parallel with the treaty system. Some, like Ralf Dahrendorf,[9] initially saw this as a source of great potential strength, recognizing the reality of interaction between sovereign states (a view of some prescience given the debates of 1991–2). Others, including the Commission, saw the avoidance of existing institutions as a retreat from Community action. But a common policy, as distinct from co-operation in foreign policy, remained only a long-term objective.

EARLY EVOLUTION

Almost immediately after its foundation the EPC system began to evolve, so that on many issues states were able to decide matters jointly and make common political action possible. This habit led to a European 'reflex' of co-ordination among states, and a 'collegiate sense in Europe' became a real factor in international relations.[10] States welcomed the pragmatic mechanisms of EPC, and its flexibility, and the usefulness of concerted action. As the system evolved, ministers decided to meet more often, agreed that the Political Committee should meet as often as necessary (usually monthly) and set up a Group of 'Correspondents'. As part of this process of greater intensity of consultation, the COREU system was also established, namely a telex liaison system between the departments of foreign affairs.

A Foreign Ministers Report in September 1973 reaffirmed the 'purpose of the consultation is to seek common policies on practical problems' and each state agreed 'as a general rule not to take up final positions without prior consultation with its partners' within the framework of EPC. Perhaps in recognition of certain tensions that had arisen between EPC and the Communities' external relations both in policies and organization, the Copenhagen Report allocated a specific section to the relationship between EPC and the Community system. This recognized the inter-governmental nature of EPC as compared to the Community structure of the treaties, but was rather vague as to the distinctiveness of subject-matter in each context. It was acknowledged that the Commission could make known its views on activities which had 'an incidence on Community activities'. Additionally, although it never happened, the Council was to be informed, through the President of COREPER, of the agreed conclusions obtained in Political Co-operation, where these conclusions had an interest for the work of the Community.[11]

This problem of discrepancies between EPC and the EC system was epitomized in November 1973 when the foreign ministers met in Copenhagen in the morning as the 'Conference of Foreign Ministers' for EPC, only to have to travel to Brussels in the afternoon for an EC Council meeting. This and other developments led to the abandonment of twin-sited meetings and to a blurring of the distinctions which had been created. By the summer of 1974 the system was introduced of holding political co-operation meetings 'within the margin' of the Council meetings and at the same place.

April 1974 saw the introduction of the so-called *Gymnich* meetings, informal gatherings of foreign ministers without officials in convivial surroundings allowing wide-ranging but informal exchanges of view and attitude. A further development was the evolution of the 'troika' arrangement *vis-à-vis* the presidency, namely that the incumbent presidency responsible for the EPC would be aided by its predecessor and would have representation from its successor in order to aid continuity. Perhaps more important as a portent for the future was the decision of the Paris summit of 1974 to create the European Council, as an institutionalization of the previous periodic summits and a mechanism whereby at the very highest level EC and EPC matters could be discussed together. The European Council was also meant to provide momentum for integration by the injection of political will at the very highest level.[12]

This activity and interest in the early 1970s, accompanied by the rhetoric about European identity and European Union, was belied by the absence of the political will to move forward in a fundamental way. That absence was caused by, and symptomatic of, the uncertain environment in international politics and economics generated by the Arab–Israeli conflict of October 1973 and the resultant energy crisis of the 1970s. Contrary to expectations that external crises might stimulate centripetal behaviour, it instead produced centrifugal pressures for each state to seek to arrange its own deal to its best advantage. The system also had to cope with the enlargement of 1973, bringing into the Community some states that were more hesitant about these matters.

In this atmosphere it is not surprising that the members produced only a thin document on 'European identity' in December 1973.[13] In it they undertook to define 'progressively' their identity and to 'strengthen their own cohesion and contribute to the framing of a genuinely European foreign policy', but the reality was much more lukewarm. This was seen again in the 1976 reaction to the Tindemans' Report on 'European Union' of December 1975.[14] The second half of the 1970s saw disillusionment, and a further report by 'three wise men' in 1979 noted that 'the present time seems to us ill-suited to futuristic visions which presuppose a profound and rapid transformation of attitudes within the Community. The chance of such transformation in the next few years seems to be exceedingly slight.'[15]

None the less, progress had been made in EPC in the 1970s. These years saw the system of EPC evolve informally, most importantly with respect to the development of the habit of working together and the embryonic reflex of co-ordinated action; on some issues states had begun to take the system for granted and to recognize and accept that there were common European interests. There were also growing European doubts about the United States' performance as leader of the Western world. A consequence was a growing acceptance of the need for greater room for European manoeuvre from the United States and greater freedom for consultation among themselves about what were increasingly perceived as their own interests. In addition, there was the related concern to reinforce Europe's capacity to act as a single entity in world affairs. On the other hand, there remained a suspicion that EPC had 'reached a plateau',[16] and that there was a need for further development of both the mechanics and scope of the system.

ATTEMPTS AT DEVELOPMENT

In the 1970s and 1980s various efforts were made to make the loose, informal arrangements of EPC somewhat more formal, structured, binding and coherent. These efforts included the London Report of 1981,[17] and the Genscher–Colombo initiative, which led to the Solemn Declaration of Stuttgart in 1983.[18] The London Report both confirmed and built on previous practice, and also reflected a concern that perhaps the system was too reactive, responding to rather than instigating events, and needed, therefore, to take on a 'longer-term approach to certain problems'. The debate over the London Report became controversial because of a German wish to include defence questions within the ambit of EPC. This was ruled out, but it was agreed that the political aspects of security could be discussed as they had been for many years. Given the role of non-alliance member Ireland, and the hesitations of several other members, the narrow interpretation of security was upheld in the London Report – that is, EPC was identified with the political aspects of security, although it was quite clear that the distinctions between the political, economic and military aspects of security were difficult, if not impossible to maintain in the real world. The Report noted that 'having regard to the different situations of the Member States' (which Dublin interpreted as a nod in the direction of its apparent neutrality), ministers had agreed to maintain 'the flexible and pragmatic approach which has made it possible to discuss in political co-operation certain important policy questions bearing on the political aspects of security'. Discussions on the Genscher–Colombo proposals also raised the question of whether defence should be included in this 'security' dimension, but the issue was again ducked. These discussions merely enlarged the 'political aspects' to 'the political and economic aspects of security'. These debates appeared to culminate in the arrangements laid out in Title III of the Single European Act (SEA) of 1986, which contained the basic organizational structure and operational parameters of EPC up to the Gulf and Yugoslav crises of 1990–3, and the Maastricht decisions of December 1991.

EPC AND THE SEA

The SEA[19] reasserted the distinct juridical base of the EC and EPC systems (the Preamble and article 30.3), although article 30.5 provides that the 'external policies of the European Community and the policies agreed in European Political Co-operation must be consistent'. The SEA confirmed the existing practices and ensured that the commitments remained political rather than legal, if only in the sense that there was no way of enforcing them, although EPC was at last provided with a legal basis by the SEA. Despite the view of the Irish Supreme Court in April 1987 that the SEA Title III on EPC constituted a 'solemnly covenanted commitment' and involved 'a programme which would trench progressively on Ireland's independence and sovereignty in the conduct of foreign policy'[20] (a view that caused some amazement in other states), how were commitments to 'endeavour jointly to formulate and implement a European foreign policy', to 'inform and consult', and 'to take full account of the positions of the other partners' and to give 'due consideration to the desirability of adopting and implementing common European positions', to be legally judged or enforced?

Under the SEA, EPC remains inter-governmental, and consequently subject to individual vetoes and, in case of blockage, unilateral actions. The organizational scheme (Title III, article 30) confirmed the existing practice:

> the central role of the Presidency; the (at least) quarterly meetings of foreign ministers; the innovative, preparatory role of the Political Committee; the responsibility of the European Correspondents' Group for monitoring the system and studying organizational issues; and the role of the working groups on specific matters under the direction of the Political Committee.

A new advance was the establishment of a secretariat, based in Brussels, to 'assist the presidency in preparing and implementing the activities of European Political Co-operation and in administrative matters'. It was to carry out its duties under the authority of the Presidency. This temporarily ended the 25-year-old argument about the structure and location of such a secretariat and its role.

It was reiterated that EPC covered only the 'political and economic aspects of security', and by implication not the military aspects. Security was among the last issues to be settled in the negotiations. The Italians favoured the creation of a mechanism for consultation between EPC and the Western European Union. At that time the United Kingdom, and to some extent France, Germany and the Netherlands, favoured primarily using NATO and the WEU. This subject caused difficulties for the Danes and Greeks, who were not members of the WEU, but most particularly for the Irish, given their rhetorical neutrality and non-adhesion to NATO and WEU. In a further harbinger of things to come the SEA acknowledged that those who wished were to be free to pursue 'closer co-operation in the field of security . . . within the framework of the Western European Union or the Atlantic Alliance'. The SEA again acknowledged the need to promote 'a European identity in external policy matters', as well as the need to 'maintain the technological and industrial conditions necessary for . . . security', albeit within the framework of existing competent institutions.

The debate about security raised questions of definition. It is clear that the EPC system worked well, for example, during the Conference on Security and Co-operation in Europe (CSCE) meetings, which dealt with among other things, military confidence-building measures. The history of EPC and the EC shows quite clearly that it is not possible to draw rigid demarcation lines between the political, economic and military aspects of security, or indeed between the EC and EPC systems and policies. The dividing line between the two has often been blurred. An example from the early 1980s was the EPC decision to condemn the Soviet invasion of Afghanistan and the EC decision to ensure that Community products did not replace the grain sales cut off by the United States as part of the co-ordinated Western response. It was not all plain sailing. There was nit-picking in April–June 1982 over the question of sanctions against Argentina after the invasion of the Falklands, although the initial Community decision to embargo imports from the Argentine for the first time referred in its preamble to the agreement reached in EPC on the taking of economic measures.

The SEA did not end the debate, however. The Italians, for example, felt that the SEA did not go far enough towards political co-operation, while the Danes suffered the embarrassment of their parliament, the Folketing, which narrowly rejected the reforms and demanded a renegotiation, a possibility ruled out by the other member states. It went to a referendum, which saw a 56.2 per cent Yes majority. In Ireland too there was the constitutional hiccup over foreign policy and a referendum (with a 69.9 per cent Yes), which delayed the entry into force of the SEA in the EC until July 1987. The SEA position on EPC was, of course, overtaken by the 1991 Inter-Governmental Conference (IGC) on Political Union, but the arrangements outlined in Title III provided the basic framework of EPC in the crises of 1990–2.

CONFLICTING PRESSURES

The member states of the Community prior to these events increasingly had been viewed from the outside as a coherent force in international relations. It may also be argued that the cumulative collective actions of the member states had gradually begun to give the appearance of constituting a policy line from which it appeared increasingly difficult for the member states to depart, and that as the London Report put it, political co-operation had become 'a central element in the foreign policies of all member states'.[21] These tendencies were most pronounced at forums such as the UN General Assembly, where the presidency routinely speaks for the Twelve in major policy debates. Such successes have stemmed from the habit of consultation producing the 'European reflex', which allowed the members to see the 'collective dimensions' of issues, and made it 'normal' to seek consensus. Indeed, EPC can be characterized as exhibiting a tendency towards 'groupthink', in that those involved have tended to develop an *esprit de corps* and to take a convergent view.[22]

There have been a number of pressures, both exogenous and endogenous, pushing the member states to play a wider, more coherent world role. The exogenous factors have included its economic weight in the world, its relationship with the African, Caribbean and Pacific states, and the fear that it would be an economic giant but a political dwarf. The external world expects it to take a coherent view, and friends such as the United States are exasperated when it does not. Equally important are the endogenous pressures. After all, one of the underlying imperatives for integration was the desire for a united Europe to play a major role in the world, the desire for a specifically European influence in the world. As noted previously, as early as the Messina conference there was agreement that unity was 'indispensable if Europe is to maintain her position in the world, regain her influence and prestige'.[23] As the sources and centres of power have become more diffuse, so Europeans have had to come to terms with the fact that in general they have more influence when acting together, a factor that is apparently appreciated by most Community citizens (see Figures 10.1, 10.2, and 10.3).

There is, moreover, the commitment to the ideal of European unity. It is also true that several 'internal' policies of the EC, particularly agriculture, have external repercussions, as has been clearly seen in the Uruguay Round GATT saga, and that the development of internal policies can be undertaken only with cognizance of the external dimension.

It must be concluded, however, that the record on EPC prior to the events of 1990–2 was at best mixed, that there was really no

Over half the European Community's population (51 per cent) favours a joint foreign policy for the Community, while just over a quarter (26 per cent) is against. This is one of the findings of a Eurobarometer opinion survey in the twelve member states of the Community in autumn 1990.

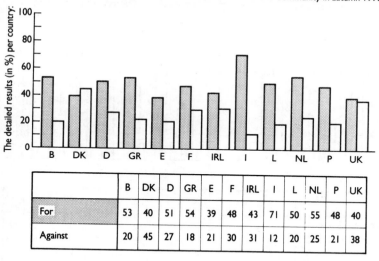

	B	DK	D	GR	E	F	IRL	I	L	NL	P	UK
For	53	40	51	54	39	48	43	71	50	55	48	40
Against	20	45	27	18	21	30	31	12	20	25	21	38

Figure 10.1 *Joint foreign policy favoured*

The chart shows the findings of an opinion poll conducted during the Gulf crisis in spring 1991. Support for joint action ranged from 80 per cent of interviewees in the United Kingdom to 58 per cent in Denmark; the Community average was 74 per cent. On the creation of a European intervention force, 62 per cent were in favour, 11 per cent more than in autumn 1990.

The Europeans and a common foreign policy (%)

☐ For a common foreign policy

▨ For a common military intervention force

Figure 10.2 *Joint action in international crises*

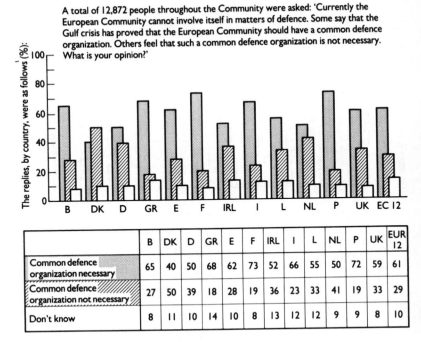

A total of 12,872 people throughout the Community were asked: 'Currently the European Community cannot involve itself in matters of defence. Some say that the Gulf crisis has proved that the European Community should have a common defence organization. Others feel that such a common defence organization is not necessary. What is your opinion?'

	B	DK	D	GR	E	F	IRL	I	L	NL	P	UK	EUR 12
Common defence organization necessary	65	40	50	68	62	73	52	66	55	50	72	59	61
Common defence organization not necessary	27	50	39	18	28	19	36	23	33	41	19	33	29
Don't know	8	11	10	14	10	8	13	12	12	9	9	8	10

Figure 10.3 *Support for Community defence?*

common European foreign policy, since while a pattern of solidarity could be detected, it was by no means complete or wholly predictable. A notorious example was the failure to condemn the Soviet Union for shooting down the South Korean Boeing 747 (KAL–007) in 1983. Despite repeated efforts at official and ministerial level to agree a statement condemning the Soviet Union, no such statement could be agreed because the Greeks refused to join in any condemnation and unanimity ruled. A number of states have fairly consistently maintained their freedom of manoeuvre. The issues the Community states have disagreed on have been among the most important in international relations. This trend was confirmed by the Gulf and Yugoslav experience.

That divisions occur on such issues is not surprising. Roger Morgan noted perspicaciously many years ago that the development of a common foreign policy was likely to be hampered by the legacies the member states brought with them into EPC, especially their centuries of distinctive experience. He identified four distinct problems, namely:

1. The states in the Community were far from agreement on many aspects of their internal arrangements, and that some of those disputes had external repercussions (for example, was Europe progressing towards a federal system or retaining inter-governmentalism?).
2. The inevitably divisive factor of straightforward commercial competition.
3. The differing geographical perspectives from which they viewed the outside world, a factor specifically relating to the varying but long-standing historical traditions of each state's view of its place in the world.
4. The different substantive interests of the EC members in the international system as a whole, and in both economics and strategy.[24]

In addition, mention must be made of the sovereignty issue, especially in the sensitive areas of defence and security.

This legacy of which Morgan writes reflects, for example, the different experiences of colonialism undergone by Britain, France and Ireland; the different wartime experiences of Britain, Ireland and the continental states; and the profoundly differing post-war political experiences of Spain, Portugal and Greece compared to the Nine of 1973. The diversity engendered by this type of input into national political cultures has not unnaturally led to divergences in perceived national interests on a range of issues within EPC, and the EPC policy-making system is not always able to cope given the requirement of consensus and unanimity. The colonial experience seems to have been particularly significant, with divisions in EPC appearing on Namibia, Rhodesia, apartheid and sanctions against South Africa, decolonization and Third World issues, especially the New International Economic Order, although the nuclear powers have also diverged on questions of disarmament.

On many issues the divergences are submerged to some extent, given the highly declaratory nature of EPC, the fact that it consists largely of statements and has few other instruments. This has been coupled with a tendency for the participants to unite 'behind a common position sufficiently loosely defined to allow each to add his own interpretation, so producing some forward movement without confronting the major obstacles ahead'.[25] Furthermore, as Jacques Delors explained in connection with the Yugoslavia crisis in 1991, EPC only had three weapons at its disposal in crises such as Yugoslavia: public opinion, the threat of withholding diplomatic recognition and economic sanctions.[26] He had earlier observed in March 1991 during the Gulf crisis that 'the Community had neither the institutional machinery nor the military force which would have allowed it to act as a Community'. This remains so, and it was this vacuum that prompted his call for the new treaty to allow for common defence issues to be dealt with by the European Council, as well as a number of other measures.[27]

THE DEBATE ON THE EVE OF MAASTRICHT

The foregoing provided the environment within which individual states, societies, policy-makers and institutions had to determine their responses to the debate about the nature and scope of EPC in the context of the IGC on Political Union. It had already been agreed (in Strasbourg, 1989) that there should be an Inter-governmental Conference on Economic and Monetary Union in 1991. The preliminary decision to call a parallel IGC on Political Union was taken at the special April 1990 Dublin European Council, and was a response not only to the sweeping events unfolding in Eastern Europe, including the approaching unification of Germany, but also to the renewal of the stumbling debate within the Twelve in the 1980s over their political future. The crises in the Gulf and Yugoslavia added a compelling, urgent and complicating factor to the debate about the unity, coherence and motivation of the EC's international action, and for a re-examination and revitalization of EPC.

Initially, it seemed as if the debate would focus on improving the organization of EPC and perhaps extending its scope. However, it became clear that a number of member states wished to elevate the importance of the issue in response to the Gulf and Yugoslav crises, the Gulf crisis changing the parameters of the debate on EPC in a very profound sense. The appearance of an 'out-of-area' threat and the possibility of war lent urgency to the discussion of EPC and a foreign and security policy. There were two main themes in the debate on EPC reform. The first was the call for a common foreign and security policy, which would represent a 'quantum leap forward'. With varying degrees of priority Italy, Germany, Belgium, the Netherlands and Greece declared their interest in this first approach.

The second approach was a concern to improve the internal workings of EPC, a gradualist approach. Britain, Ireland and to some extent Denmark and Portugal voiced reservations about departing too far from the current arrangements for co-ordinating policy by consensus and avoiding defence matters usually left to NATO and WEU. The Irish had problems with their rhetorical attachment to neutrality, and noted that the SEA did not cover the military aspects of security. The Danish parliament had long been loath to endorse political union and the development of a strong security profile by the EC.

The United Kingdom did not support developments that undermined NATO or WEU, and showed little enthusiasm for majority voting in this area, being clear that decisions should be consensual. It accepted that some lessons might have to be learnt from the Gulf, but felt it was wrong to catapult the EC into a defence role for which it was not prepared. In the UK view the defects in the Community's common response to the Gulf War were not caused by the absence of machinery, but by differences in view on substance. What was needed, therefore, was a greater unity of analysis and an event-by-event approach, gradually working towards a more effective common policy.

Apart from the problems of EPC already discussed, one of the difficulties facing European states was the problem of which institution should do what, and how to rationalize the activities of a number of defence-related institutions in Europe with overlapping functions and heterogeneous memberships. (See Figure 10.4.) For example, France has remained in NATO but outside the integrated military commands. It had also refrained from direct involvement with the Eurogroup (a grouping originally created in 1968 to informally articulate and promote European interests and views), although it is in the IEPG (the Independent European Programme Group). All of the EC12, except Ireland, are in NATO, but France is not the only one to have a form of 'special status'. In addition, there are the differing commitments under the NATO and Brussels Treaty (BTO), the foundation of the WEU, arrangements. The latter

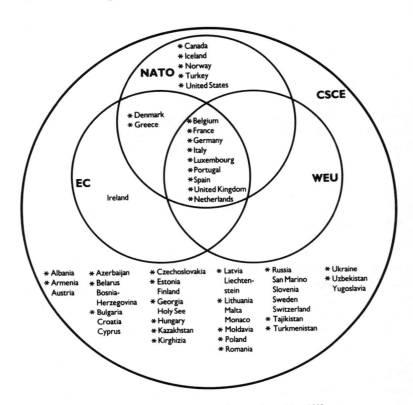

* Membership of North Atlantic Co-operation Council as at 5 June 1992

Figure 10.4 *Security in Europe: membership of international organizations (1992)*

obliges states to provide miltary assistance, while the former only requires that they provide the help they deem necessary.

The Gulf and Yugoslav crises focused attention on the Western European Union (WEU). The WEU, with the accession of Spain and Portugal in 1988 had nine of the EC12 as members, but not Ireland, Denmark or Greece. Moribund for many years, it was revived in 1984 precisely because of the perceived need to agree and articulate a European view on security.[28] The WEU was almost thrust into a role in the Gulf crisis by default, given the EC's reluctance to become involved too directly in military affairs and the refusal of NATO to take on out-of-area responsibilities. The WEU had some success because its treaty permitted out-of-area action, which was particularly important to the NATO members, who wanted a mechanism for co-ordinating such issues. The WEU played a role in attempting to work out an agreed European response, in providing an umbrella under which states could contribute, and in co-ordinating the activities of NATO's European members. The WEU also sought to show that the Europeans were interested in intervening in matters that affected both their own and international security more generally.[29]

France was especially keen to see a WEU role and sought to underline the close links between the WEU's security interests and the broader process of European integration. It did this, for example, by inviting all twelve members of the EC to attend a WEU meeting in August 1990, even though only nine of the twelve were members. Denmark and Greece agreed to send observers, while Ireland declined the invitation.

Also in the minds of those discussing a CFSP were the deliberations of NATO, which led to the NATO summit in Rome on 7–8 November 1991 just a few days before the Maastricht meeting. Rome produced the 'Declaration on Peace and Security' and the Alliance's 'New Strategic Concept'.[30] The Rome Declaration on Peace and Co-operation confirmed the Alliance's belief that the Alliance would continue to play a key role in European security, but was clear that in the new security environment NATO, the CSCE, the EC, the WEU and the Council of Europe all complemented one another, and all had a role to play if instability was to be prevented. It stressed that appropriate links would have to be established between NATO, WEU and the Twelve to ensure that all were adequately informed about decisions that might affect their security. The NATO states said they welcomed the prospect of the reinforcement of the role of the WEU, 'both as a defence component of the process of European unification and as a means of strengthening the European pillar of the Alliance'.[31] These two processes were regarded as mutually reinforcing, with the Alliance seen as the buttress of strategic unity and indivisibility of security.

Before turning to the Maastricht outcome it is worth noting other ingredients in the debate. One was the hesitancy of the United States with regard to any emergent European identity. While always supporting the idea of Europeans doing more to help themselves, and supporting the idea in principle of a European Union, as the talks began to take off in 1991 the United States became more and more anxious about the economic and strategic implications of European unity, and feared that it might be excluded from certain key developments.

Equally important was the issue whether it should be 'Atlantic European defence' (i.e. predominantly NATO) or 'European European defence' (i.e. predominantly WEU in the short term, but EC in the longer term). Reflecting on the Gulf experience and the approaching IGC, in March 1991 Jacques Delors, while acknowledging that a European common defence policy had to be built on what existed, namely the WEU, also noted the divisions which existed on its role. He summarized these as: 'should it be a forum for increased co-operation between the countries of Europe, a bridge to the Atlantic Alliance, or should it be a melting-pot for a European defence embedded in the Community, the second pillar of the Alliance?' For Delors, only the second option was acceptable, it being the goal which separated the approaches.[32] Still others believed that in the changed situation post-1989 any defence or security arrangements should be focused on the pan-European level, namely the post-Paris November 1990 revived CSCE.

Another fundamental division underlay the discussions. For the French it is prudent for Europe to make preparations independently of the United States; from a British standpoint, that is the kind of attitude that will make the United States leave. This divide took on particular edge in 1991–2 with the Franco–German proposal to develop their joint brigade (currently 4,200 soldiers of two French regiments and two German battalions) into a joint corps of 35,000–40,000 by 1995, which could be the nucleus of, or model for, a future European army. Belgium, Italy, Luxembourg and Spain were all reported to be interested in being involved.

These debates became embroiled in the IGC on Political Union, and the discussions within NATO on re-orienting the organization, and on re-structuring its forces. In some minds the pervasive uncertainty surrounding the new European environment counselled the cautious view that institutions and arrangements that had served them well should not be tampered with.

THE GULF

The major factor in the environment which provided the backdrop to Maastricht was the mixed performance, at best, of the Twelve during the Gulf and Yugoslav crises. Initially the analysis from EC officials on the response to the Gulf crisis was upbeat. Its reaction had been 'light years ahead of any of its previous actions to major international crises both in speech and in content'.[33] Supporters of this view pointed to the aid effort to the front-line states, the trade embargo, the concord at the UN and the series of declaratory statements.

Sceptics rather than looking at the rhetoric, however, saw resurfacing of old national positions and divergences of interests and views. They pointed to the limitations in the Community's response, and particularly the clear divergence between those who were reluctant to back any policy and the more resolute British attitude.

One concern was over initiatives by former statesmen, including Willy Brandt, and Edward Heath. This prompted a declaration by the EC heads of state and/or government at the European Council meeting in Rome in October 1990 of 'their determination not to negotiate with Iraq the release of foreign hostages and to discourage others from doing so'.[34] Despite this, within hours the German political leaders were meeting to discuss how the Federal Republic could support Brandt's visit with minimum diplomatic damage. What appears to have been decisive for Bonn was not EC solidarity, but concern at opposing an apparently humanitarian visit by a respected elder statesman of German politics and public opinion with an election only weeks away.

The proposed visit caused outrage in a number of European capitals, partly because it came so soon after the Rome Declaration, and partly because it was a devastating example of the kind of national interest and concern that undermined the goal of united action and, indeed, the rhetoric of unity. The Germans tried to put a brave face on it, as well as belatedly seeking to surround the visit with an EC and UN mantle. A caustic British comment was that it was a 'bad example of governments deciding on a policy in conclave and then one of them deciding to do something else and trying to persuade other European governments to copy its bad example'.[35] The Belgians and Dutch called for an emergency EC foreign ministers meeting, and this led to another declaration, including reaffirmation of the Rome Declaration not to bargain with Baghdad.

Another problem was the French last-minute initiative to avoid war, although that too was soon overtaken by events, by the fact of war. On 14 January 1990 the French had made new proposals to the UN Security Council calling for an Iraqi withdrawal from Kuwait, but also stating that a peace conference would be held on the Middle East at some appropriate time. Not only was there displeasure at the nature of the French proposal, but more particularly at its Community partners not being informed. There had been a meeting of foreign ministers the morning of the French proposal and nothing appears to have been said about the initiative. Indeed, the ministers seemed to have agreed that there was no point in sending a peace mission to Baghdad, regretting that 'the conditions for a new European initiative do not exist as of this moment'. The same day the British Prime Minister, John Major, lunched with President Mitterrand, and again nothing overt appears to have been said. The French claimed that they had mentioned the idea but had not gone into detail because the text was still being worked on.

There were twelve different contributions to the international coalition effort in the Gulf from EC members, no two states contributing in the same way (see Table 10.1). The Gulf crisis exposed the fragility of European co-operation. After the war the Twelve sought to revive coherence, in some degree, in their response to John Major's initiative for a UN force to provide Iraqi Kurdish refugees with protection.

Yet just as the EC states were seeking to come to terms with their performance over the Gulf over the previous eighteen months, and were beginning to enter serious negotiations in the context of the IGC on Political Union, on the possibilities of a 'common foreign and security policy', even a defence role for the Community, and its relationships with the Western European Union and NATO, another issue raised the stakes.

YUGOSLAVIA

Yugoslavia[36] raised even more fundamental questions about cohesion, and whether the exhortations contained in the SEA, and

Table 10.1 *Contributions to the coalition effort in the Gulf*

	Belgium	Denmark	France	Germany	Greece	Italy	Luxem-bourg	Nether-lands	Portugal	Spain	United Kingdom
Took part in offensive air operations in Iraq and Kuwait			●			●					●
Took part in offensive land operations in Iraq and Kuwait			●								●
Took part in offensive naval operations in the Gulf			●			●		●			●
Took part in naval embargo operations		●	●		●	●		●			●
Took part in mine-clearing operations			●	●		●		●			●
Defended key areas in Saudi Arabia			●								●
Deployed medical units	●	●	●	●		●		●			●
Provided practical or financial assistance to the coalition	●	●	●	●		●	●	●	●	●	●
Took part in defensive operations in the NATO area	●			●	●	●		●	●	●	●

Note: Ireland agreed to allow refuelling of US planes at Shannon airport.
Source: Statement on the Defence Estimates: Britain's Defence for the 90s, Vol. 1, Cm. 1559–1, (London: HMSO, 1991), p. 9.

subsequently agreed at Maastricht, regarding common stances on foreign policy and security, had any real relevance with regard to the issue of diplomatic recognition of, for example, Croatia and Slovenia. Increasingly, the issue became whether the Community could act as one on the question of diplomatic recognition, precisely the sort of issue that EPC had apparently been coping with for almost two . decades.

As early as July 1991 the Germans decided to shift their policy in favour of diplomatic recognition of the two breakaway republics. Increasingly restive on this matter, the Germans did accept for some months that, while inevitable, recognition should come from the Community as a whole. For several months the other member states managed to ward that off.

By November Germany was pushing for full recognition of the breakaway republics by the end of the year, although it still toed the official EC line that saw recognition as part of a peace treaty and a new political settlement. Most other EC states felt recognition to be premature, fearing that Croatia would then press for military assistance, which would make the crisis more intractable. They also feared that recognition without safeguards for minorities throughout Yugoslavia would only increase the bloodshed.

Germany came to believe that if it acted it would not be alone, thinking it would have support from the Danes, while the Belgians and Italians were wavering. The French, British and Dutch were opposed, the Dutch partly because they saw German pressure and action as incompatible with the Maastricht process. Strenuous efforts were made to keep the Community together, by seeking to agree a timetable and the conditions which Croatia and Slovenia and others would have to meet before being recognized. At the insistence of Greece, again illustrating that individual states' concerns were important, it was also agreed that the republics must abandon territorial claims on their EC neighbours, that is, the issue of Macedonia. It was agreed that if they passed these tests the EC states would recognize them on 15 January 1992. Bonn, however, decided not to wait, and the German President, von Weizsäcker, recognized the two republics on 23 December 1991, although as a gesture to its partners it announced it would open diplomatic relations with the two new states on 15 January. The Germans maintained that they did not need to wait to see if the EC tests had been passed as they had assurances from the Croats and Slovenes. Germany's partners remained profoundly unhappy with the Germans' behaviour. This was doubly so when a report on whether the two republics had met the required tests early in January cast substantial doubts on whether that was so. None the less, the other EC states fell into line on 15 January 1992.

Divergence among Community states attracted great attention. It can be argued in support of the Community, however, that it tried to bring peace in an impossible situation. It contributed through the sending of monitors to try to observe the ceasefires and by convening the protracted peace conference but there was little that any outsider could do. It did stop Germany breaking ranks for a long period. None the less, it was the sort of issue that demonstrated that if the member states wish to move to a common foreign and security policy, changes of attitude would be required. The cumulative impact of the Gulf and Yugoslavia gave pause for thought about the future and did influence the discussions at Maastricht.

THE TREATY ON EUROPEAN UNION AND CFSP

Maastricht agreed to establish a CFSP, although Title V in the treaty and article J both promised rather more than was actually produced.[37] CFSP was to be one of the pillars of the European Union (see Chapter Twelve). Article J.1 is careful to refer to 'the Union and the member states' as defining and implementing a CFSP, a signal to its inter-governmental nature. The pertinent part of the new Treaty on European Union, the CFSP, like Title III of the Single European Act, is not part of the Community system *per se*, and not subject to the same decision-making procedures, nor subject to judicial review by the ECJ.

Article J.1.4 of Title V gives responsibility for determining that the principles of the CFSP are complied with to the Council. In addition, article J.8.2 makes it clear that 'The Council shall act unanimously, except for procedural questions', and where it has unanimously agreed 'matters on which decisions are to be taken by a qualified vote' (article J.3.2). If there is no agreement, then only peer and Commission disapproval, and a general weakening of confidence prevents a member state from going it alone. The provisions of Title V do not require any amendment to the existing treaties and could just as well come into effect by purely political decisions by the member states.

The objectives of the policy (article J.1) were unsurprising: safeguarding common values, interests and the independence of the Union; strengthening security; promoting international co-operation; and enhancing democracy. These were to be pursued by 'systematic co-operation between Member States' and the gradual implementation of 'joint action', where the member states have common interests. (Although not attached to the official Final Act Declarations published with the Treaty on European Union, it was agreed at Maastricht by the European Council that with the entry into force of the treaty, the CSCE process, arms control and disarmament in Europe, nuclear non-proliferation, and the economic aspects of security, especially arms transfers to the Third World would be areas of 'joint action'. The Council was instructed to identify further areas of possible joint action *vis-à-vis* particular groups of states, and the foreign ministers were instructed to prepare for the basic elements of policy for the Union by January 1993.) The signatories agreed to refrain from actions which impaired such policies or the Union. Member states agreed, as always, to consult and to seek by concerted action to exercise their influence as effectively as possible.

A crucial statement is contained in article J.4, in which it was agreed that a CFSP 'shall include *all* questions related to the security of the Union, including the eventual framing of a common defence policy, which might in time lead to a common defence'. This implicitly drew a distinction between a joint, collaborative defence policy, and the more expansive idea of common defence *per se* as mooted by Jacques Delors and recognized as the ultimate goal.

It appeared that the Twelve had effectively subcontracted 'decisions and actions of the Union which have defence implications' to the WEU by requesting it 'to elaborate and implement' decisions of the Union which had such implications. This could be interpreted as a separation of CFSP among the Twelve from defence in the WEU and the Alliance, but the WEU is described as an 'integral part' of the European Union (EU), so the question remains about how separate these activities will be. There is also the curious wording that the WEU is 'to elaborate and implement' defence orientated actions, which seems to avoid a direct statement of who will take such decisions, it being implicit that it is the Council of the European Union. Given this, it is perhaps not surprising that Council of the Union and the WEU were to agree suitable practical arrangements to govern their relationship.

Concomitantly, the nine members of the WEU (all of whom are members of the EC), agreed a 'Declaration on the Role of the Western European Union and its Relations with the European Union and with the Atlantic Alliance'. In this the WEU Nine agreed to develop 'a genuine European security and defence identity and a greater European responsibility on defence matters'. They noted that the WEU was integral to the development of European Union, but immediately linked this to the Union's contribution to enhancing solidarity within the Atlantic Alliance.[38] WEU states agreed with article J.4 of the European Union treaty, adding that such common defence was to be compatible with the Atlantic Alliance. Most importantly of all, the WEU Nine said the WEU was 'prepared, at the request of the European Union, to elaborate and implement decisions and actions of the Union which have defence implications'.

The WEU states proposed synchronization of WEU/European Union meetings, closer co-operation between staffs, and harmonization of the presidencies. But to balance this, working links between WEU and NATO were also to be strengthened, as was the contribution, role and responsibility of the WEU Nine within NATO. It is worth noting that having agreed to be the defence arm of the European Union and to implement its decisions, they also agreed that 'WEU will act in conformity with the positions adopted in the Atlantic alliance'.

In a new development the WEU Nine agreed to try to co-ordinate their policies on Atlantic issues, such as to seek to introduce the 'joint positions agreed in the WEU into the process for consultation in the Alliance', reiterating that the alliance was *the* vehicle for security and defence matters under the North Atlantic Treaty. To increase the WEU's operational role they agreed to establish, 'a planning cell; meetings of WEU Chiefs of Staff; a study of military units answerable to WEU and closer co-operation with the Alliance in logistics, transport, training and strategic surveillance.'

The WEU Nine also agreed to consider enhanced co-operation in the field of armaments with a view to creating a European armaments agency, and making sure that the WEU's stronger operational role was compatible with NATO. All of this endeavour was to be fully compatible with the military dispositions necessary to ensure the collective defence of all the allies. In addition, the WEU Council and secretariat would move to Brussels, and Alliance and European Union representatives would be 'double-hatted'. In a further

Declaration the WEU Nine invited the three European Union non-members of the WEU (Ireland, Greece and Denmark) either to join it or assume observer status. Norway, Turkey and Iceland, as European members of NATO, but in neither European Union nor WEU, were invited to become associate members of WEU.

Given that these arrangements did not really resolve the 'Atlantic European defence' as against the 'European European defence' issue, it is not surprising that in article J.4.6 of the Treaty on European Union, the Twelve agreed to review the European Union/WEU and CFSP components of the treaty in 1996. Here they were taking advantage of the fact that the original Brussels treaty of 1948, which laid the foundation of the WEU, was to remain in force only until 1998.

The Maastricht text leaves a central ambiguity in interpretations of the goal of a 'common defence', viz. is the long term objective of the Union to change the basis of defence from membership of the Alliance to membership of the Union itself? Until this is settled there remains an underlying tension in all the discussions about European security and defence. Is it true, as Genscher said in April 1991, that the 'development of a common European foreign, security and defence policy is not intended to create an ersatz NATO, but to reinforce the European pillar. . . . A growing sense of identity in Europe does not make the Atlantic wider'?[39]

Having made this linkage with the WEU, a linkage reciprocated by the WEU Nine in their declarations, the Twelve in article J.4 of the European Union Treaty went on to say that their policy should 'not prejudice the specific character of the security and defence policy of certain Member States', nor the obligations of signatories of the North Atlantic Treaty. Presumably the former was a rather indirect sop to Ireland, with its traditional policy of non-alliance involvement, and perhaps also an acknowledgement of both the nuclear and Security Council roles of Britain and France. It was also agreed that bilateral co-operation was permissible between states, as long as it was compatible with all the above.

The presidency was to represent the European Union in matters relating to CFSP, as well as implementing common measures (not including defence), and representing the EU in international organizations and conferences. The troika arrangement was to continue and the Commission was to be associated with all the work carried out in the CFSP field. Where not all member states were members of an international organization those that were (including members of the Security Council) were to keep them fully informed and where possible promote the interests of the Union. The presidency also had responsibilities to keep the European Parliament informed of the main choices and aspects of CFSP.

How were decisions to be made? It is clear the Council 'shall act unanimously' (although an attached declaration noted that they had agreed that where decisions required unanimity 'Member States will, to the extent possible, avoid preventing a unanimous decision where a qualified majority exists in favour of that decision'). However, procedural matters were subject to qualified majority voting, and the Council, acting on the basis of unanimity, could 'define those matters on which decisions are to be taken by a qualified majority'. It was also agreed that where circumstances had changed, after joint action had been agreed, it would be reviewed by the Council, but as long as the Council had not acted, 'the joint action shall stand'. Joint actions were to be regarded as committing the member states, although it was accepted that considerations of urgency, etc. would allow member states to take necessary measures. It was also agreed that the 'joint actions' should be discrete and time-limited, not permanent arrangements.

There still remains some residue of the debate as to whether the EU states should follow an institutional approach, which believes that the strengthening of the institutions of the Twelve and of the Community, and seeking to arrive at 'binding' procedures, will necessarily advance the common interest; and the 'problem-oriented' approach, which attempts to sort out which problems are most amenable of solution or influence by the Community, and tries to bring the collective weight of the Community to bear on them.

CONCLUSION

At Maastricht it was not possible to resolve the underlying debates about a European security identity or CFSP. There is no resolution of the alphabet soup of institutions, of the definitive role of EU, WEU and NATO, of 'Atlantic Europe' or 'European Europe', of whether the future is to be inter-governmental or federal, a common defence policy or common defence, incremental drift or real change. Maastricht left as an open question what the role of the European

Union was to be. A further complication is the impending membership of Sweden, Finland and Austria, the former European neutrals, in the Union and CFSP.

The real issue, perhaps, is not institutional, whether to have joint integrated commands or corps, the lead played by NATO, WEU or EU, but whether there is an emergent identification of common political and security interests that guarantees unity. Effective institutions, alliances and policies in CFSP area require potent military capability, a working consensus on the conditions under which the capabilities should be used, and a credible willingness to act when agreed conditions exist. Do these exist?

The current situation cannot continue indefinitely. By accident or design the ingredients will have been changed in the next decade. If it is to be by design, and there is to be a European CFSP or a European voice in the world, choices will have to be made. In determining those choices cognizance will need to be paid to:

- a German inclination to assert greater influence, and certainly not to accept any longer a subordinate role;
- the question of a 'German Europe' or a 'European Germany';
- the US position, caught as it is between the aspiration to leadership and profound resource and domestic difficulties;
- the fact that in the years ahead, the Europeans are not likely to find need for US protection, and especially leadership;
- the realization that, as the Gulf demonstrated, the Europeans are still short of coherence, and even logistics, and in their hearts know how valuable the years of NATO defence planning and rehearsing were to success;
- the Eastern dimension.

The one certain prediction in the next few years is the continuing presence of uncertainty and unpredictability.

11 Attitudes of the Member States to European Integration and the Treaty on European Union

There has been a number of important debates about the nature and shape of European integration. These debates took on contemporary importance during the negotiations surrounding the IGCs on EMU and EPU in 1991. This chapter briefly examines the main imperatives behind the attitudes of the member states to European integration over time and with specific reference to the Treaty on European Union.

All twelve member states joined the Community for their own reasons and in their own perceived interests. Some joined later than others: Denmark, Ireland and the United Kingdom in 1973, Greece in 1981, and Portugal and Spain in 1986. Others will probably follow from about 1995 until the end of the century. In many cases, but not all, the different interests, concerns and circumstances that affected the original decisions are still of some relevance today, and had some influence on policy positions in the Inter-Governmental Conferences, and at the subsequent Maastricht, Lisbon, Birmingham and Edinburgh meetings in 1992, as well as in the domestic debates about ratification of the Treaty on European Union.[1]

While this chapter will examine the attitudes of member states in order of their accession to the Community, this is not to imply that those acceding at any one point shared an identity of interests. Among the original Six, for example, there have been significant divergences of outlook about the future shape of the Community, its domain and scope, and the destination of the enterprise. In the current debates, the Federal Republic of Germany, in the light of its own history and contemporary experience, has identified federalism as a decentralizing concept. The Benelux states, along with Italy, have been convinced federalists at least in rhetoric, while the French have been supportive, if a form of federalism encompasses a dominant Franco-German axis, as well as catering for French national interests. On financial questions such as Delors II, only Luxembourg and the Netherlands have been really supportive, the others wishing to see spending scaled down, although even here there are divergences as some, Belgium, France, and Italy, have favoured more support for the poorer states, which as perceived 'paymaster' the Federal Republic has opposed. Of those joining in 1973, Ireland has been much more *communautaire*, largely it could be argued because it has been a clear net financial beneficiary, and has seen Community membership as a vehicle for escaping suffocating British influence. It has supported the movement to a single currency, Delors II, and a leading role for the Commission as a protector for small states. Both the Danes and the British have retained much of the original reserve which characterized their attitudes as non-members, and remain more wedded to an inter-governmental approach, both wishing to 'opt out' of commitment at this stage to a single currency, the United Kingdom from the social chapter and Denmark from common defence. They both favour the return of powers to the member states. Greece provides an example of a state that joined 'late' and which, with successive changes of government and transfers of resources via Community subsidies, has moved from agnosticism to selective belief. The last members, Portugal and Spain, while generally having a similar outlook, have differed over whether there is a need to reduce the power of Brussels, which Portugal would like to see, and over a Community role in defence, which Portugal would prefer not to see.

Given such differences any negotiation over the future of the Community was, and is, bound to be difficult. It is worth recalling that the original negotiations over the future were not trouble-free either: the EDC Treaty was derailed by France in August 1954, and the negotiations before the Treaty of Rome founding the EEC nearly floundered. There was argument about the extent of centralized power in the context of how to reconcile French hesitations with the belief that it was necessary to go beyond the unanimity rule which prevailed in other organizations. Differences over agriculture meant that the final text only states general objectives to be attained by the end of the transitional period, leaving the details to be worked out by the new Community itself. A difficult issue during the negotiations in 1956–7 was the relationship between the Six and their overseas territories, that is, former colonies. This was only resolved at the last minute by a heads of state/government meeting, and only then, because the French were able to argue that without a satisfactory arrangement there was little prospect of ratification. It is perhaps also worth recalling that Norway signed the Treaty of Accession in January 1972, only to have to withdraw following a referendum, in which the voters refused to endorse that decision.

The previous difficulties are especially relevant perhaps given the traumas of the 1992 ratification process. In addition to the traditional attitudes and interests of the twelve member states 1992 also saw the debate take place against a background of recession and apparent public disaffection from the European Community and with national governments apparently unable to turn the economic tide. The Community appeared remote and irrelevant to many people, fearful of unemployment, and the debates about EMU did not seem timely to those current concerns. Given the civil war in Yugoslavia and the recognition of the potential for more troubles in Eastern Europe, many in Western Europe lacked confidence in the future and were fearful also of a wave of apparently uncontrolled immigration. Nationalism began to appear to be respectable.

One ought not, therefore, to fall into the trap of seeing an inexorable uniform pattern of progress towards some clearly defined predetermined goal. In fact, the record of the Community might be better characterized as one of 'stop–go', or of the proverbial 'two steps forward one step backwards'. In 1990–2 the question became whether it was to be 'two steps backward one step forward'.

THE BENELUX STATES

These three states had in some ways been the precursors of the EEC. Their governments in exile in London agreed in 1944 to create a customs union after the war, eliminating all customs barriers between them and introducing a uniform tariff for imports. This agreement came into effect in January 1948, and had the effect of demonstrating to those involved that they could profitably co-operate at the economic and political levels. None the less, this was not to be an end in itself, and the states concerned were interested in co-operation in a wider field, at least partly because they had direct experience of

Table 11.1 *Maastricht and the EC's future*

If there were a referendum on whether to agree to the Maastricht Treaty or not, would you vote for or against?

	Belg	Dk	Ger	Gre	Spa	Fra	Irl	Ita	Lux	NL	P	UK	EC 12
For	53	43	44	58	34	45	55	55	56	62	43	26	43
Against	11	48	30	15	16	38	24	10	22	18	11	43	27
Undecided	35	9	26	28	50	17	22	35	23	20	47	31	30

If you were told tomorrow that the EC had been scrapped, would you be very sorry, indifferent or very relieved?

	Belg	Dk	Ger	Gre	Spa	Fra	Irl	Ita	Lux	NL	P	UK	EC 12
Very sorry	41	48	44	53	45	47	53	58	60	55	44	25	45
Indifferent	43	29	32	33	41	32	34	29	28	31	43	41	34
Very relieved	6	16	12	5	8	14	7	4	5	6	3	28	12
Don't know	9	8	12	10	6	8	6	10	7	9	10	7	9

Source: Eurobarometer, November 1992

war on their territories. In keeping with these twin motivations of peace and trade, these states played a vital part in the '*relance européenne*' when, on 20 May 1955, they jointly proposed to the other members of the ECSC the creation of a European atomic energy organization and a customs union, with trade, agriculture, energy and transport under the guidance of a common authority. The Benelux memorandum played an important role at Messina and subsequent events, and the Belgian Foreign Minister, Paul Henri Spaak, chaired the committee which drew up the draft treaties. It is noteworthy too that Belgium was the first member state to make concrete proposals for a IGC on political union in 1990.

Belgium has had a generally uncritical view of integration for most of the post-war period. One observer has noted that 'Being at the crossroads of Latin and German cultures, Belgium needs agreement and peace more than anyone else.' Europe provides a meeting point for most of the innumerable Belgian parties and for the two sides of the Flemish/Walloon divide. Moreover, as a free trade nation by tradition and by conviction, Belgium sees her relationship with Europe as a 'marriage of love and reason'.[2] Much the same applies to the traditional position of Luxembourg. Geography, heavy dependence on external trade and small size all contributed to a positive attitude to integration. These factors held true for the Dutch too, but while supportive in general, they perhaps have not always been quite so enthusiastic, partly because there has been throughout the post-war period a rather stronger 'Atlanticist' element in their policy, and a belief in the necessity for NATO and the American presence. They had, for example, reservations about the European Defence Community proposal.[3]

On most of the major issues surrounding the Treaty on European Union the three states held similar positions. They all favoured the movement to a single currency expecting to be among the initial participants in economic and monetary union. Similarly, they favoured the 'federal goal', which was regarded as an essential element of European development, the Netherlands insisting that it must go hand in hand with economic integration. Belgium supported federal moves partly because of a lack of a strong national identity and their new federalization.[4] For Luxembourg, it was a mechanism for defence of its autonomy, reflecting the belief that the Community helped protect the small against the powerful, a view shared by the Netherlands. In line with their attitude to federalism Belgium and the Netherlands supported in principle the so-called 'tree' approach to integration rather than the 'temple' approach. Luxembourg, while supportive of fully fledged union, held the presidency in the first half of 1991 and during the initial discussions on the new treaty. Loyal to its role in the presidency, it kept a low profile with respect to its own views, seeking to maximize progress and areas of agreement. In its famous 'non-paper' in April 1991, therefore, it based its proposals on its perception of the dominant tendencies of the prevailing discussions and proposed the three pillar temple approach, the pillars being EC, CFSP and home affairs and judicial concerns. The succeeding Dutch presidency caused surprise with its proposals in September 1991, when it abandoned the temple and opted, in line with its own predisposition, for a unified treaty structure, that is, the tree approach, bringing all the branches into the EC system. Only Belgium supported this shift, having been critical of the Luxembourg 'non-paper'. Luxembourg did not; correctly seeing it as unlikely to win general support.

All three supported more majority voting, and the creation of a common foreign and security policy (with maximum discipline among the Twelve). For Luxembourg a CFSP was a priority, and it wanted a CFSP backed by resources for decision and implementation. Belgium and the Netherlands too favoured developments in this area, with the need for qualified majority voting to avoid inertia. The three were also against the separation of CFSP and the Community's Treaty of Rome defined external role. The Netherlands was sensitive about the inclusion of defence as a Community competence stressing that any move should be compatible with NATO developments and role, and as presidency it also looked for compromise. Belgium and Luxembourg were more positive about a European dimension.

Belgium and the Netherlands were enthusiastic advocates of reducing the 'democratic deficit' and of greater powers for the European Parliament, their own parliaments making it clear at one stage that this was a precondition for ratification. Belgium was happy, as it had been in the SEA negotiations, with the the European Parliament having the right to elect the Commission President, revoke Council legislative decisions and having greater power in the area of co-operation and consent procedures. Luxembourg was much less enamoured since it only has six MEPs out of the 518. The states, however, shared concern at any possible erosion of the Commission's right of initiative, which they regarded as another defence for the small. In general, they all favoured maintaining the existing institutional balance between Commission, Council and member states fearing that any increase in Council power would increase inter-governmentalism. The Dutch were particularly fearful of any suggestion of a great power directorate emerging, being concerned at Franco-German hegemony.

All three tended to favour the expansion of Community competencies into new policy areas. Belgium was most keen, especially on social policy, a real industrial policy and measures designed to show the Community was more than a capitalist club. The Netherlands was wary of the potential costs. All three broadly supported Delors II, the Netherlands arguing that it could be the basis for agreement, Luxembourg that it should be supported and more should be given to the poorer states, and Belgium that while more should be given to the poorer states, Delors II might also be scaled down.

As can be seen, the basic positions of these states were not that dissimilar on the major issues, although there were differences of emphasis and tactics. The basic Belgium position was set out in a memorandum of 19 March 1990. In this the Belgium government set out its agenda as:

- strengthen the existing institutional machinery in order to make it more effective;
- increase the democratic component of the institutional machinery by reinforcing the powers of Parliament and developing the Community's social dimension;
- developing convergence between political co-operation and Community policy; here, the policy towards Central and Eastern Europe could be the first opportunity to put this into practice.[5]

The Dutch did not submit a memorandum of its own position in this way,[6] but the priorities for it were to maintain institutional balance, while addressing the question of democratic legitimacy by enhancing the powers of the European Parliament, and to bring the CFSP into Community competence.

FRANCE

If the Benelux has some claim to be a precursor of the European

Community, France may rightly claim a large responsibility for its origin and original nature, particularly through the seminal initiative and endeavour of Jean Monnet and Robert Schuman.

Like the Benelux states too, France has a central geographical role in Europe having land borders with five other Community states and being just 22 miles from the United Kingdom. It too has had first hand experience of war, especially of defeat and occupation, given the traumas of 1870, 1914–18 and 1939–45, especially 1940. Its geographical position and history have placed its relations with Germany, divided or united, at the centre of French concerns in the post-war period. This traditional concern was given a new dimension with the events of 1989 in Europe and the unification of Germany on 3 October 1990.

It was the concern with Germany that played a significant role in the impetus behind the ECSC, with fears of renascent German heavy industry. Four years later fears about rearming Germans played a key role in the French Assembly rejection of the EDC. But under the influence of Monnet and others, in the late 1940s and 1950s it was perceived that France needed to tie Germany into a political, security and economic relationship with France and other West European states, a perception reinforced by the looming Soviet threat.

Because of the EDC débâcle, France lost the lead on European matters to the Benelux states in the mid-1950s, but signed the Treaty of Rome in 1957. By this time a number of apprehensions about the Community were very apparent in France: fears over sovereignty and French national identity being lost to supranationalism; fears of German growing economic and industrial power; and concern at the underlying economic philosophy of the Treaty of Rome. Against these, however, were the memories of blood and war, and the high priority accorded to peace and stability, as well as the desire to see Europe as a distinctive entity. It might also be argued that the French have long felt that their true vocation was to be a – or the – European power.

Just a year after the signing of the Treaties of Rome, de Gaulle came to power in France and he dominated French policy for a decade. De Gaulle wanted France to be at the centre of Western Europe, but his vision extended to a Europe that extended from the Atlantic to the Urals, a freer, less bipolar, wider and more genuine Europe. De Gaulle's Europe might be summarized as a Europe of independent states, independent of the United States, dominated in foreign policy by France and open to Eastern Europe. His view of the future of the Community system was encapsulated in the Fouchet proposals for an inter-governmental political union, in which decisions would be made through a Council of heads of state or government on political, economic, cultural and security matters. The key concern was that there should be no surrender of national sovereignty. As de Gaulle put it in a press conference of 9 September 1965: 'nothing of any importance either in the initial planning or the later operation of the Common Market' should be decided except by the national governments. Otherwise the member states would lose their national identities and 'be ruled by some sort of technocratic body of elders, stateless and responsible to no one'.[7] These elements came together in the decision in 1966 to withdraw from NATO's integrated military structure, and the EEC French 'empty chair' crisis and boycott of July 1965 to January 1966 (see Chapter Two).

De Gaulle's immediate successors, Pompidou and Giscard d'Estaing, paid some lip-service to Gaullist rhetoric, but in practice followed very different policies. One immediate difference was seen at The Hague summit in December 1969 which opened the way for enlargement, paved the way for the development of common policies and reaffirmed the state's political commitment. Georges Pompidou seems to have been more interested in practical questions and specific policies and tasks. Valéry Giscard d'Estaing also contributed positively to European integration in his role in the development of the European Monetary System with Helmut Schmidt of the Federal Republic and Roy Jenkins of the Commission.

Interestingly, and reflecting continuing French concerns, the first Commission memorandum on economic and monetary union was by Raymond Barre, a French Commissioner in February 1968. (Barre later became Prime Minister of France.)

Collaboration on EMS has not been the only example of Franco-German leadership in the Community. There were a number of joint Franco-German proposals and memoranda to their partners in 1990–2 on the questions raised by the IGCs. They have also developed the Franco-German military brigade which may be developed to corps strength. In the early 1980s French policy towards the Community entered a new phase with the election as President of François Mitterrand, who was to be a key player in the debates about the future of the Community. In the early 1990s as his second seven-year mandate drew to a close, however, voter disillusion with his government grew and the European policies which the government upheld were not sufficiently explained. Furthermore, European integration seemed to some of the population, already worried by the perception of excessive immigration, to threaten to denature France. The idea that foreigners might vote in French municipal and European elections went hard in a country where since 1789 sovereignty had belonged to the people.

In the IGC debates France officially supported the movement to the single currency and economic and monetary union, and wished it to take place sooner rather than later. It expected to be an initial participant in the system. France believed that there should be political control of economic and financial policies, and opposed the ideas of an independent European Central Bank on the Bundesbank model. Fearful that the newly united Germany might, as an economic giant, dominate Europe and the proposed EMU, France argued that EMU had to be complemented by further political integration and Political Union, and was one of those who argued that the two IGCs must be held in parallel.

In June 1990 Mitterrand told his partners that the Union must have a 'federal finality',[8] but France did not mean quite the same thing as others by this phrase. Mitterrand, at other times, was more inclined to 'confederation'. It is also clear that the perceived need to contain a unified Germany pushed the French to favouring deeper political integration. None the less, France certainly favoured the temple rather than the tree approach, indeed the temple approach was a French idea. It was not keen on anything that presupposed France losing its leading role in Europe or its sovereignty. France was thus keen on inter-governmentalism and welcomed the structures proposed for CFSP and home affairs. CFSP had a high priority for France, especially the notion of a strong European security and defence identity firmly anchored within the new European Union, with the emphasis on a 'European European' defence and an autonomous European security and defence identity (see Chapter Ten). France favoured inter-governmentalism on matters of principle for CFSP, and retaining the right for states to be free to continue to adopt national policy initiatives in this area. However, they did favour a move to qualified majority voting in the implementation phase.

France was reluctant to see any increase in the power of the European Parliament or Commission, favouring instead the strengthening of both the Council and the European Council, itself a French creation. They still felt it was unthinkable to transfer power to centralized institutions. They ended by reluctantly making some concessions on institutional questions, especially on the European Parliament, and the increase of cases of putative majority voting, whereby a member state might be outvoted. One interesting aspect of the French case on the European Parliament was the idea that it should be matched by a Senate or Diet, but although never completely abandoned, when it became clear that it had no significant support from others, it was not pressed very hard. The French idea involved a Diet, comprising of MEPs and members of national parliaments, having supremacy over the European Parliament and setting legislative guidelines for the Community. In general, France wished to maintain the prevailing institutional balance, or at least not see any significant shift to the centre.

On the other hand, France was willing to see movement into new policy areas, a view that reflected some of the lingering interventionist tendencies of the Socialist government. In an early joint letter to the Italian Prime Minister, Andreotti, on 6 December 1990 Mitterrand and the German Chancellor, Helmut Kohl, proposed that the competencies of the Union be 'deepened and enlarged, particularly concerning the environment, health, social policy, energy, research and technology, consumer protection'.[9] However, as France moved to being a net contributor to the Community budget, it also began to be cautious about some of the new policy proposals. On Delors II it held that the plan should both be scaled down and more found for the poorest states. A quixotic feature of the French debate was the referendum on 20 September 1991 on the question: 'Do you approve the law presented to the French people by the President of the Republic authorizing ratification of the Treaty on European Union?' This was constitutionally unnecessary, since the necessary three-fifths majority of a 'congress' of the combined National Assembly and Senate had approved the treaty on 23 June 1991. It very nearly ended the Maastricht process, given that the final outcome was 51.04 per cent Yes to 48.95 per cent No on a 69.7 per cent turn-out. But Mitterrand, largely for domestic political reasons, namely to boost his flagging popularity and to embarrass his divided opponents, decided to appeal to the people. He also hoped to demonstrate French commitment to the European ideal after the blow it had received from the Danes in June 1992. The main opposition was led by Philippe Séguin and Charles Pasqua of the Gaullist *Rassemblement pour la République*, whose leadership supported a Yes vote. Arguments against related to the view that a No did not mean the end of the Community, the franc would become simply part of the DM zone if EMU went ahead, the promised million jobs would not materialize, there would be a European tax, that the 'democratic deficit' had not been addressed, and indeed that it could only be addressed by reducing the power of the Commission and returning power to national parliaments, with the reminder that de Gaulle had claimed that 'democracy is inseparable from national sovereignty', and the belief that events in the former Soviet Union and Yugoslavia showed that multinational federations were worthless.

A more strident right-wing view was espoused by Jean-Marie Le Pen of the *Front National*, who campaigned against the end of France, more immigrants, more taxes, more unemployment and more drugs. Also active were the farmers, who were complaining more about the reforms of CAP than Maastricht. A complicating feature of the campaign and voting was that the referendum was seen as on Mitterrand himself, rather than the treaty.

THE FEDERAL REPUBLIC OF GERMANY

In 1949 the Federal Republic (West Germany, FRG) and the Democratic Republic (East Germany, DRG) were created and the two Germanies existed until unification in October 1990, when the five Länder of the communist German Democratic Republic acceded to the FRG.[10] Throughout this period, and for some even since, the 'problem' of Germany has been at the heart of the European enterprise.[11] It was the problem that prompted Monnet to take his initiative in 1950, fearing that there was an 'increasing acceptance of a war that is thought to be inevitable' not because Germany 'might initiate something, but because other countries were treating her as the stake in their power games'.[12]

Response in the FRG was not unanimously favourable, some seeing the Schuman Plan as a method of stopping the revival of German industry, reflecting France's desire for cheap German coal from the Sarre and a brake on the recovery of steel-making in the Ruhr. For the SPD it was an attack on workers' rights and a real threat to the prospects for unification, which at that time was high on the German agenda. The decisive policy-maker, however, was Konrad Adenauer, elected Federal Chancellor on 17 September 1949, and Chancellor for the next 15 years. Adenauer placed a premium on Western values, had a profound distrust of the Soviets and their various unification offers, which invariably had conditions attached, such as the neutralization of a unified Germany, and also favoured the European ideal over the discredited nationalism which had besmirched Germany. There was also the belief that identification with Western European developments offered a path to moral, political and economic rehabilitation, would strengthen the new democracy through interaction with other democracies, as well as strengthening national security, given the perceived threat from the communist East, especially the Soviet Union. There was real debate, however, over the relative priorities to be given to a Western orientation as against a hope of unification, but the distrust of the Soviets and the desire to be under a security umbrella provided by the West led to the opting for the Atlantic Alliance and European integration. The FRG was thus a founder member of the ECSC, and once hesitations at home and abroad over German rearmament had been overcome, a member of NATO in 1955. In the late 1950s the SPD moved away from their original opposition so that by, and from, the early 1960s there was a degree of consensus in West German European policy. West Germany for a generation was one of the strongest supporters of both political and economic integration, although at times this has taken different forms and particular issues have provoked reservation. In the 1970s an economically powerful Germany increasingly felt able to adopt a more independent policy and provide European leadership. For example, Helmut Schmidt, who became Chancellor in 1974, was originally hostile to the Brussels bureaucracy and its works. Favouring inter-governmentalism, by the end of the decade, he was co-operating closely with the French Prime Minister, Giscard d'Estaing, on the creation of EMS as a way of managing the economic turmoil of the 1970s. In the 1980s Foreign Minister Genscher was the principal author of the Genscher–Colombo initiative, designed to promote European Union, provide it with clear political objectives and a comprehensive political and legal framework capable of development, including the expansion of the definition of security to include defence. An accompanying statement on economic integration called for a functional internal market and closer co-ordination of economic policy.

A positive attitude to European integration was aided by the fact that, domestically, the CAP was helpful in German politics. It had the effect of taking added value off the urban and industrialized parts of Germany and recycling it, via Brussels, to the agrarian parts, notably Bavaria. Since this did not involve budgetary processes in Germany, it was a money laundering operation, which might otherwise have provoked criticism. Moreover, as citizens of a federation – of Anglo-French creation – German leaders had no difficulty with a wider federation of Europe. In the German Basic Law, the competencies of government – *Kreis*, *Land* and *Bund* – are more or less clearly apportioned and the addition of a European layer is conceptually easy. But it is also a condition of the system that there should be democracy at every level. Accordingly, the European layer needs to be subject to a democratic control, represented in German eyes by the development of the European Parliament.

The velvet revolution in Eastern Europe in 1989 transformed the context of German policy, and for some of its neighbours raised the ghost of Germany past. An initial British response, for example, was that German unification was not in prospect. The response of Chancellor Kohl, who won round President Mitterrand, was to try to tie the new Germany firmly into a network of interdependent relationships and into deeper European integration. Thus 19 April 1990 saw a joint letter from Mitterrand and Kohl to the Irish presidency, noting that the 'far-reaching changes in Europe', and the completion of the internal market, made it 'necessary to accelerate the political construction of the Europe of the Twelve' and to transform relations into a 'European Union' as envisaged by the Single European Act. They called, therefore, for intensified preparations for the IGC on EMU and for the Dublin European Council to

> initiate preparations for an inter-governmental conference on political union . . . the objective is to: strengthen the democratic legitimation of the union – render its institutions more efficient – ensure unity and coherence of the union's economic, monetary and political action, define and implement a common foreign and security policy. . . . We wish the inter-governmental conference on political union to be held in parallel to the conference on economic and monetary union . . .[13]

Germany was keen to demonstrate that unification would not

weaken its commitment to integration, that the aim was 'a European Germany, not a German Europe'. The Dublin Council endorsed German unification and agreed to an examination of the question of a second IGC. Franco-German leadership was vital to the IGC's developments, although they had several differences of view (even on CFSP, on which they made several joint proposals, Germany being a little more cautious about a European defence identity than France), and Germany in particular was anxious not to marginalize the United Kingdom. To give effect to the Franco-German relationship, the Germans were willing to compromise to some extent on economic and especially monetary policy by agreeing to pool authority for it, while demanding a high degree of fiscal and exchange rate rectitude from those who aspired to share it. As joint architects of the EMS and its ERM, France and Germany had a stake in sustaining it when it ran into trouble in 1992, and the German authorities were prepared to go to very considerable lengths to help the franc, lengths which were the envy of other weaker currency states.

Chancellor Kohl personally has been deeply committed to European integration, although he has come up against the limits of internal support for certain aspects of the process, especially the increasing concern over the costs to Germany of a number of current and proposed policies and the perceived challenge posed to the mark by EMU and the single currency. Germany officially has championed these developments, but insisted that those moving to the third stage of EMU would need to meet tough convergence criteria and also insisted on the independence of the proposed European Central Bank System from political control, on the Bundesbank model.

German influence can also be seen in the priority accorded to price stability in the new arrangements. Neither the Bundesbank nor the public seem to be as convinced of the benefits of the new arrangements as the government.

In the ratification process the government bowed to public pressure and agreed to make a German move to the third stage of EMU and the single currency, subject to the approval of a two-thirds majority of both Houses of Parliament. Problems also arose when several *Länder* claimed that the Federal government had negotiated away some of their rights, and claimed the government had no right to do so. In June 1992, fortified by the Danish 'No', they threatened to veto ratification in the *Bundesrat*. Eventually, a compromise was reached which allows the *Länder* to be directly represented in future Community negotiations on areas falling within their competence such as education, culture and the police. This is an example of the German determination that federalism should not be equated with centralism, but rather had to be seen as a decentralizing concept both in Germany and in the Community. This was a crucial factor in German support for subsidiarity, which the *Bundesrat* made a condition of support for Maastricht in November 1991.

A key feature of the German position was the importance attached to a rectifying of the 'democratic deficit'. Kohl made movement on this matter and increased institutional strength a condition for approval of EMU. Germany wanted real powers for the European Parliament. It should have an equal say with the Council on legislation, should have a right of initiative and be involved in the appointment of the Commission and its President. While happy to see a reduction in central power in light of subsidiarity, Kohl made the European Parliament dimension something of a crusade and was also prepared to see an extension of qualified majority voting in the Council. The new powers for European Parliament fell short of German demands, and they had to wait until Edinburgh for the question of extra seats in the Parliament for the new Germany to be resolved.

Adherence to subsidiarity influenced the German approach to the granting of more competencies to the Union, as did a considerable preoccupation with costs and a belief in a non interventionist approach to a number of matters, especially economic. New areas were to meet the test of subsidiarity, and the areas Germany pushed hardest for were in the fields of asylum seekers, visa applications, cross-border crime and counter-terrorist policies, all of which were dealt with inter-governmentally at Maastricht. The German government opposed the scale of the Delors II proposals, being preoccupied with the cost of integrating the five eastern *Länder*. Germany upset many of its partners in the winter of 1991–2 with its assertiveness over the recognition of Croatia and Slovenia, and its determination to press ahead on this matter regardless of the views of other member states (see Chapter Ten). In 1992, its domestic anti-inflation policy of high interest rates put breaking strains on the ERM.

In an ironic development in 1993 Germany's ratification of the Treaty on European Union was put in doubt by a legal challenge

before Germany's Constitutional Court. Whilst the political establishment remained in favour of the treaty, an unusual mixture of
Greens, far-right Republicans, and, most notably, a former German
senior Commission official, challenged the constitutionality of the
treaty under German law. The crux of the complaint was that in the
treaty Germany gave too many of its powers to Brussels. In the
summer of 1993 the Court asked the government a series of questions
about the influence that the German state would continue to have in
the Community if the treaty were ratified. The Court, however, has
generally sought to avoid causing international embarrassment for
the government and has often tempered technicalities with political
reality.

ITALY

Like Germany, Italy had a practical and psychological need to
overcome its past, as well as rehabilitating itself and re-establishing
its credibility. Like the Federal Republic too, Italy, which for nearly
thirty years was concerned at the power of the Communist Party of
Italy (PCI), and a number of other destabilizing tendencies, sought
to protect itself by intimate involvement with the Community,
NATO and the West in general, perceiving a linkage between such
involvement and political stability at home. There was thus a
pragmatic as well as an idealistic element in the original Italian choice
to support integration.

There was a belief in some quarters in the European ideal, the past
having discredited the nation state and sovereignty as a concept.
These influences are reflected in the post-war Constitution, which
envisages agreeing 'on conditions of equality with other states, to
such limitation of sovereignty as may be necessary for a system
calculated to ensure peace and justice between nations . . .',[14] in the
early activities of Foreign Minister Sforza, who sought in 1947 a
Franco-Italian customs union, and in the life and work of the
federalist Altiero Spinelli. This mixture of pragmatism and idealism
is one reason why it is not just in recent years that there has been a
'contradiction between the prevalence of pro-integrationist rhetoric
in Italian political circles and their marked inability or unwillingness
to translate this into policy action'.[15] This has been apparent on a
number of occasions in the last 40+ years, most recently in the fact

that according to the Commission, in 1990, Italy had implemented fewer internal market directives than any other state, as well as paying least attention to judgments given against it in the European Court of Justice.[16] Similarly apparent has been a difficulty in matching France and Germany in terms of political weight, and indeed, concern at the recurring prospect of a Franco-German hegemony. This concern was one factor in Italian support for British membership of the Community and more recently has been evidenced in the seeking of links with the British and the Spanish.

A number of reasons can be adduced for the lack of Italian political weight in the Community: internal political instability of governments has reduced the authority of Italian policy-makers in the higher circles of Community policy-making; there have been problems in policy co-ordination within the governmental system and a lack of preparation; policy has often been reactive rather than proactive; and these difficulties have been compounded by recurring economic weakness. This latter has caused a number of difficulties for Italy, which were neatly summed up in the context of the EMS debate in 1978–9 by Guido Carli, President of Confindustria: 'Italy cannot afford to join this scheme, and she cannot allow herself to remain distant from it.'[17] There has been on this and other occasions considerable concern at possible exclusion from the core of European developments and a fear of a 'two-speed' Europe with Italy in the slow lane. Italy has, however, on a number of occasions taken initiatives and been diplomatically active. Colombo, for example, played a role in resolving the 1965–6 crisis as well as in the Genscher–Colombo proposals of the 1980s. The Milan European Council, under Italian presidency in June 1985, was crucial in bringing about the IGC that led to the Single European Act.

In the 1970s the Community gained greater priority in its own right in Italian policy, partly because the energy crisis and the enlargements to include Greece, Portugal and Spain focused more attention on the Mediterranean arena. Italy strongly supported these enlargements as shifting the centre of gravity in the Community more towards the south, and has as well promoted the idea of a Mediterranean CSCE. None the less, Italy has not been able to influence many of the internal Community policies. For example, despite the importance of agriculture to the Italian economy over the last forty years, it has been others who have taken the lead on the issue and made it predominantly a policy for temperate agriculture.

It was at the end of the Italian presidency in 1990 that the two IGCs were convened. Italy had already intimated a day after the Belgian memorandum in March 1990 that it supported an IGC on institutional reforms, and their foreign minister at the time, De Michelis, conformed to the pattern of ardent Italian rhetorical support for integration and federalism. At Dublin in June 1990 the Prime Minister, Andreotti, called for a 'federative union'.[18] Not surprisingly, in principle they favoured the tree approach to integration, although recognizing the reality of the situation, they joined in voting the Dutch draft of September 1991 down. There is also some evidence that they gradually shifted to a position that was differentiated according to the question in hand, that is a blend of federalism, confederalism and inter-governmentalism.

Late in the summer, after the Iraqi invasion of Kuwait, the Italians made CFSP a priority, calling it in a memorandum of 18 September 1990 the 'most visible objective to be realized in the Inter-governmental Conference on Political Union'.[19] For them the Gulf showed the Twelve must 'extend the competencies of the Union to all aspects of security without limitations' and the September memorandum went on most radically to propose the 'transfer to the Union [of] the competencies presently being exercised by WEU', since this would imply a security guarantee among members, involve defence ministers in the work of the Union, and enable the Union to concert policy on crises outside Europe. They made other significant proposals on this matter on 5 February 1991 and with the British on 5 October 1991, these being something of a compromise, and clearly representing a move in the direction of an 'Atlantic European defence'. On CFSP the Italians clearly believed that there should be qualified majority voting by foreign ministers on implementation after general principles and guidelines had been laid down by the European Council and a firm obligation to cohesion once decisions had been made. On Community matters generally they believed there should be majority voting across the board.

The Italians took a radical line in regard to the European Parliament, their own parliament having said it would not ratify the Treaty unless the European Parliament accepted it. They had earlier supported the European Parliament's 1984 Draft Treaty (which was based on Spinelli's work) and in 1989 88 per cent of voters had agreed that the European Parliament should be allowed to draw up a European constitution. In 1990–2, they took the view that the

European Parliament should have co-decision with the Council, a right of initiative, and the right to approve both the Commission President's appointment and that of the Commission as a whole, and perhaps eventually the powers of a national parliament. The Italians were firmly against French proposals for a Diet, since it elevated the position of the national dimension, and suggestions which emphasized the primacy of the European Council, or inter-governmentalism, although as early as October 1990 a Kohl–Andreotti meeting apparently endorsed the idea of a representative body for the regions. On many of these issues Italy behaved almost as a small state, seeing integration as a protection for itself and as a way of enlarging its own scope of action. There was also support for 'deepening' on the grounds that it might delay the next enlargement, an enlargement that poses some practical problems for the Italians, especially in relation to Austria and Switzerland, as well as tying the unified Germany firmly into the Western European orbit.

Italy strongly supported the movement to EMU and the single currency, but opposed the German insistence on tough or mechanical convergence criteria, because of the difficulties Italy would have in meeting them, especially because of its public deficit, and the dangers of the transition to the third stage in fact leading to tiers among the Twelve and the two-speed Europe it had always opposed. Although for most of the period there was little real debate on the IGC negotiations, it was this aspect which occasioned most debate, especially after the Economic Affairs Commissioner warned the other eleven member states in November 1991 that Italy's economy presented a considerable risk to EMU. But for an Italy which aspired to be a charter member of the European Union, and which increasingly was subject to internal problems of corruption and a sharpening of the North/South tension, a monetary authority, standing aloof from the political battle, looked like the most promising way of emerging from short-termism and political chicanery.

The Italians strongly favoured the wide extension of the competencies of the Union, being particularly keen on the social policy. Rather than the principle of subsidiarity being the touchstone, the Italians tended to believe that a range of policies should be dealt with at the Community level, although as time went on they were cautious about Delors II, taking the position that it should be scaled down, although they wanted more to go to the poorer states.

Italy was moving towards joining Germany, the United Kingdom and France as a net contributor to the budget.

IRELAND

Of the three states that joined in January 1973, Ireland has been by far the most *communautaire*. Yet until 1973 its history, its location and its economic dependence on the United Kingdom made it impossible for Ireland to join. Within Ireland the real watershed in attitudes was in the period 1958–61. Up to then it had been outside the mainstream of European politics, having been a non-belligerent in 'the Emergency' (that is, the Second World War), and so pre-occupied with the Partition of the island of Ireland that it had both refused to join NATO in 1949 and pursued the so-called policy of the 'sore thumb' in European institutions it did belong to, especially the Council of Europe (i.e., the Irish single-mindedly thumbing their noses at British occupation of Northern Ireland). 'Neutrality', Partition, irredentism, the claustrophobic relationship with Britain and protectionism were the key features of Irish policy.

In the late 1950s a sea change began in Irish politics. One factor was the growing perception that protectionism had not succeeded. Another, related factor was the dramatic change in the external environment brought about first by the discussions of a free trade area in Western Europe, by the creation of the EEC and subsequently EFTA, by Ireland's exclusion from both (the latter largely at Britain's doing since Britain argued that EFTA was for developed states only and should exclude agriculture), and most fundamentally, by Britain's decision to apply for EEC membership in the summer of 1961. Many felt Ireland faced 'Hobson's choice' in 1961, it being clear that if Britain applied, 'we also will apply', since if Ireland's trading partners joined 'together in an economic union, we cannot be outside it'. It was not a choice of joining or leaving things as they were since the status quo was disappearing. If Britain did not join, neither would Ireland.[20] Ireland's bid was stillborn because of de Gaulle's attitude to the United Kingdom.

When the climate for Britain changed, so too did the climate for Ireland, and by 1969 it had had a number of years to seek to adjust to the new requirements that it would face. On 10 May 1972 the Irish people voted 83 per cent to 17 per cent in favour of membership, with a turnout of 71 per cent. In the debate the key arguments for were: the British decision, fear of jeopardizing trade if they did not join, a belief that membership would free them from the suffocating relationship with Britain, the prospect of agricultural markets with guaranteed prices, the prospect of foreign investment, the alleged benefits of Protocol No. 30 in the Treaty of Accession, (which recognizing the economic and social imbalances that existed in the Community between the regions, noted that they would need to be removed, a statement the Irish interpreted as a commitment to far-reaching regional policy), a vague hope that it might contribute to ameliorating 'the troubles' in Northern Ireland, and that there was no commitment to joining any alliance, and according to the proponents of membership no threat to neutrality. The 'pro' campaign enjoyed the support of both major parties, Fianna Fail and Fine Gael.

The opposition was disparate and divided. The main opposition came from the Irish Labour Party, but also involved were Official and Provisional Sinn Fein. Labour attacked the terms, the capitalist orientation of the EEC, the problems posed to traditional Irish industries, as well as disputing the benefits to agriculture. They bitterly contrasted the Irish alleged preparedness to enter military alliances and abandon neutrality with the principled stand of Austria, Sweden and Switzerland, who all said membership was incompatible with neutrality.

Table 11.2 *Irish voting in referendums on EC membership, the SEA and the Treaty on European Union*

		Yes(%)	No(%)	Turn-out (%)
EC	1972	83.1	16.9	71
SEA	1987	69.9	30.1	44
TEU	1992	68.7	31.3	57

The initial years were like a honeymoon, as Ireland benefited from the CAP and other transfers to the tune of £500 million. Garret FitzGerald, the Foreign Minister, summed up the Irish position in November 1975, noting that since Ireland would be 'to a remarkable degree a net beneficiary of Community policies . . . Ireland must be careful not to appear too much in the role of constant '*demandeur*' . . . Ireland must seek to compensate for this by playing a positive and constructive role in the present running and future development of the Community'.[21] Not surprisingly, therefore, Ireland supported the Commission and was anxious about any inter-governmental tendencies, especially any that smacked of a 'directorate' or Franco-German hegemony, such as the EMS genesis, or of ideas related to two-tier developments. Partly for such reasons, and given substantial side payments, Ireland joined the EMS at its commencement. On 30 March 1979 adherence to the EMS brought about the break with the link with sterling for the first time in 150 years, and was the final demonstration to many of Irish independence from the United Kingdom.

Fifteen years after entry the Irish people were again consulted in a referendum about Irish membership, the occasion being the ratification of the Single European Act. The referendum was necessary because the Irish Supreme Court took the view that Title III of the Act on EPC was contrary to the Irish constitution's prescription that the government should be unfettered in its foreign policy. In the referendum, 69.9 per cent of those voting voted in favour of ratifying the Single Act, but in what many saw as significant, only 44 per cent of the electorate voted. The honeymoon was over and there was much disappointment with the CAP and concern over its reform, and especially the Social and Regional Funds and the lack of genuine cohesion. None the less the arguments that had been relevant before were still decisive. For example, it was now calculated that between 1973 and 1986 Ireland had received IR£5,744.6 million in net receipts from the Community, and that in 1986 the net budgetary transfers were equivalent to 13½ per cent of current government revenue. No wonder it was argued that to leave the Community would be 'economic suicide'.[22] Given that EPC had occasioned the referendum, neutrality played a role in the debate. To counter accusations that they had given up Irish neutrality, the government appended to their instrument of ratification a declaration affirming that in Irish eyes,

> the provisions of Title III do not affect Ireland's long established policy of military neutrality and that coordination of positions on the political and economic aspects of security does not include the military aspects of security or procurement for military purposes and does not affect

Ireland's right to act or refrain from acting in any way which might affect Ireland's international status of military neutrality.[23]

In October 1990, the Taoiseach, or Prime Minister, Charles Haughey, told the Dail, the Irish Parliament, that the four principles that guided Irish policy on the IGCs – maintaining the link and balance between political integration and social and economic integration; that the Community should play a positive political role; it should be deepened and made more efficient; and cohesion – were crucial.[24] Ireland has always favoured political integration as a protection for small states against larger neighbours. But given its relatively recent independence it has also been sensitive to not going too far in the federalist direction, although it has argued that integration enhances Irish influence in Europe and the world. It was prepared in the IGCs to let others take the lead on this matter. It strongly supported subsidiarity, especially in the social and environmental areas, although simultaneously it was worried that the principle could be abused and inhibit the development of policies in Irish interests.

Ireland supported EMU and a single currency, being fearful of any second division in which it might find itself again closely tied to the British economy. It wanted the transition to the third stage to be irreversible and short. Ireland anticipated moving to the third stage in the first wave of states.

Not surprisingly firm commitments to cohesion were a priority for Ireland in the negotiations. Ireland was the first state to make firm proposals in this area, although it did not press its demands as stridently as Spain. Cohesion was important, given the economic realities of Ireland, their view of the original commitments and since otherwise EMU was perceived as widening the regional disparities that already existed, especially in peripheral areas. The Irish insisted on inclusion of economic and social cohesion in the treaty, and were rewarded with Title XIV on Economic and Social Cohesion as well as Protocol 15 on the same topic. Also not surprisingly Ireland strongly favoured the creation of the new Cohesion Fund, seeking IR£6 billion in structural and cohesion funds over the next five years, and subsequently supported the Delors II proposals, which provided for the Fund.

Ireland favoured the current institutional balance and distribution of powers for the same reasons as other small states, but while paying lip service to increasing the powers of the European Parliament, they were not as enthusiastic as some given fears over its possible urban composition and the small numbers of Irish MEPs. It supported more majority voting, but was also cautious, especially in the area of social policy. It favoured those aspects of social policy which touched on employment and workers rights, but was anxious lest there be any movement into areas touching upon issues of personal morality. Thus Protocol 17 attempted to make clear that nothing in the current treaty nor any Community treaty affected the 'application *in* Ireland of Article 40.3.3 of the constitution of Ireland', that is the prohibition on abortion and the equal right to life of child and mother. There was later some confusion over what this meant, and whether it affected travel abroad for abortions or the right to information. Formal amendment initially was rejected by the other members, who did not wish to open up the prospect of renegotiation, but in May 1992 they approved a 'solemn declaration' to be attached to the treaty saying that 'it was and is their intention that the Protocol shall not limit freedom either to travel between member states or . . . to obtain or make available in Ireland, information relating to services lawfully available in member states.' Confusion, however, persisted for the rest of 1992 and was unresolved by an Irish referendum on the abortion issue late in the year.[25]

CFSP proposals were always delicate for Ireland, given its history and the declaration attached to SEA on Ireland's military neutrality. It favoured the continuation of unanimity for CFSP decisions, but came to accept the agreed procedure of unanimity for the first step, followed by the possibility of majority voting if all agreed on questions of implementation. It accepted the merging of EPC and General Affairs meetings. Ireland has always opposed membership in existing alliance systems, but in line with its long standing policy it did accept that it would participate if the Community developed its own security system. The Minister of Defence in November 1991 acknowledged that Europe must have its own common defence system, which would not be subservient to the United States and that Ireland would need to play a role in determining that system. Again it was fearful of being in a second tier of development, and so, although it opposed the Italian idea of a merger between the European Union and WEU, it finally did accept the Franco-German idea of the European Council deciding on defence questions, with the WEU implementing those decisions. Ireland took the view that these matters had effectively been subcontracted to the WEU. Ireland could afford to be somewhat relaxed on this issue because it did not believe that any major decisions were imminent, and the Treaty on European Union, echoing the London Report of 1981, did say (article J.4.3) that the proposals 'shall not prejudice the specific character of the security and defence policy of certain member states'. Furthermore, real progress was to wait until another IGC in 1996, and any changes would require unanimity. Meantime, CFSP was purely inter-governmental. Ireland was still not committed to an alliance, or to a mutual defence commitment. Despite these reservations on defence, Ireland was quite keen to see the European Union play a more active and coherent role in international politics.

On 18 June 1992 68.7 per cent of Irish voters voted in favour of ratification in a turnout of 57.3 per cent after a campaign emphasizing the economic benefits of membership, the prospect of IR£6 billion to come and warnings of losses in foreign investment.

DENMARK

The Danes have had four referendums on EC questions (Table 11.3). Although turn-outs have been high on these occasions, the lack of enthusiasm towards membership is reflected in the Danish turn-outs for direct elections to the European Parliament in 1979, 1984 and 1989, namely 47.8 per cent, 52.3 per cent and 46.1 per cent respectively. The 1979 and 1989 figures placed Danish participation above that of the United Kingdom, but below that of all of the other member states. Indeed, Denmark, along with Britain, has been consistently the most sceptical of the member states. Part of the reason has been its geographical position between the Baltics, Scandinavia and Western Europe, and another had been its close ties with the UK market. Also, it has been said that it is possible to characterize Danish policy as reflecting the tension between 'two opposing tendencies, towards involvement in and withdrawal from international politics'; while historically there has always been a concern with its 'political relations with the great power neighbour'.[26] It was a founder member of the OEEC and Council of Europe and was generally sympathetic to the British position. It was not involved in discussions on the ECSC, since coal and steel were of no relevance to Denmark. Of more relevance were Nordic efforts in 1947 and

1948–9 seeking to bring about a Nordic Customs Union and a Nordic Defence Union. These negotiations were unsuccessful but a passport union was agreed. At the time of the ECSC negotiations the Scandinavians were involved in discussions on a Nordic Council, which came into existence in 1952, but which because of the previous difficulties avoided questions of high politics and was avowedly inter-governmental. Originally, the Council had no statutes, permanent headquarters or secretariat, and it has no power to oblige governments to comply with recommendations. The Danes have often looked north as much as south, and this has been a continuing feature of their policy.

Table 11.3 *Danish voting in referendums on EC membership, the SEA and the Treaty on European Union*

		Yes(%)	No(%)	Turn-out (%)
EC	1972	63.3	36.7	90.1
SEA	1987	56.2	43.8	74.8
TEU	1992	49.3	50.7	82.3
TEU	1993	56.8	43.2	86.2

The Danes were one of those states that took the initiative in the OEEC to try to establish a free trade area that would include the Six, but to no avail. At other times too they sought to be a bridge between the Six and others, especially EFTA, also to no avail. The Danes were founder members of EFTA in 1960, although they would have preferred a wider free trade area with agriculture included. They received a shock in 1958 when a Danish government commission questioned whether Denmark was ready for free trade or EEC membership without severe economic dislocation.[27] In 1961 the Danes applied for EEC membership following the British application. Given the importance of the British (and German) market to them, the Danes wished to participate in the evolution of the CAP. Their application and negotiation was overshadowed by the British, and floundered when the United Kingdom's did. 1962 saw the codification of Nordic co-operation in the Nordic Council and some very limited institutional development. In the 1960s Denmark's EFTA membership benefited the Danish economy and the diversification of its markets. Again, circumstances outside its control transformed the situation in 1969 with The Hague summit and subsequent British application. The Danish negotiations were not difficult, indeed the Danes proposed full membership without a transitional period; an offer rejected by the Six. Some difficulty was caused over the Faeroe Islands and Greenland[28] in relation to fisheries, and the Danes were also anxious about their former EFTA partners who were not applying for EEC membership.

The Danish constitution allows for the transfer of power to international organization, if five-sixths of the Parliament (Folketing) agree, or failing that if a simple majority of the Folketing is supported in a referendum. To avoid making the question of membership an election issue in the winter of 1971–2, however, it was agreed that the issue be put to a referendum. In a vote in the Folketing in September 1972, a few weeks before the referendum, the opposition managed to muster more than one-sixth of the vote. In another twist, the Norwegian referendum took place a week before the Danish people voted, and produced a No. The real issue was summed up as 'Ever since the Six was formed, the Danes have faced the predicament of having a too significant economic interest in the Common Market to ignore it but too many restraining factors to join alone,'[29] hardly a ringing endorsement. Denmark joined because it felt it could not afford to be out; it was an economic decision to join a customs union, conditioned by the policies of others and external developments. It was not a vote for European political integration or federalism; and there was always reservation about 'deepening'. Ironically, there was support for increasing the scope of integration to include social, environmental, industrial, regional and economic, trade and monetary policy. The Danes were positive about the CAP and against major reforms; against other protectionist tendencies in the EEC and barriers to trade; and for fixed currencies and the EMS. The oil, energy and economic crises of the 1970s combined to reinforce the lack of enthusiasm for membership, especially as it had been sold on economic grounds. They also had great difficulty with the common fisheries policy, being regarded as the least conservation-minded. In the 1980s the Danes continued to be comfortable with the economic dimension of integration, and supported moves to the internal market. They pushed hard on the environmental question, finally being satisfied that they could maintain their own high standards. Political integration continued to be a problem. The Danes were a 'footnote' state in the Dooge Report (that is, they expressed a number of reservations in footnotes), and voted against the calling of an IGC at the Milan European Council in 1985. They had earlier resisted the Genscher–Colombo proposals, especially those seeking to integrate security, defence and foreign policy into the EC system, and were later against the linkage being made between the single market and institutional reform. They took the view that 'the difficulties facing the construction of Europe resulted from a failure to implement the existing treaties fully and could be remedied by the strict application of the Treaties.'[30]

Having been obliged to participate in a treaty revision they did not want, the Danes made the best out of a bad job by positively encouraging the IGC to strengthen Community competence in social affairs and in the protection of the environment. Their motives were mixed. They hoped and expected that the Community would be obliged to work for standards which were closer to those that Denmark had for long applied, thereby reducing whatever was the competitive disadvantage which Denmark might have inflicted on itself. But the government also wished to put some brakes on internal demands for further – and costly – improvements in the Danish welfare state, by deploying the argument that Denmark must not, in its own self-interest, get too far ahead of its partners. Denmark also secured, in a quiet way, the first of the opt-outs which were later to become a feature of the Community's constitution. This was the so-called Danish clause of the Single Market article of the SEA. Article 100a, para.4, enables a member state to maintain higher standards than those accepted by the Community to protect the environment or the working environment, provided its higher standards do not restrict trade. In practice, the Danes never applied to the Commission to use this facility – nor did any other member state.

The Folketing rejected the SEA in January 1986 by 80 to 75 votes on the grounds of the erosion of national sovereignty, and asked the government to seek to re-negotiate. The other member states refused, and the subsequent referendum endorsed the SEA, the government arguing a No would put Danish membership of the EC into question, and strongly playing the economic card, Denmark being a large beneficiary of the Community budget. Denmark, however, consistently has been one of the states to emphasize the upholding of national sovereignty.[31]

In October 1990 Danish parties representing 75 per cent of the Folketing agreed on a memorandum which was submitted to the other member states, and which set out the basic Danish position on the IGCs. It was clear that 'the principle of subsidiarity should be stated as a basic principle in the preamble and should be applied in each specific area'.[32] Although not mentioned by name there was a clear antipathy to federalism in the document, with talk of 'gradual deepening' and 'gradual development' and several references to strengthening the existing Community. Later in the context of the proposals of others, the Folketing demanded explicit references to a federal goal or vocation be dropped, and the Danes opposed the new Dutch draft of September 1991. On the other hand, after German unification the Danes were worried about the power of their neighbour, and some of them saw European Union as a way of containing Germany. The October 1990 memorandum argued that the institutions had coped 'satisfactorily' in the past, there, therefore, being 'no need to consider any fundamental changes in the *natural* balance'.[33] Thus majority voting should only be introduced in some areas particularly the environment and in social policy and labour market matters where Denmark wanted progress. The memorandum argued for the strengthening of the role of national parliaments, and drew especial attention to the role of the Folketing Common Market Committee. Its proposals on strengthening the European Parliament were modest, allowing greater scope for the co-operation procedure (but not co-decision), allowing the European Parliament to require the Commission to put forward proposals called for by the Parliament, and allowing it to hold hearings in member states that had not complied with or implemented EC legislation. An ombudsman was to be responsible to the parliament. Mention was made of increased openness in the institutions, and of the possibility of some Council meetings being in public. The Danes would accept a reduction in the size of the Commission and referred to a 'Committee . . . under the auspices of the Council . . . to enable the regions to be given a hearing'. If cautious on the IGC on Political Union, the memorandum supported EMU, seeing it as a 'natural extension of the creation of the internal market', and believing that it should be based on tough criteria. The Danes hoped that EMU would help keep inflation under control, and that the ECSB would be an alternative to domination by the Bundesbank. It accepted the case for an independent ECSB, but worried about democratic accountability, which should balance 'the necessary independence' of the ECSB. While accepting price stability as a supreme goal, the Danes wanted explicit references to the goals of full employment and environmentally sustainable development. They also wanted to make sure that in regard to 'fiscal and budgetary policy of the individual Member States the Treaty must reflect the principle of subsidiarity'.

On new competencies the Danish memorandum made the enhancement of environmental policy a priority, along with social policy 'as a means of distributing the benefits deriving from the internal market. . . . It is important that solidarity . . . be shown.' There was a call for a series of minimum standards to be laid down in this area. They were anxious to avoid social dumping by multinational companies. There was also a call for an examination of the introduction of minimum rates of income tax, VAT and other taxes (Denmark is heavily taxed). Other desiderata included: state aid regulations to be tightened up; consumer protection to be made a priority; decisions on development aid to be taken by qualified majority vote; a legal basis for the consideration of health policy to be introduced where necessary; and a specific basis for education and cultural policy. With typical caution the Danish memorandum accepted 'investigating the possibility of and scope for greater co-ordination of the economic, political and security aspects of external policy' but 'rejects the idea that European Political Co-operation should come to include co-operation in defence policies, *inter alia* the setting-up of common military forces'.

Denmark, of course, still had not joined WEU and remained pro-NATO and Atlanticist, despite some reservations about NATO policy in the 1980s.[34] It favoured the continuation of consensus in EPC/CFSP. It saw the need for greater co-ordination between EPC and EC both institutionally and practically. It also called for the Community to be open to third countries, especially in Europe, and for enlargement to proceed.

During the IGCs the government was kept in constant check by the Folketing, which, for example, made the inclusion of a Protocol forbidding the sale of summer houses to foreigners a condition of support (it was included in the treaty as Protocol I, and allowed the Danes to maintain the status quo). In March 1991 the government submitted a number of proposals, keeping CFSP as a second pillar and in practice endorsing the temple approach. The Council was to be the decisive body in this area.

As Maastricht approached, some of the Danish consensus began to erode, especially on the single currency. This led to Protocol 12, which noted that the Danish constitution might 'imply a referendum in Denmark prior to Danish participation in the third stage of Economic and Monetary Union . . . [and] in the event of a notification that Denmark will not participate in the third stage, Denmark shall have an exemption. . . .'[35] The Danish government, however, still said that it wished to take a full part in EMU, and noted that Denmark already fulfilled the convergence criteria. Only two small Danish parties opposed the deal agreed at Maastricht, and the Folketing on 12 May 1992 supported it by 130 to 25. Yet in the referendum on 2 June 1992 it was rejected by a margin of 46,269 votes (50.7 per cent to 49.3 per cent).

The opposition was composed of a variety of disparate interests, but is perhaps best summed up in an old Danish saying, '[be] prepared to sit next to someone but not on his lap', a saying that had a particular salience given Danish views of Germany.

- The fears included a loss of democracy, uncompensated for by a remote European Parliament.
- An acceptance of the internal market, but no belief in the need for political union – 'Ja til Europa, Nej til unionen', linked to traditional concerns about independence and sovereignty.
- Concern that the treaty did not go far enough on social and environmental matters, such that it would undermine the Danes' own higher standards;
- That it went too far on immigration and citizenship.
- An exaggerated fear of young Danes being conscripted to a European army, even worse an army dominated by Germany.

Against such fears the government and others tried to argue that there was a danger that the other eleven would go ahead with European Union leaving Denmark on its own, and that there was no possibility of renegotiation. In fact, after the 'no' vote it was made clear the eleven would not proceed without the Danes, and in the second half of 1992 there was much negotiation about the treaty.

After a pause for reflection, and to await the vote in the French referendum, the government put together a package, which seven of the eight parties in the Folketing accepted as a national compromise in October 1992, the opposition Socialist People's Party accepting but the Progress Party still saying no. The national compromise looked more radical on paper than in practice. It required a declaration making clear that Denmark was not committed to the third stage of EMU, including a single currency (the treaty already contained a provision for a Danish referendum). Denmark would not accept any obligation to join the WEU or a common defence of the European Union, again despite the fact that references to this in Maastricht imply no commitment to such defence. Other questions involved the treaty's provisions on European citizenship, the closer co-operation on home affairs and justice, assurances that nothing will be done to force Denmark to lower its existing national social and environmental protection standards, and a call for greater openness in EC decision-making, more explicit attention to subsidiarity and a strengthening of the role of both national and European Parliaments. A further problem was the call that 'Danish agreement must be juridically binding for all Twelve Community member states'. It was this that proved to be so difficult at the Edinburgh European Council in December, although the Danish government and their Community partners, as is elaborated in Chapter Twelve below, believed that the Conclusions reached in Edinburgh squared the circle.

BRITAIN

If the Danes have proved to be something of a thorn in the flesh of their partners, the United Kingdom has also been 'An Awkward Partner'[36] for the other member states, and this awkwardness too has stemmed from deep-seated roots in British political culture.

One element of the problem has been the difficulty in adjusting to the secular loss of relative power and declining economic base since the mid-nineteenth century.[37] This trend accelerated as a result of both world wars, and with the loss of empire. The problem was exacerbated in so far as the trend was obscured by being on the winning side in both world wars, by the award of a permanent seat on the UN Security Council with its accompanying veto, by the possession of the largest empire ever seen, and by the military power Britain still enjoyed in 1945, a power soon to be enhanced by the acquisition of the atomic bomb. Britain had also been the leading West European power on the allied side during the 1940–5 period. There was a widespread perception that Britain had 'won' the war, that it was a global power and a pervasive belief in Britain's greatness. While there had been a 'Descent from Power',[38] that descent had been somewhat obscured, and given Britain's position in 1945 somewhat exaggerated.

The United Kingdom still had a global view of its position. Others might think almost exclusively in terms of European reconstruction and influence, but Britain believed that it was 'not solely a European power',[39] and therefore had wider considerations on its mind. Indeed, in the 1960s Harold Wilson as Prime Minister could still talk of Britain's frontiers being on the Himalayas, and in 1987 Mrs Thatcher could still talk triumphantly of British troops being present in over thirty states in the world. But within this global context there were three spheres of influence that were regarded as particularly crucial to Britain: the 'special relationship' with the United States; its colonial heritage and inheritance, and the balance of power concern with developments in Europe. The problem for Britain was that the secular economic decline meant increasingly that it was unable or unwilling to provide the resources necessary to sustain these interests and roles, such that increasingly it began to focus on the European dimension, while still occasionally hankering after a wider and larger role.

The 'special relationship' stemmed from shared values, culture and language, although these were never quite as shared as sometimes imagined. There were also close personal ties stemming from wartime collaboration. The British had been desperate to sustain these ties and US involvement in Western Europe after 1945 as they saw US power as the only real guarantee against the perceived colossal power of the Soviet Union, and of European peace and stability. For the British, American involvement in the North Atlantic Treaty was a triumph of diplomacy. The relationship was deeply strained by the British Suez fiasco in 1956 and by the ascent of the United States into superpower status. May 1960 saw the last of the four power summits, and after the Cuban missile crisis of October 1962, the two superpowers conducted their relations on a bilateral basis. The United Kingdom was to become increasingly concerned that the United States would look to a strong EC as its major partner in Europe.

As this relationship was gradually transformed, so too was that with empire and what became the Commonwealth. Decolonization, accelerating from the mid-1950s, reduced British influence. This transformation was not always easy or painless, as the new states wished to stress, even exaggerate, their newly found independence from Britain. Britain in its turn found that the Commonwealth was not really an alternative market to that appearing on the continent, partly because the Commonwealth was relatively poor. The relationship was exacerbated by Suez, by the crisis engendered by apartheid in South Africa and by the problems in Britain's handling of the Rhodesian crisis after the unilateral declaration of independence in November 1965.

Meanwhile Britain had been observing the developments in Western Europe with some anguish. In the late 1940s Britain had played a role in West European developments, being a founder member of the OEEC, the Council of Europe, the Brussels Treaty Organization and NATO. Many in Europe had looked for British leadership on the question of European reorganization, given Britain's wartime leadership and its role in the liberation of Europe.

These hopes were reinforced by the famous speech Winston Churchill made in Zurich in September 1946, when leader of the opposition. Churchill called 'for a kind of United States of Europe', but reflecting British concerns of the day and its paternalism, he went on to explain that Britain and its Commonwealth, the United States and perhaps the Soviet Union were to be 'the friends and sponsors of the new Europe', but not – although this point initially eluded many in Europe – an integral part of it.[40] In 1953, Churchill explained that Britain's relationship with Europe 'can be expressed by prepositions, but the preposition "with" but not "of" – we are with them but not of them.'[41] To be too involved would have meant sacrificing Britain's vision of itself, as expressed by the Foreign Secretary Anthony Eden in 1952 in explaining why Britain could not become involved with the proposed EDC:

> This is something which we know, in our bones, we cannot do. . . . For Britain's story and her interests lie far beyond the Continent of Europe. Our thoughts move across the seas to the many communities in which our people play their part, in every corner of the world. These are our family ties. That is our life: without it we should be no more than some millions of people living on an island off the coast of Europe, in which nobody wants to take any particular notice.[42]

Perhaps most importantly for Britain's attitude to European integration was its very different wartime experience from that of defeated and occupied nations. Far from believing that the war showed the need for a radical overhaul of the state and consequently of sovereignty, for Britain the British state had been vindicated by the years 1939–45. There was thus not the same perception of the need for radical readjustments such as federalism and the relinquishing of sovereignty. Therefore, British policy-makers firmly opposed such developments, with no willingness to 'transfer control of the British economy, or other aspects of policy, from the British government to a European body, either through the delegation of power or the acceptance of majority voting.'[43] These reservations were shared by members of the first Labour majority government, and across the political spectrum. Many agreed with Attlee when he argued that they were 'not prepared to accept the principle that the most vital economic forces of this country should be handed over to an authority that is utterly undemocratic and is responsible to nobody'.[44] The preferred model was strictly inter-governmental co-operation in limited fields. Her Majesty's Government would have to acquiesce before any decisions were made in any organization to which it belonged. It had already made that clear in the debate over the structure and powers of the Council of Europe, and the North Atlantic Treaty too relied on consent, before any action could occur.

This attitude was deeply ingrained and the British never really appreciated the 'depth of drive towards real unity, as distinct from intergovernmental co-operation on the continent'.[45] This failure was profound and enduring, although to some extent the gradual realization that the Europeans did care, did mean business, and were making progress towards their objective (see Chapters One and Two) was an important factor behind the gradual movement of British policy towards applying for EEC membership.

This realization was abetted by the failure of the Maudling talks under the auspices of the OEEC in 1957–8. This British attempt to create a free trade area between the Six, who had just signed the Treaty of Rome, and the other members of the OEEC, floundered. Britain briefly considered threatening to withdraw from NATO and Europe to teach 'little Europe' a lesson, but instead began to realize that it might have to shift its own position. In the interim the British government proceeded to negotiate with some of the other non-EEC OEEC states, and these negotiations led to the signing of the Stockholm Convention in January 1960, which founded the

European Free Trade Association. EFTA was purely inter-governmental, involved only limited co-operation, excluded agriculture and was limited to free trade, with no supranational bodies or powers. It was hoped EFTA could still build some kind of bridge to the EEC.

But just as EFTA was coming into being, questions began to be asked about the validity of that and other assumptions. It came to be appreciated that in any negotiations the Six were likely to insist upon a customs union. If so, the question became whether Britain would be better off joining the EEC. Other factors working in the same direction were the recognition that the Six was not a flash in the pan, but was becoming a reality; that the British trading position faced real dangers since neither EFTA nor the Commonwealth were viable alternatives; that the British economy was not performing satisfactorily; and that the 'Descent from Power' was continuing. Fundamentally, it became a question of making the best out of a bad job, as other avenues for progress, prosperity and influence were closed off or downgraded. It was not a radical shift of sentiment, but a pragmatic recognition of reality.[46]

In the winter of 1959–60 a senior civil service committee, the Economic Steering Committee, re-examined the options for Britain in its relations with the Six, and opted on political grounds for British membership of the EEC. On the one hand they feared instability in Europe, which Britain could counter, while at the same time fearing a strong EEC would lead to the marginalization of British influence. Economically, they hoped the cold douche of competition would spur the British economy and saw the merits of a larger market. Gradually, these arguments won the day, although the political argument was stronger than the economic case. After much internal debate and consultations with EFTA partners, the Commonwealth, the United States and the Six, the Prime Minister, Harold Macmillan announced on 31 July 1961 that the government had 'come to the conclusion that it would be right for Britain to make a formal application . . . for negotiations with a view to joining the Community if satisfactory arrangements can be made to meet the special needs of the United Kingdom, of the Commonwealth and of the European Free Trade Association', it being added that there was no guarantee of success, and there could be a situation where the cost outweighed the potential gains, especially if Commonwealth relations were disrupted. The Commonwealth was still at that time a potent force in British politics since the 'old' Commonwealth had helped Britain to defeat its enemies in two world wars. The House of Commons was told that Britain would have 'no influence' in Europe if outside the Community, this being one reason why membership was being sought rather than association, and that there was 'a tendency towards larger groups of nations acting together in the common interest'. The application was lodged on 10 August 1961. Both Macmillan and Hugh Gaitskell, leader of the opposition, emphasized their antipathy towards federal developments. For Gaitskell there was 'no question whatever of Britain entering a federal Europe now'. Conservative anti-marketeers agreed.[47] The official position of the Labour Party was enunciated a year later, when the National Executive Committee laid down five conditions that needed to be satisfied: (1) safeguards for the Commonwealth; (2) freedom to pursue an independent foreign policy; (3) fulfilment of pledges to EFTA partners; (4) the right of Britain to plan its own economy; and (5) guarantees for British agriculture. It would only pass judgement on the actual terms, not on the abstract principle of membership.

The Conservative government appointed Edward Heath to negotiate to see what terms were on offer, and made clear that it accepted the Treaty of Rome objectives. The major issues were the Commonwealth, agriculture and EFTA, as well as the length of the transitional period. The negotiations were, however, brought to an end by de Gaulle's unilateral 'non' in January 1963. De Gaulle's objections were not to the terms but to the prospect of French hegemony in the EEC being challenged.

In 1966 the Labour government that had come to power in 1964 announced that it would seek membership of the EEC again, 'provided the right conditions . . . are established'.[48] All the previous factors came into play, plus the new recognition that technology demanded large markets. The formal application was made on 11 May 1967, although many in both the Cabinet and the Parliamentary Labour Party were unenthusiastic. The Conservative Party was not united, but its leader, Edward Heath, worked hard to gain support and limit the numbers of outright opponents in the party. The Commons voted 488 to 62 in favour of applying. It remained true that the economic arguments were finely balanced, while the political arguments were seen as compelling.

The negotiating issues were similar to those previously: agriculture and the financing of the CAP; the Commonwealth, especially New Zealand and the sugar-producing states. With a Labour government there was now also concern about the freedom of a Labour government to pursue industrial and social development in the less favoured UK regions.

These concerns and the internal debate were again rendered superfluous by another de Gaulle objection in November 1967. De Gaulle again argued that the United Kingdom was not really committed to Europe, that the CAP was incompatible with Britain's relations with the Commonwealth, and that following the devaluation of the pound a few weeks earlier, the British economy was too weak to sustain membership.

The situation changed with the change of government in both France and Germany. At The Hague summit in December 1969, the Six agreed to enlargement if the applicants accepted the treaties, their political finality and the *acquis communautaire*. A British White Paper in February 1970 was cautious about the economic consequences of membership, but there was still seen to be no alternative. Wilson now argued that 'on fair terms we can stand and profit' by entry, but he warned that 'should the negotiations not lead to acceptable terms for entry, Britain is and will be strong enough to stand on her own feet outside'.[49] Before real negotiations could start the June 1970 general election intervened, and the Conservatives returned to power. The new government was committed to negotiations and to seeking a fair settlement. The debate over the next few years revolved around whether the terms of entry were right. The government was headed by Edward Heath, who had made his maiden speech in 1950 welcoming the Schuman plan, and had led the 1961–3 negotiating team. Britain again made clear that it accepted the treaties and the *acquis communautaire*. Labour would determine its position once the terms were known. The main phase of the negotiations was completed in June 1971 and a White Paper in July argued the key question was whether British influence would be greater inside or outside the Community. The 'joint strength' of the Community was greater than that of its individual members, membership involved participation in Community decisions and a sharing of sovereignty, while unanimity protected Britain's vital interests. There would be no federation. On the economic side, membership was seen as a stimulus to improvement, although that improvement would not be automatic nor easy. The cost of food would increase because of the CAP. Transitional arrangements were made for New Zealand, and the sugar question was postponed. The new Commonwealth was offered association.[50]

The Conservative conference supported membership and the terms by about 8 to 1, but this understates the opposition. Labour was more equally divided, a majority coming to the view that the terms were unacceptable. Embarrassingly both the Labour Deputy Leader, Roy Jenkins, and the initial negotiator in 1970, George Thomson, stated publicly that a Labour government would have accepted them.[51] The Labour conference opposed membership on the terms attained by a majority of 5 to 1. In October 1971 the House of Commons debated entry and supported membership on the terms negotiated by 356 to 244. Despite a three-line whip to vote against, 69 Labour MPs voted in favour, including the current (1993) Labour leader, John Smith. The Conservatives had a 'free vote' and 39 of them voted against their own government. A new theme for Labour was the failure to consult the British people, as had happened in the other applicant states, and they also announced that a Labour government would seek to renegotiate the terms, especially the CAP burden, the blow to the Commonwealth and the threat to regional policy.

The European Communities Bill, giving domestic effect to the Treaty of Accession, had a tortuous path through the Commons and a Labour amendment calling for an election and the 'express consent' of the British people was defeated, as was a rebel Conservative call, supported by most but not all of Labour (Jenkins, Thomson and Lever being the principal opponents), for a consultative referendum. The Bill was finally passed by a majority of 17, and the United Kingdom became a member of the European Communities on 1 January 1973.

The decision was made, but significantly there was the lingering feeling that, Heath and a few others apart, there was no deep enthusiasm for the experiment of uniting Europe, a feeling reinforced by the party divisions on the European question. The British sojourn to Europe was motivated not by enthusiasm, but by the lack of visible alternatives:

> [T]he important thing about Britain's entry into Europe was that it had every appearance of being a policy of last resort, adopted, one might almost say, when all other expedients had failed. There was no suggestion

of it being hailed as a brilliant success . . . the impression remained that it was brought about in humiliating circumstances and when other options in foreign policy had lost their convincingness.[52]

This set the tone for British attitudes and policies towards the Community in the years that followed entry.

Entry did not resolve the debate about the nature of Britain's relationship with the Community. In February 1974, Labour fought a general election arguing that entry on the Heath government's terms was a mistake, and calling for renegotiation of those terms, particularly as regards the CAP, the financing of the Community and retention of British control over regional, industrial and fiscal policies. Labour said they would give the British people an opportunity to express their views through either a general election or a consultative referendum. If the renegotiation was unsatisfactory Labour would not be bound by the terms of the treaty, but if successful, Labour would play a full part in Europe. The election resulted in a minority Labour government, which immediately lodged the demand for renegotiation, citing problems with the goals of economic and monetary union and European Union, and with the CAP, trade with the Commonwealth and developing states, the budget and certain regional and industrial policies. The other member states demurred. Labour became a majority government in October 1974, with a majority of 3, and the renegotiation took place between then and March 1975, when it culminated at the first European Council in Dublin. Harold Wilson, the Labour Prime Minister, claimed that his government had been successful, arguing changes to CAP would reduce prices; that there were guarantees for Commonwealth sugar producers and New Zealand; a corrective mechanism for British budgetary contributions was to be introduced (although it never operated and was soon forgotten); that there was progress on industrial and regional matters; and that it was now clear that EMU had been tacitly abandoned.[53] Seven Labour Cabinet members disagreed, including the future Party leader Michael Foot, as well as the leading anti-marketeer, Tony Benn. They felt food was still too dear, the budget was unfair and little had been done to ameliorate problems for Asian states or the balance of payments. More important still was the undiluted challenge to British democracy and sovereignty. In a key Commons debate in April 1975, while 396 to 170 MPs supported the recommendation that Britain should remain a member, a majority of Labour MPs on a free vote voted against the motion, including 7 Cabinet ministers and 30 junior ministers. Even more embarrassingly, a special Labour Conference voted by nearly 2 to 1 to oppose continued membership. The Conservatives, under their new leader, Mrs Margaret Thatcher, overwhelmingly supported continued membership, only seven MPs voting against. Mrs Thatcher argued membership allowed the influence of being in a larger club, contributed to peace and security, and provided a secure source of food, whereas withdrawal would be a leap in the dark – and was not a genuine alternative.[54]

The referendum question on 5 June 1975, in Britain's first ever national referendum, was: 'Do you think that the UK should stay in the European Community (Common Market)?' The government and the pressure group 'Britain in Europe' reiterated previous arguments, stressing the availability of veto and that traditional sovereignty was a chimera. Membership provided a say in decisions. Parliament would still have the right to repeal membership at a later date. The 'no' campaign was headed by the National Referendum Campaign which claimed pre-entry promises about jobs and prosperity had proved to be false and that the British were being asked to give up ruling themselves. They stressed the power that North Sea oil now provided Britain, such that Britain could 'go it alone', and that there was an alternative to membership in a free trade area. The referendum result was 17,378,581 Yes, 8,470,073 No.

Table 11.4 *The British referendum*

Yes (%)	No (%)	Turn-out (%)
67.2	32.8	64

Of 68 voting areas, only the Western Isles and the Shetlands voted no, with a general pattern of greater support in the south than in the north. Wilson claimed 'the debate is now over' and called for past divisions to be laid aside.[55] These hopes proved to be pious, particularly in his own party where many contended that the referendum had been an unfair contest, given the disparity of resources between the two sides. The Community also became an issue in the internal Labour Party divisions for the next ten years. The party executive secured control of the manifesto for the first direct elections in 1979, and called for fundamental reforms in the Community, as well as repeating old claims. There was to be national parliamentary control over Community legislation and the possibility of withdrawal was again raised. The Conservatives in 1979 were much more positive about Europe, but in a harbinger of things to come, began to stress the need for a 'common sense Community which resists bureaucracy and unnecessary harmonization proposals, holding to the principles of free enterprise which inspired its original founders'. The CAP should be reformed and 'National payments into the budget should be more closely related to ability to pay'. The power of the European Parliament was not to change.[56]

Overshadowed by the earlier referendums on Scottish and Welsh devolution, and the general election of May 1979, the first direct elections in the United Kingdom were an anti-climax. Only 32.1 per cent of the electorate voted, compared to the Community average of 61 per cent. The Conservatives' success in the election did nothing to endear the Community to Labour supporters, and it again featured in internal party arguments. By the 1983 general election, Labour, led by Michael Foot, took the official position that 'British withdrawal from the Community is the right policy for Britain', since membership was an obstacle to serious socialist policies.[57] Under their new leader after the election defeat, Neil Kinnock, Labour gradually moved to a pragmatic view that membership was a reality and that it was necessary to work constructively within the Community for what one wanted. By the late 1980s and early 1990s Labour was focusing on the need for a European dimension to tackle common problems, and they now saw the advantages of the social dimension of the Community. It remained wary of federalism and EMU.

But after 1979 British policy towards the Community was made by Conservative governments and has seen a continuation of the predominantly suspicious British attitude to European integration, although it was now accepted that the question of membership was closed. The pervasive concern became, therefore, the attempt to remodel the Community in the British image, that image reflecting certain features common to both major parties and to traditional British post-war policy, although there were also distinctive Thatcherite elements.

This attempt to remodel the Community was originally hampered by the problem of the British budgetary contribution, which occupied the years 1979–84. The details have already been discussed (pp. 44–5), but it is important to note here that many of Britain's partners saw it as a continuation of special British pleading. The environment did change as they realized that there were wider problems and that the Community needed to raise more money to finance its objectives. Reform needed the support of all and gradually linkage was established between an increase in resources, the reform of the CAP, budgetary discipline and a permanent formula for resolving the problems of budget imbalances – the British problem. The real issue was the question as to whether Britain was willing to become more *communautaire* in orientation and policy. Its partners pointed to failure to join the Exchange Rate Mechanism (ERM), the continuing exchange over the CAP, and the obvious lack of enthusiasm for the various proposals for institutional reform in the 1980's. Britain clearly had a different vision of the future from the one held by many of its partners. While Britain favoured proposals relating to improving EPC, it opposed all reforms of the institutions that would strengthen the centre or radically alter the current institutional balance. Britain opposed the call for an IGC in 1985 at Milan and participated in the IGC because it knew that any treaty change required unanimity. Any treaty amendments would have to be on a pragmatic and limited basis to have British support. Britain had made clear earlier that it strongly supported the single market dimension of the discussions. It had called as early as 1984 for the creation of a 'genuine common market in goods and services', for the removal of the 'remaining obstacles to intra-Community trade' and the harmonizing of standards, all of which could lead to the creation of 'what is potentially the largest Single Market in the industrialized world'. It also supported the 'development of a vigorous, efficient and cost effective industrial sector' able to compete with others.[58] Parts of the SEA, therefore, fitted in very well with the Thatcher government's emphasis on deregulation and market forces, and reflected a British preference for measures of negative integration, that is, 'the removal of discrimination as between the economic agents of the member countries', as distinct from positive integration, namely 'the formation and application of coordinated and positive policies on a sufficient scale to ensure that major economic and welfare objectives are fulfilled'.[59]

Enthusiasm for the Single Market did not extend to all aspects of the SEA, not all of which seem to have been fully appreciated in 1986–7. Britain, for example, was not enthusiastic about the 'social dimension' which as well as new measures to alleviate unemployment, also gave weight to workers' rights to consultation and to participation, and about the revived notion of monetary union going beyond the EMS.

In September 1988 Mrs Thatcher articulated her vision of the future in a famous speech at the College of Europe at Bruges. Some of this reflected the specifics of contemporary Conservative thinking on the free market, but some also reflected very traditional British policy, although expressed in Mrs. Thatcher's own style. Britain had contributed to Europe for centuries, not least in bringing freedom in 1944–5. It sought no alternative to the Community, but did not want a European super-state. Attention was to be given to specific tasks in hand, not 'arcane institutional debates', which were 'no substitute for effective action'. Mrs Thatcher went on to offer some 'guiding principles for the future' development of Europe:

- There must be 'willing and active co-operation between independent sovereign states'. It was not possible to 'suppress nationhood and concentrate power at the centre of a European conglomerate'. Europe should seek to speak with a single voice on more issues, but this did 'not require power to be centralized in Brussels or decisions to be taken by an appointed bureaucracy'. Success for Europe lay, as in Britain, in 'dispersing power and decisions away from the centre'. Britain had 'not successfully rolled back the frontiers of the state . . . only to see them reimposed at a European level, with a European super-state exercising a new dominance from Brussels.' She wished to see 'Europe more united', but this had to be done in a way that 'preserves the different traditions, Parliamentary powers and sense of national pride in one's own country'.
- 'Community policies must tackle present problems in a practical way' – for example, although progress had been made in reforming the CAP it remained 'unwieldy, inefficient and grossly expensive'.
- Community policies must 'encourage enterprise' and there must be a greater awareness that the Treaty of Rome 'was intended as a Charter for Economic Liberty'. The aim should be deregulation,

free markets, wider choice and reduced government intervention. Rather than debating whether there should be a European central bank, there should be a focus on immediate practical requirements, such as making easier the movement of goods and services.

However, it was a 'matter of plain commonsense that we cannot totally abolish frontier controls', because of problems relating to drug traffic, terrorism and illegal immigrants.

- 'Europe should not be protectionist.'
- Europe 'must continue to maintain a sure defence through NATO', although again Mrs Thatcher made the point that this was 'not an institutional problem. It's not a problem of drafting. It's much more simple and more profound; it's a question of political will and political courage.'

In concluding her speech, Mrs Thatcher reiterated that it was 'not enough just to talk in general terms about a European vision or ideal', and 'new documents' were not required. It was necessary to make decisions, rather than being 'distracted by Utopian goals'. In sum, the British wanted a 'family of nations, understanding each other better, appreciating each other more, doing more together but relishing our national identity no less than our common European endeavour.'[60]

The European issue continued to cause trouble for British political parties, especially, now, the Conservative Party. In July 1990, Nicholas Ridley, then Secretary of State for Trade and Industry, was forced to resign over anti-German remarks. More substantially the Chancellor of the Exchequer, Nigel Lawson, resigned in 1989 over the conduct of government economic policy, especially as regards the exchange rate and disagreements with Mrs Thatcher over the ERM. The real crisis, however, was generated by the resignation from the government of the Foreign Secretary, Sir Geoffrey Howe, in November 1990. He revealed that there were deep and continuing divisions over European policy, especially over monetary policy within the government, and that he and Lawson had only been able to persuade the Prime Minister to make a specific commitment to joining the ERM, albeit with conditions, at the Madrid European Council in June 1989 by threatening to resign. Britain joined the ERM on 8 October 1990 at 2.95 DM (with a ±6 per cent fluctuation band with a commitment to move to the narrower band when appropriate), three weeks before Howe's resignation, but he felt that the Prime Minister was still not really committed to the idea. She clearly continued to have reservations, at least partly because of identifying the pound with sovereignty. At Rome in late October 1990, Mrs Thatcher had been isolated in her opposition to an early move towards the second stage of EMU and it was clear that she would resist the possible ultimate introduction of a single currency. There was a growing feeling that her trenchant negotiating style was now becoming counter-productive, both at home and abroad. Conservatives also had other concerns about the direction of the government.

In the leadership elections, John Major defeated the pro-European Michael Heseltine, although Europe was not the decisive issue. Major shared some of Mrs Thatcher's views on Europe, and had made known as Chancellor his antipathy towards the Delors path to EMU, proposing instead a gradualist approach via the introduction of a parallel optional currency, the 'hard ecu'. He seemed, however, to believe that it was more productive to argue one's case positively and by seeking to be constructive than by continually adopting negative tactics and rhetoric. He had to be mindful that many in the party shared the Bruges views of Mrs Thatcher, indeed had formed a 'Bruges group'. In May 1991, for example, 105 Conservative MPs, led by the anti-federalist Bruges group, signed a Commons motion calling on the Prime Minister to reject moves towards EMU, and in June in the United States Mrs Thatcher again attacked those trying to create an artificial state by taking away the power of national states. She continued to denounce fixed exchange rates as taking away a crucial economic weapon from the government, and advocated the creation of a free trade Atlantic Economic Community. The new Prime Minister, therefore, had to approach the IGCs in a rather cautious vein.

Not surprisingly, Britain was adamantly opposed to the federal vocation espoused by many. John Major made it clear that reference to it had to be removed when it appeared in the preamble of the Luxembourg draft, and insisted again on its withdrawal in the Dutch draft. He told the House of Commons in November 1991 that 'We will not [therefore] accept a Treaty which describes the Community as having a Federal vocation.'[61] Its deletion from the draft Maastricht text was seen as a British success. There was political hostility across the Labour and Conservative Parties to the 'F-word'. The British much preferred to stress the principle of subsidiarity. For example, speaking to the European Parliament in July 1992 Douglas Hurd, the Foreign Secretary, argued:

> In the wide areas outside the exclusive competence, the Community should ask two questions: is it necessary for the Community to act; if so, to what extent? Even in the areas where national governments have by treaty given the Community exclusive competence, the institutions of the Community should ask to what extent do we need to act to secure the full objectives of the Treaties, bearing in mind that excessive intrusion is one of the accusations most often brought against it?[62]

The British position was that the two questions were applicable in all areas, and should be answered in a minimalist fashion. Britain regarded subsidiarity as 'bottom up' and therefore acceptable, and 'federalism' as centralization, and therefore unacceptable. Throughout 1992 in the political debate in the United Kingdom much was made of 'subsidiarity', although the government was careful usually to refer to article 3b with its specific reference to 'member states' rather than the article A reference to 'as closely as possible to the citizen'. This was because of the dangers the principle held for the internal political debate in the United Kingdom about greater independence for Scotland. The government advocated the temple approach to the treaty, and welcomed the fact that CFSP and home affairs and judicial co-operation would be on an inter-governmental basis, so that they were outside the purview of the Court of Justice and supranationalism. The government wanted unanimity to be retained for CFSP and that even where joint action was being sought, although the British would endeavour to seek consensus, there had to be a right to take national decisions, if they were regarded as essential for the pursuit of British policy objectives. A number of difficulties in agreeing to majority voting on implementation were also raised. Britain would really have preferred to keep the current EPC system, albeit with slight modifications in its mechanisms. It did recognize that there were advantages in the Twelve speaking with one voice, but as noted in Chapter Ten, felt joint analysis and objectives had to proceed new institutional arrangements.

It was the same on defence. Britain continues to believe in the primacy of NATO and that nothing must call into question the US presence in and commitment to Europe. While Europe could do more for its own defence, the United Kingdom strongly opposed new structures as unnecessary and even worse as duplicating and undermining NATO. Britain, therefore, had little sympathy with the Franco-German approaches, and joined with the Italians in October 1991 with a set of proposals to build up the WEU as a European pillar of NATO, not as an alternative to NATO. WEU was to 'develop its role in two complementary directions: as the defence component of the Union and as a means to strengthen the European pillar of the Alliance', but there was to be no challenge to NATO. There could, however, be some WEU development, including the development of a planning cell and a European reaction force for operation outside the NATO area.

The British position on EMU was already clear by mid-1991. Britain believed in the necessity for strict convergence criteria before moving to the third stage, but would not accept a firm commitment on its part to a single currency. The decisions about joining and when to join were to remain matters for separate decision by the British parliament. When pressed by opponents to EMU as to why the government did not block this part of the treaty, the government replied by showing nervousness that the other eleven might go ahead in this area on their own, leaving Britain on the sidelines. The key decisions in this area were arrived at prior to the Maastricht meeting, and the Treaty on European Union contained Protocol 11, which recognized 'that the United Kingdom shall not be obliged or committed to move to the third stage of Economic and Monetary Union without a separate decision to do so by its government and Parliament'.[63] The United Kingdom was later to be opposed to the Delors II proposals, was not enthusiastic about cohesion, and wished to see a firm lid kept on Community expenditure.

Britain also stood aside from the decision by the other eleven to proceed by agreement on social policy in order to implement the 1989 Social Charter, which it had not accepted. The Conservative government felt these proposals would undo much of their labour and social policy of the 1980s, as well as costing jobs.

Conservative supporters of the government's position later made much of M. Delors' reported remark that British self-exclusion from the social chapter made Britain a paradise for foreign investment. This issue was fiercely contested at Maastricht. Britain was generally unenthusiastic about new policy areas for the Community, and held firmly to the belief that the principle of subsidiarity should apply in any such developments, and that areas such as health and education, while open to some European co-operation, were primarily national matters. Major believed that 'We must constrain the extension of community competencies to those areas where Community action makes more sense than national action or than action on a voluntary, inter-governmental basis.'[64] He did support developments to make the Single Market effective and accepted that pollution, for example, knew no frontiers. But all policies had to be judged in the light of its own political philosophy, and that meant a preference for the free market and non-intervention in industrial practice, union relations and wage bargaining.

The government did not support any proposal that the European Parliament should have the right to initiate legislation, nor be co-equal in determining Community law. What it would accept was greater powers for the Parliament in monitoring the unelected Commission, and in approving the appointment of the Commission, although it should not have the right to dismiss individual Commissioners. Parliament could also have some greater blocking power over matters currently subject to majority voting under the Single European Act and should have a more powerful voice in auditing Community expenditure. It did support the Ombudsman proposal. In line with traditional British thinking, the government's basic position on institutions was to support inter-governmentalism, and partly for that reason it was keen that nothing be agreed that would make enlargement more difficult.

Immediately after Maastricht John Major described the negotiations as 'game, set and match for Britain', and on 19 December 1991 the House of Commons supported the negotiated outcome by 339 to 253. It repeated this verdict early in 1992 on the second reading of the European Communities (Amendment) Bill by a majority of 244. But this did not end the discord. On 5 November 1992, the government had a majority of only 3 on a motion inviting the House to proceed to further consideration of the Bill, a general election (won by the government), the Danish 'no' and the narrow French 'yes', plus 'Black Wednesday' in September 1992, when the pound was forced out of the ERM by currency speculation and devalued, having radically changed the environment. This majority was only achieved with great difficulty and the progress of ratification faced significant other problems. Some opposed on principle for much the same reasons as before, some opposed because there was to be no referendum or direct consultation with the British people on what was seen as a move curtailing sovereignty, and some opposed because of the 'opt out' on social policy. Labour was ambivalent because of that 'opt out' but did not wish to see the Treaty on European Union defeated.

In the first half of 1993 the European Communities (Amendment) Bill continued its tortuous and tortured path through the House of Commons, finally overcoming that hurdle in May 1993, just after the Danish referendum. Over 600 amendments had been tabled on the Bill and the Committee stage alone lasted 23 days. The strongest challenges continued to be over the Social Chapter 'opt-out' and the case for a referendum, whilst the government was defeated on an opposition amendment that required that the persons appointed to the new Committee of the Regions must be elected local authority members. Even after completing this Commons stage the Bill faced two further hurdles. One was its passage through the House of Lords, where renewed attempts which failed were made to force a referendum. The other was a legal challenge by Lord Rees-Mogg, who argued that: Parliament had not specifically approved new powers for the European Parliament, that the government could not ratify the social protocol via Royal Prerogative, and that the treaty involved the Crown transferring its foreign policy powers, which it was not entitled to do. These arguments were rejected by the British courts and the UK ratified the treaty.

Britain has remained a 'reluctant European', but at least officially coming to the view that the events of 1992 in Denmark, France and elsewhere, the emphasis on subsidiarity, plus the prospect of enlargement may mean that the Community is moving in a direction favourable to the long-standing British position of antipathy to all forms of centralization. Britain as a late entrant has found it difficult to adjust politically and psychologically to a system it did not create. Other late entrants have not experienced those problems to anything like the same degree.

THE SOUTHERN OR MEDITERRANEAN ENLARGEMENT

In the 1980s three more states joined the Community, Greece in 1981 and Portugal and Spain in 1986. The three had many experiences in common, especially recent experience of dictatorship, and levels of economic development which were well below the Community average.[65] Their accession also posed new issues for the Community, raised the importance of others and appeared as if it would shift the centre of gravity of the Community from the established democratic, industrialized northern states.

Greece

The Greek accession in January 1981 marked the beginning of the 'Mediterranean' or southern enlargement. Given its geographic position, chequered political history and relatively low levels of socio-economic development, Greece had not been involved in the mainstream of European integration, although it was a founder member of the OEEC, joined the Council of Europe in 1949 just after its foundation, and NATO in 1952. It lacked a common frontier with the Six.

In 1959 it requested an association agreement with the Six against a background of domestic economic crisis and in 1961 the 'Athens Agreement' was signed. The Greeks favoured the EEC link over EFTA because they wished to strengthen their ties with the West and consolidate their internal political situation. There had been civil war in the 1940s and communist sympathizers received 25 per cent of the vote in the 1958 election. Some, therefore, saw the EC as a contributor to stability. There were also hopes of the CAP, of some financing for economic development and the attraction of foreign investment. Critics from the left saw the link as ending sovereignty and involving imperialist links with capitalist powers. There were also more widespread fears that Greece would suffer in the competitive economic environment.

The 1961 Association Agreement was seen by both the Six and the Greeks as a first step towards membership, and not just as a trade arrangement. As a consequence it covered not just trade but a number of measures designed to bring the Greek economy closer to that of the Six. The agreement was for a customs union for industrial products, but there was a two-stage transition period, with some Greek manufacturing products being protected for 22 years. It also envisaged some financial aid. A major problem with the agreement was over agricultural harmonization, and especially over the Greek aspiration to be directly involved in the making of CAP policy.

A hiatus in the development of relations occurred with the Colonels' coup of 21 April 1967, and in the following period the

Community 'froze' the agreement. It was reactivated after the return to democracy in July 1974 when the Junta was replaced by a Greek conservative government headed by Prime Minister Karamanlis, who remained in power until 1980.

As early as August 1974 the new government expressed its intention to apply for membership, and in June 1975 it applied. The political case was important to both sides: membership would mark a return to political respectability and the Community would buttress Greek democracy. The economic case was not undisputed, and indeed the Commission initially expressed a number of reservations on socio-economic grounds and because of the position regarding Greek–Turkish relations. Such reservations were brushed aside by the Council for political reasons, although there were some attempts to postpone the issue; threats which in turn led the Greek government to threaten to withdraw its application. Despite somewhat protracted negotiations the Treaty of Accession was signed in May 1979. The delay was largely for internal Community reasons, relating to its difficulty in adjusting quickly to the changed environment, the institutional implications of a broad enlargement (including Portugal and Spain) and a lack of Community political confidence and direction, as well as disputes over particular aspects of the negotiations, such as Greek–Turkish relations and agriculture. There was also some attempt to link the three applications in 'globalization'. Once the political will to negotiate seriously was established, the negotiations were not too difficult.

The situation again changed when ten months after accession there was a new government in Athens, formed by the PASOK party (Panhellenic Socialist Movement). PASOK had boycotted the accession vote because it did not wish to provide legitimacy for what it deemed to be an attack on Greek sovereignty, and in opposition in the 1970s had adopted a nationalistic radical position. It had pledged it would hold a referendum on the membership issue, although no such referendum took place. In practice in government PASOK's opposition to the Community became reduced, but they were never enamoured. They never sought a formal renegotiation, but in March 1982 issued a memorandum calling for the Community to be more sympathetic to Greece's economic problems, low level of development and to the principle of the harmonization of development and economic convergence. The response over the next few years in terms of substantial funding and economic aid lessened

266 *Understanding the New European Community*

further PASOK's hostility to the Community, although they never became fully converted to the concept of political union or EPC. They were another Dooge footnote state, having already reserved their position on aspects of the Stuttgart Declaration relating to majority voting and EPC. They remained opposed to institutional development, especially any enhanced role for the Commission or European Parliament. In 1983 they argued, 'we cannot easily abandon traditional principles . . . [and] it would not be expedient for us to give the outside world the impression that we are obliged, since our accession to the Community, to adopt views diametrically opposed to those we have hitherto held' (this reaching its nadir at the Athens Council meeting in 1983, during the Greek presidency, when the Greeks refused to allow the Community and its member states to condemn the Soviet Union for shooting down the South Korean Boeing). By 1988 the Greeks were arguing that their presidency would see 'every effort to ensure full application of the Single Act, especially working out common positions, devising common measures and strengthening the principles of solidarity, mutual agreement and cohesion.'[66]

By the time of the airing of the possibility of the IGC on Political Union there was a new Greek government, the New Democracy Party, which had taken Greece into the Community returning to power. On 15 May 1990 it issued a 'Contribution to the Discussions on Progress Towards Political Union',[67] which reflected the decisive shift that the new regime brought to these matters. The memorandum made clear Greek support for further development of the Community, calling for rapid progress towards Political Union, which they linked to increased democracy within the Community, as well as playing a role in stabilizing Eastern Europe. The European Parliament was to be made into a 'real legislative and monitoring body' with an extension of the 'assent' procedure, recognition of a right of initiative and extension of the co-operation procedure to all legislative Acts. The Parliament was to have the right to appoint the Commission's President and to agree Commission membership with the member states and the President, and the right to censure individual members of the Commission. The Greeks wanted some extension of majority voting in the Council and restriction of the principle of unanimity, although they were sensitive on issues like frontiers. Interestingly, they proposed a reduction in the number of different Councils to increase cohesion in decision-making. The

Commission was to have more executive power. The memorandum also proposed European citizenship and the recognition of basic human rights by the Community. The Greeks wished to see an emphasis on 'People's Europe'. Every effort was to be made to bring about what had already been agreed, especially 'cohesion' (the resource transfer), and new policies were to be adopted in the areas of culture and education, the 'social dimension', environment, and cohesion. All these, however, were to be based 'on the principle of subsidiarity'. They now spoke of strengthening the Community's voice in the world and the incorporation of EPC into the Community system, with its secretariat being merged into the Council secretariat. They favoured abandoning restrictions on types of security issues that could be discussed, and the inclusion of defence. In general, although not mentioned in the memorandum, the Greeks tended to the Franco-German position on security and defence, and the Franco-German corps, and at one point seemed to threaten a veto of the whole exercise if they were not admitted to the WEU. This was important to them because of increasing Balkan instability and their apprehensions regarding Turkey, against whom they wanted a security guarantee. They, therefore, welcomed the Maastricht decision that 'States, which are members of the European Union are invited to accede to WEU . . . or become observers if they so wish'; whereas Turkey as a NATO but non-European Union member, was only offered 'associate' membership of the WEU.[68] Greece in the IGCs favoured the implementation of CFSP being a matter for qualified majority voting.

Greece at the time of the IGCs was an enthusiastic supporter of both the federal goal and the tree approach. This reflects the view that unless Greece commits itself fully to political integration it could be left on the EC's economic and political periphery. Political union was to be based on subsidiarity and was to progress in parallel with EMU. They supported the movement to a single currency, despite knowing that they had little hope of joining in the twentieth century and do not expect to join the ERM before 1994. The Greeks were unhappy with what they regarded as prematurely strict convergence criteria and know that fulfilling them is going to be a long hard haul. They staunchly reject the suggestion of a two-speed Europe and fear economic marginalization. They obviously supported Delors II in 1992, and pressed hard on the cohesion fund, believing that Maastricht had involved a commitment to a transfer of resources to the structural funds of the Community. Of importance at Edinburgh in December 1992 was that the other states should not recognize 'Macedonia' under that name. The Greek Prime Minister briefly left the European Council negotiations to be able to tell his people that his partners had not recognized this name, and indeed the Declaration refers to 'the former Yugoslav Republic of Macedonia'.[69]

Portugal

Portugal experienced a dictatorship from 1932 to 1974. During this time the regime was profoundly nationalistic and was strongly committed to the Portuguese African empire. It was relatively isolated, but being reasonably benevolent, was tolerated by West European states, although excluded from the Council of Europe. It was a member of the OEEC, and because of its strategic position, as well as that of the Azores, was a founder member of NATO. Virulent anti-communism and attachment to colonies made Portugal very Atlanticist. It also was a founder member of EFTA in 1960. There was a gradual change in policy outlook in the late 1950s and 1960s as the elite saw the external environment begin to change with integration in Western Europe, decolonization pressures in Africa and pressures for change at home. EFTA membership was no sign of commitment to the European idea, but rather reflected the importance of trade with Britain and becoming isolated. Portugal, given its nationalistic outlook, favoured inter-governmental co-operation. EEC membership was at that time still ruled out by the nature of the regime and by Portuguese fears of supranationalism, and of potential EEC exploitation of its colonies. The colonial aspect was a powerful factor in Portuguese policy considerations, and hindered the development of policy in other areas, but gradually there came a growing awareness of problems in that relationship, of the increasing importance of imports from EFTA and of foreign investment, and that the old policies were not working. Crucial was the trade dependence on the United Kingdom, which was such that until 1973 Portugal's position was determined by the United Kingdom's position.[70] With the British decision in 1961, Portugal had to ask for negotiations on trade links with the EEC, and in 1969–70 it again had to improve its relations with the Community. In July 1972, along with other EFTA members, it signed a vital free trade agreement with the Community. This encompassed the elimination of tariff barriers to exports from Portugal by July 1977 and some concessions on agricultural exports, although on the industrial side there were exceptions for about one third of Portuguese exports, notably textiles, which were particularly sensitive. The agreement also contained an 'evolutionary clause', which provided for its revision and expansion.

The context of Portuguese policy and opportunities completely changed with the revolution of 25 April 1974, which ushered in the liberation of the colonies, and, after a period of apparent anarchy, democracy. Portuguese policy-makers had to re-evaluate a range of external policies, while pursuing the revolution at home. Domestic convulsions caused a number of problems, but also caused Western Europe to rush in with emergency aid and concessions for Portuguese exports. These states took the political decision to seek to consolidate democracy in Portugal. Portugal applied for membership in March 1977, four months before Spain, with negotiations beginning simultaneously in 1978. The Treaty of Accession was signed in June 1985, Spain and Portugal becoming members of the Community on 1 January 1986. There was during this period little political debate, with the public mostly appearing indifferent. As can be seen the negotiations were very protracted. Partly, as in the Greek case, this was because of internal Community difficulties on other matters, only some of which touched on enlargement. But there were also difficulties again on the whole question of agriculture and the perceived threat posed to French and Italian interests. More importantly, the Portuguese application became caught up in the greater difficulties of Spain, it being intended that the two should enter together. In the interim the Community provided Portugal with substantial pre-accession aid from 1980 on.

Membership is seen in Portugal as having been a success, contributing to rapid change, a transformation in the state's infrastructure and an economic growth rate above the Community average. There is little opposition to membership, but much of the public remains indifferent. The Portuguese have been cautious about political union, the tone of their attitude being encapsulated in their memorandum of 30 November 1990 which starts by saying that progress must be

(a) pursued gradually, (b) be based on a pragmatic view of political, economic and social realities in Europe, (c) respect national identities and diversity, (d) preserve the existing institutional balance, (e) ensure the correct application of the dual aspects of subsidiarity and solidarity.[71]

The Portuguese wished the Community to be closer to the citizens of Europe, and were strong supporters of European citizenship. Related to these concerns they saw it as necessary to extend the range of Community policies. Policies to which they drew attention included those 'transcending' the purely economic, such as the environment, energy, major trans-European networks (which they saw as of benefit to them directly), social questions, health and education. Importantly, they argued that the 'principle of economic and social cohesion . . . will have to permeate all Community action and also act as a driving force for European integration and the harmonious development of the Community area.' In the negotiations they linked these aspects to their support for EMU and movement to a single currency. They have opposed suggestions of a two speed Europe, fearing being placed in perpetual relative disadvantage. The Portuguese were strong supporters of Delors II. Portugal believes that in 1993 the equivalent of 3.7 per cent of its GDP would come from EC aid. Cohesion was one of their priorities, and they felt there was little substance to the European rhetoric about integration if there was not a greater effort to reduce regional disparities. In the same vein the Portuguese advocated the principle of 'sufficient means', namely that new tasks and policies should be properly funded.

Subsidiarity was important, but was not to be an obstacle to Community development and therefore was only one criterion to be considered. They were one of the states opposed to references to 'federal' vocation. Also relevant to bringing the Community closer to its citizens was the democratic legitimacy issue, although the current institutional balance was not to be challenged. Their proposals on the Parliament were, therefore, modest, involving the extension of co-operation procedure and minor expansion of the assent procedure. The Commission was to maintain the right of initiative and have stronger executive powers, and although responsible to the Parliament for its broad programme, the latter was to have no clearly defined role in the appointment of the Commission. Their way of addressing the problem of democracy was to float the idea of a European Congress, bringing together national delegations, parliaments and the European Parliament.

The Congress was to focus on the broad aspects of policy, including foreign policy, macro-economic policy, constitutional questions and the People's Europe. They wished to see the European Council strengthened and playing a greater role in terms of initiative. There was support for the extension of majority voting as long as there were exceptions.

The Portuguese favoured the abolition of the demarcation between external relations and EPC, but were very cautious on CFSP decision-making, which should be based on unanimity on all major aspects, only gradually moving to some sort of majority voting. It was not to be normal majority voting, but one state one vote, with a blocking group of three. Defence was not mentioned explicitly, but the general tenor of the remarks was a clear preference for current arrangements, especially NATO's primacy, and the remaining importance of Portugal's Atlantic location. WEU was to be a European pillar of NATO, not a pillar of European European defence. In general, Portugal was willing to accept some political developments as the price for gaining economic and financial advantage.

Spain

Spain applied for EC membership on 28 July 1977. It had been excluded for many years from consideration because of the nature of its regime, and through having been too close to the Axis powers. It was also excluded from the UN, the Marshall Plan, the OEEC, the Council of Europe and NATO. Spain was not invited to take part in the movement towards closer European integration. Not surprisingly its economic policy was self-sufficiency, and it looked to a vision of a community between it, Latin America and parts of North Africa, rather than to Europe. In 1953 it did make a bilateral defence deal with a United States consumed by fear of communism, and in 1955 as part of a package deal it joined the UN. By the mid-1950s it was acquiring some acceptability on the Western side, but there remained many reservations on both sides.

By the mid-1960s the question of Spain's relations with the rest of Western Europe needed to be addressed, as within Spain itself the policy of self-sufficiency and of resistance to change had been shown to be flawed. Modernization became the key word, and it in turn became identified with Europeanization. Europe was seen as offering access to wider markets, especially for agriculture and sources of investment capital. Britain's decision to apply was important too given the size of the UK market for Spanish agriculture. In 1962 the Spanish floated the idea of association with the aim of full integration into the Community, but this was still not acceptable to the Six. 1970, however, saw the signature of a preferential trade agreement, providing for free trade but not for Spanish eventual membership. The Spanish saw this as a major political development, but for the Community it was a purely commercial arrangement. It was, however, part of the Community attempt to construct a global Mediterranean policy, a policy that could not exclude such a major trading partner as Spain. The 1970 agreement had a chequered career, with Spain being disappointed by the limited progress in its agricultural exports. The agreement formally lapsed when it was not adjusted to take into account the enlargement of 1973, but both parties continued to observe its major provisions. In 1975 political reform began in Spain, although a storm was created in October 1975 when the regime executed five Basques for terrorism, despite appeals for clemency by the Nine.

The real turning point was the death of General Franco in November 1975, and in February 1976 the first post-Franco government announced that Spain wished to accede to the European Community. The initial reaction from the Community was favourable, and the formal application followed on 28 July 1977. While different groups in Spain had their own motivations for membership an over-arching objective was to complete the process of emerging from the political shadows, and a necessary precondition was the return to pluralist, representative democracy. The Spanish saw the possibility of preference within the EC for Spanish agricultural produce, free access to the Community market, the possibility of attracting foreign investment, and both common cause with democracy and Christian Democracy. Given the return to democracy, it might have been thought that the negotiations would be quick, but in fact they were protracted. This was because the Community had its own internal problems, and because of disagreements in the negotiations over agriculture, fisheries and the reduction of tariff barriers for Spanish industrial goods. The Greeks at one point had also caused a hitch by linking progress on the application to their demands for aid to assist their own economic development, and with what came to be known as the 'integrated

Mediterranean programmes', a reservation only lifted in the spring of 1985. This allowed the Accession Treaty to be signed on 12 June 1985 and accession into the Community in January 1986. Within Spain there was general agreement with the decision. All parties emphasized the political dimension of the Community, and the opportunities for internal social and economic reforms.

In November 1988, along with Portugal, Spain joined the WEU. This was significant since the 1980 announcement by the centre-right government that it wished Spain to join NATO, which Spain did in 1982, had been bitterly contested by the socialist opposition. Spain also negotiated special arrangements subsequently which involved opting out of NATO's integrated military structure. The socialists promised a referendum on the issue and under Felipe Gonzalez Marquez came to power in October 1982. They modified their position on NATO and the subsequent referendum saw a 52.55 per cent vote in favour of NATO membership, with 39.8 per cent against (7.65 per cent abstained). This vote, along with Community and WEU membership, put Spain firmly in the West European camp, and in the initial year of membership, 1986, Spain signed the Single European Act in February 1986. In June 1989 Spain joined the ERM, a decision which culminated a successful presidency in the first half of 1989, and by which Spain demonstrated its European commitment. During this time too it had played a positive role in EPC.

Accession to the Community, along with resource flows and heightened international respectability, hastened the transformation of Spain from the Church-ridden, tightly controlled society of Franco's time. But it also brought problems. A rapid inflow of foreign capital, attracted by cheap labour and commercial opportunities, stoked up inflationary pressure and an anti-inflationary policy of high interest rates made the peseta an attractive speculative investment. For a period in 1990–1, the peseta was the currency which set the ceilings and floors in the ERM, but the high interest rate maintained to defend the value of the currency had damaging effects on growth. Spain wanted to be a charter, or at least early member of a monetary union, and for this and other domestic reasons embarked in 1991 on a programme of austerity measures, which ensured political unpopularity for the Socialist government. Although European policy took its share of the blame, there was no strong opposition to ratification of the Treaty on European Union.

Spain made an important contribution to the IGC outcome and

the text of the Treaty on European Union when its Prime Minister circulated texts in September 1990 and February 1991 on European citizenship. He suggested that the Community had not unnaturally previously concentrated on economic questions, but that now it was appropriate to move to create a European citizenship which would provide 'special rights and duties that are specific to the nature of the Union'. Crucial were 'freedom of movement, freedom to choose one's place of residence and the right of establishment'.[72] The proposed rights included the right to vote in European elections at the place of residence. There should be an Ombudsman to protect citizens' rights. The IGC should also examine the provision of consular and diplomatic provision by member states of each others nationals. The February 1991 proposal made clear that provision for human rights and fundamental freedoms should also be acknowledged by the union. Not unnaturally this view also led to the view that such rights would be created in parallel with the acquisition of new policies by the Community in the areas of social policy, health, education, the environment and consumption. It was important, therefore, that the Community pay for these developments. These views came together in the emphatic Spanish insistence on economic and social cohesion. For them, 'If Europe is only a single market, Spain does not have an awful lot to gain in this operation.'[73] In March 1991 Spain presented its views on the issue in a paper to partners.[74] The memorandum traced the history of the concept in the European Community and noted that it had also been theoretically accepted as well, yet by comparison there had been a paucity of concrete action to back genuine political, economic and monetary union. So far the Community had acted as if the existing structural funds were an adequate solution, but these had not been sufficiently directed to those states that most needed help. The case for action was now particularly strong given the prospect of EMU. Spain supported EMU and a single currency. It claimed not to see cohesion as compensation for involvement, but rather as a 'necessary political balance between efficiency, stability and equity'. It identified itself, Portugal, Greece and Ireland as having special problems of economic disparity, and called for a special fund to help implement cohesion, as well as a significant increase in structural funds within the budget. It argued that VAT was regressive and therefore hurt the poorer members. It feared that it might soon become a net contributor to the Community budget unless changes were made, as it was already seeing its net benefit from the Community reducing. The matter of cohesion was regarded as crucial to Spain, and it argued in November 1991 that unless there was a satisfactory outcome on this issue they would block the negotiations on other matters. Spain was successful in this area at Maastricht, but was aggrieved at the amounts of money proposed. Felipe Gonzales very nearly brought the Edinburgh European Council meeting to collapse on this issue, and made progress on all other issues conditional on obtaining satisfaction. After hours of haggling he was moderately successful. Rather like Portugal, Spain also emphasized the principle of sufficiency of resources for new policies.

The Spanish supported the federal goal and were wary of subsidiarity as a potential mechanism for some members to pursue their own interests. They took the view that the enterprise was about sharing sovereignty rather than losing it. Spain supported some co-decision for the European Parliament, but this was to be in carefully selected areas. The Parliament should, however, be involved in appointing the Commission and the Commission President and have some rights of initiative in legislation where the Commission had not acted. Otherwise, Spain largely preferred to maintain the existing institutional balance, and while supporting a consultative 'committee of the regions' was sensitive as to its powers and composition given the sensitivity of the separatist question within Spain itself.

On CFSP Spain tended to support the inclusion of all aspects of security within it, including defence. It wished eventually to see a 'single' foreign and security policy, but accepted that that might not be possible in the short or medium term. It did want EPC to be integrated into the Community framework, and the European Council to establish a list where 'common action' would take place among the Twelve. On such matters unanimity would prevail, but where agreed majority voting could be used on matters relating to implementation. It was recognized that at the moment not all questions could be handled jointly. On defence Spain had few qualms about NATO, but recognizing political reality, sought to straddle the argument between European European defence and Atlantic European defence. It supported strengthening the link between the European Union and the WEU, and a European pillar of NATO. It was quite close to the Franco-German position and was the only other state to accept the invitation to attend the Franco-German dinner in October 1991 on these questions.

12 Towards European Union? The second constitutional reforms, 1987–92

The debates about models of integration and states' attitudes to associated issues came into sharp focus in the run-up to the Maastricht meeting in December 1991. This chapter traces developments in the five years leading to Maastricht and in the pivotal year of 1992, which culminated in the Edinburgh European Council meeting in December 1992 trying to salvage what had been agreed a year earlier.

TOWARDS MAASTRICHT

The Single European Act (see Chapter Three) was a compromise between those member states that had not wanted it at all and those that wanted to give substance to the 'ever closer union among the peoples of Europe', and – some of them – to the European Federation to which the Schuman Declaration of 9 May 1950 had looked forward.

The Act prefigured two further developments. It inserted into the EEC Treaty a new article 102A, under the apparently double-headed rubric 'Co-operation in economic and monetary policy (economic and monetary union)', providing that if institutional change were needed for further development in this field, there would be a new inter-governmental conference to determine the necessary changes in the treaty: the article 236 EEC procedure.

It also stipulated in Title III, political co-operation, that five years after the entry into force of the Single European Act the parties would examine whether a revision of this title was needed (article 30(12)). This would place such a review in 1992.

Any agreed proposals to amend the treaties need unanimity among the parties, ratification in accordance with their national constitutional procedures, and referendums in at least two member states.

Exhibit 12.1 *Timetable to Maastricht (1991) and Edinburgh (1992)*

---

12 March 1985
Jacques Delors, President of the EC Commission, unveils the idea of the 1992 single market programme for the economic revival of Europe to the European Parliament.

14 June 1985
The Commission publishes its White Paper on the completion of the internal market, prepared under the authority of Lord Cockfield.

28 and 29 June 1985
The European Council in Milan approves the Commission's White Paper.

2 and 3 December 1985
The European Council in Luxembourg agrees on reform of the Treaties (Single Act).

15 February 1987
The Commission adopts a programme of action for the implementation of the Single Act entitled 'The Single Act: A new frontier for Europe'.

18 February 1987
President Delors presents the Commission's action programme to the European Parliament. The challenge is one of establishing a common economic and social area, creating the conditions for stronger economic growth, acting decisively and in concert on matters of foreign policy, adapting the common agricultural policy to changing circumstances in the world, and ensuring that the financing of the Community is placed on a sound footing.

1 July 1987
The Single Act enters into force.

18 November 1987
The European Parliament approves the Commission's action programme for implementing the Single Act.

11 to 13 February 1988
The Brussels European Council endorses the Commission's programme of 15 February 1987. The agreement of the heads of state or government

after scarcely one year's negotiations leaves the way clear for the single market in 1992.

27 and 28 June 1988
The Hanover European Council instructs a committee chaired by Commission President Jacques Delors to make proposals on concrete steps leading towards economic and monetary union.

12 April 1989
The Delors Committee presents its findings in a report on economic and monetary union in the European Community.

14 to 16 June 1989
The Madrid European Council decides that the first stage of economic and monetary union should commence on 1 July 1990.

8 and 9 December 1989
In Strasbourg President François Mitterrand of France, in his capacity as President of the European Council, declares that the necessary majority exists for convening an Inter-governmental Conference under Article 236 of the EEC Treaty to draft the amendments to the Treaties needed for the final stages of economic and monetary union.

Eleven heads of state or government adopt the Community Charter of the Fundamental Social Rights of Workers.

25 and 26 June 1990
The Dublin European Council decides to convene the Inter-governmental Conference on Economic and Monetary Union on 13 December and the Inter-governmental Conference on Political Union on 14 December 1990.

1 July 1990
Full liberalization of capital movements comes into effect in eight member states. Exceptions continue to apply until the end of 1992 in four member states – Spain, Portugal, Greece and Ireland – which have not progressed as far as the others along the road to financial integration.

Start of the first stage of economic and monetary union.

13 and 14 December 1990
The Inter-governmental Conferences on Economic and Monetary Union and on Political Union open in Rome.

9 and 10 December 1991
The work of the Inter-governmental Conferences is completed a year later at the Maastricht meeting of the European Council.

7 February 1992
Foreign and Finance Ministers of the Twelve sign the Maastricht Treaty tranforming the Community into a European Union.

2 June 1992
Danish referendum 'No' by 40,000 votes.

18 June 1992
Irish referendum 'Yes'.

16 September 1992
Britain and Italy withdraw from ERM.

20 September 1992
French referendum 'Yes'.

16 October 1992
'Special' European Council meeting in Birmingham.

11–12 December 1992
European Council in Edinburgh.

Economic and monetary union took a step forward at the June 1988 meeting of the European Council in Hanover (under German presidency). The President of the Commission was asked to chair a Committee to propose concrete steps to be taken towards EMU. The Committee reported back, unanimously, to the Madrid meeting of the European Council in June 1989. It proposed the setting-up of a European system of central banks, described as being of a federal nature and charged with managing a single monetary policy characterized by irrevocably fixed parities among the national currencies. The Delors Committee did not recommend a single currency, but saw it as the natural extension of the monetary union. Meeting in Strasbourg on 8–9 December 1989, the European Council took stock, and its President, Mitterrand, concluded that the necessary majority existed to convene an inter-governmental conference on EMU under article 236 EEC. The UK government was not part of the majority. This decision gave effect to the relevant article of the Single European Act.

Meanwhile, however, there were tempestuous political events in the Soviet Union and in Eastern and Central Europe. The Berlin Wall had been torn down and German unification was imminent, fulfilling the declared policies of the NATO partners and, arguably, of the framers of the EEC Treaty, whose evocation of an ever closer union among the peoples of Europe could be held to embrace Soviet-dominated Europe as much as the western states. On 18 April 1990, on the eve of a meeting of the European Council in Dublin, President Mitterrand and Chancellor Kohl issued a statement in which they underlined that the upheavals in Europe and the fulfilment of the internal market, along with the plans for EMU, made it necessary to accelerate the political construction of Europe and transform relations among the member states into a European Union.[1] When it met again in Dublin on 25–26 June, the European Council decided that alongside the EMU conference, already decided on, there would be another conference on Political Union (EPU).

There was, however, a major difference between the methodologies of the two gatherings. The EMU conference had been comprehensively prepared and possessed an exhaustively annotated agenda, including a prediction that there would be a single currency, that the managers of the monetary institution would be fully independent of governments, that the monetary financing of public sector deficits would be prohibited and that there would be no bailouts for deficit ridden states. The EPU conference was by contrast uncharted, apart from the pre-history of work on European Union and a recent Belgian memorandum on the subject. In the terms of the Single European Act, the new EPU conference could undertake the required review of European Political Co-operation. It would also be called on to address the long-standing complaint of the European Parliament concerning its circumscribed role and the so-called 'democratic deficit' according to which the Community's legislator, the Council consisting of representatives of the governments of the member states, was effectively accountable only to national parliaments and not to any forum of European standing.

Work in the IGCs was begun by the Luxembourg presidency at the beginning of 1991 and pursued in the second half of the year by the Dutch presidency, the conferences were concluded at the meeting of the heads of state and government in Maastricht on 9–10 December 1991. The Treaty on European Union was signed, also in Maastricht, on 7 February 1992.[2]

THE TREATY ON EUROPEAN UNION

Like the Single European Act, the Treaty on European Union (prepositions are important; this is not a treaty of European Union) comprehends in a single text both the measures to create the

Economic and Monetary Union and a number of measures concerning relations among the institutions of the Community, the foundation of a Common Foreign and Security Policy and co-operation among the member states in matters of internal security. It also follows the path of the Single European Act by giving the Community new tasks.

Exhibit 12.2 *What's new in the Treaty on European Union?*

- A common European currency by 1999 at the latest.
- Rights for European citizens (Union citizenship).
- New powers for the European Community:
  A more active role in consumer protection; public health; visa policy; the establishment of trans-European transport, telecommunications and energy networks; Treaty provision for development co-operation; industrial policy; education; culture; greater importance for environmental protection; an increase in research and development; further progress on social policy (with the exception of the United Kingdom); co-operation in the field of justice and home affairs.
- Increased powers for the European Parliament:
  Involvement in the enactment of legislation; right of approval prior to appointment of the Commission; power of assent for all major international agreements.
- Introduction of a common foreign and security policy.

The Treaty, which is much criticized for its opacity, takes the form of a treaty within a treaty. An entity styled 'European Union' is created and sketchily described. It has no legal personality, no institutions of its own and no legal powers. Most of the 250+ pages concern another entity called the European Community, which displaces and abolishes the European Economic Community. In doing so, it adds some matters relating to education and training, culture, public health, consumer protection to which the EC is to contribute, and restates some others such as commercial policy, economic and social cohesion and research and technological development. These are linear developments, in the nature of tidying-up.

The response to the democratic deficit is to install a new co-decision procedure, although the word is not used. In the case of decisions to be taken under specified treaty articles, the co-operation procedure (see pp. 81–5) is strengthened in Parliament's favour. Where it foresees that in its second reading it will reject a common position adopted by the Council, the Parliament can call for a meeting of an inter-institutional conciliation Committee with the task of reaching an agreement. If successful, the outcome of the conciliation will then be adopted by the Council and by the Parliament and the legislation will be based on their joint authority. (Hitherto, legislation cites only the name of the Council, 'having consulted the European Parliament' or 'in co-operation with the European Parliament'.) If conciliation is unsuccessful, the Council can act, but its decision can be overturned by the European Parliament (new article 189b).

The treaty creates European citizenship, which confers on persons holding the nationality of a member state the right to vote and stand in municipal (not general) elections and European elections in any member state (articles 8a and 8b). Citizens of the Union are entitled to the consular or diplomatic protection of the authorities of any other member state when they are in a third country (article 8c).

ECONOMIC AND MONETARY UNION?

The EMU conference gives rise to Title VI and its annexes, which institute the economic and monetary union. The economic union imposes strict discipline on public finance, prohibiting excessive government deficits and imposing penalties on offenders – a cautionary statement ('health warning') to accompany any new issues of government paper, reconsideration of European Investment Bank policy towards the country concerned, deposits to be lodged with the Commission and ultimately fines. Strict rules for the fiscal policies which continue to be decided by national governments are the counterpart of the monetary union to which they aspire to belong (article 104c).

A cardinal rule is that the Community will not assume responsibility for the debt of a member state (article 104b). This works as a double discipline, first on the member state, which must keep its own house in order and, second, on the Union, which does not possess the power to replace or finance the public debt operations of a member state. Such a power, if provided for, is highly centralising. The deficit authorities become satellites of the centre and the latter is endowed with the vast resources it may need for rescue operations.

In its final and fully developed form, the monetary union is governed by a European Central Bank (not suggested by the Delors Committee), which works through a European System of Central Banks (ESCB), using as its agents the national central banks, whose presidents are members of the ECB, along with six full-time executives appointed by common accord of the heads of state and government. Appointments are not renewable. In parallel, legislation is to be enacted in each member state to establish the independence of the central bank from political direction. Equally, the full-time executives are independent (like Commissioners) and the institutions of the Community and the governments of the member states undertake not to seek to influence them. (There is no parallel for this self-denying ordinance in the appointment of the Commissioners.) It is for this reason that the members of the ECB have been likened to the 'philosopher kings' of whom Plato makes Socrates speak approvingly in *The Republic* and who, in their superior wisdom, govern the body politic without public participation.

The primary objective of the ESCB is price stability (article 105). It is also required to support the general economic policies of the Community. This provokes the first key question: do the governments of the member states mean to hand monetary policy over to this unelected but doubtless highly qualified body? The language of the treaty appears to confirm that that is what they mean. But President Mitterrand, addressing the nation's voters in September 1992, gave another interpretation: governments decide on the framework of monetary policy and the ESCB are the 'technicians' who apply it.

The second key question concerns membership of the monetary union (all member states automatically belong to the economic union). To be eligible for membership of the final phase, which includes the common currency, a member state must satisfy the convergence criteria set out in a protocol to article 109j. Its average rate of inflation must not be more than 1½ points worse than the average of the best three member states; the ratio of its deficit to GDP must not be more than 3 per cent; the ratio of government debt to GDP must not be more than 60 per cent; the national currency must be in the narrow band of allowable deviation (2¼ per cent) and must not have been devalued in the preceding two years; and its long-term interest rate must not be more than 2 points more than the three best performing member states. These tough tests are designed (by Germany) to protect the single currency from possible weaknesses in the performance of a participant. The question, to which ambiguous answers were given, is whether the requirements are absolute or whether there is some latitude for a state which is making an honest try.

If a majority of member states meet the conditions, the heads of state and government decide (not actually the European Council), not later than 31 December 1996, to set the date for the third and final stage. They do so by qualified majority. Otherwise the final stage starts by default on 1 January 1999, with whatever member states satisfy the conditions.

The EMU title, negotiated in a separate conference, is not of a piece with the rest of the treaty. It downgrades on the one hand the role of democratic accountability on Platonic lines, but on the other it also detracts from the powers of the national governments, which elsewhere in the treaty are reinforced.

THE BRITISH POSITION

The British government declined to accept the provisions relating to the final stage. It reserved to itself and the British parliament the right to take a separate and specific decision to join the monetary union (assuming that it met the conditions). It was concerned that, taking account of the divergence of the economic performance of the member states, the plan might be so over-ambitious as to produce only disruption in the markets if implemented, and equally damaging disappointment if not. The Danish government also reserved its position on the final stage, for which it ` ould require a referendum. The other member states accepted these reservations, possibly expecting that the monetary union would in the end prove irresistible.

The British government also declined to join with the eleven others in a programme for the development of social policy. But instead of this taking the form of the United Kingdom opting out, the Eleven declared that they would go ahead with the Social Chapter, using for the purpose the methods, institutions and legal forms of the

Community. But the measures adopted would not apply to the United Kingdom.

INTER-GOVERNMENTAL PILLARS

The Single European Act of 1987 saw the first formal treaty mention of European Political Co-operation, which had begun in 1969. The Treaty on European Union strengthens co-operation into a Common Foreign and Security Policy (CFSP) (see pp. 207–11) and recognizes and codifies co-operation among the law and order authorities in their fight against terrorism, drug trafficking, illegal immigration and international criminality. The treaty provides that the action in both fields will be inter-governmental, and not governed by the methods of the existing Communities.

Whereas in the Single European Act the obligation accepted by the parties was to endeavour to formulate a common foreign policy (article 30.1), the new treaty requires the Union and its member states to define and implement a common foreign and security policy (article J.1). They are to do so by consensus, with some expectation, expressed in a declaration annexed to the treaty, that if they reach a qualified majority the dissidents will make it unanimous. But the right to block is not removed. The Commission participates in the CFSP, as it did in the EPC, but it does not have the monopoly of initiative. The Court of Justice has no jurisdiction.

The CFSP includes the eventual framing of a common defence policy, 'which might in time lead to a common defence'. But defence policy is left skeletal, the result of divergence between those who placed the emphasis on maintaining the Atlantic alliance, including the unified NATO command structure and the positioning of US forces in Europe, and those who argued for an independent European defence capability. The instrument for defence is the Western European Union. This body grew from the Brussels Treaty of 1948 (Britain, France, Belgium, Netherlands, Luxembourg), which explicitly cited a fear of German militarism, to the WEU of 1954, which admitted Germany when it joined NATO and no longer mentioned a specific threat to security. WEU did not set up a command structure and did not have forces dedicated to it, for fear of prejudicing NATO. Spain and Portugal joined after they entered the EC. Greece and Denmark, although belonging to NATO, did not, and neither did the declared neutral Ireland. In a declaration attached to the Treaty, WEU invites all European NATO members to join it. Nothing is said about how decisions would be taken in a common defence policy, except that the rules of the CFSP would not be used. The reference to a common defence is not clarified.

The British presidency of 1986 convened meetings of an inter-governmental kind of officials and ministers, including Commission representatives, concerned with problems of immigration (see pp. 176–9). They were distinct from the so-called Trevi meetings, which had begun inter-governmentally in 1975, to co-ordinate anti-terrorist action without the presence of the Commission. The French presidency of 1990 promoted the CELAD, an inter-governmental gathering, with the Commission present, to address problems of drug trafficking and addiction. Trevi looked after itself, but the numerous and ever more frequent meetings of committees and sub-committees which took place under the other auspices were serviced by the Secretariat of the Council. Pressures of immigration and of applications, justified or not, for political asylum grew in the confused political conditions from 1990 on and this work assumed a higher profile. The Treaty on European Union institutionalizes co-operation among ministers of justice and of the interior, on lines generally similiar to those of the CFSP – inter-governmental, no Commission monopoly of proposal-making, no automatic juris-diction of the European Court of Justice, no parliamentary right of input into the deliberations. Decisions when taken are in the form of inter-governmental conventions, not Community legislation.

THE TREATY ON EUROPEAN UNION AND THE 'PILLARS'

Prior to the Treaty on European Union, European Political Co-operation and Immigration, etc., co-ordination was not taxonomic-ally regarded as belonging to the Community, and Community terminology was not used to describe it. This changes with the treaty, which provides that in these fields the member states act in the Council but it is not the same kind of animal as the Council, which also acts in that part of the new European Community which derives from the EEC and Euratom.

There is some word-play here. Article C, which is part of the treaty establishing the European Union, the shell for the European

Community, provides that the Union 'shall be served by a single institutional framework'. But the institutions of the Community are only optically single. The Community is built on several pillars, usually counted as three, but the institutional peculiarity of the EMU makes the count four. The first is the classic Community, using what used to be described as the Community method – independent Commission with a monopoly of initiative, Parliament with the right to be consulted and limited right to reject, Council, representative of member states, taking the decisions, historically unanimously, but after 1987 by qualified majorities especially for single market measures, the Commission again monitoring member states for compliance with the law, the Court of Justice applying the provisions of the treaties. The second is the monetary union, with its own institutions, independent of the Commission and of the other institutions and (ostensibly) of the governments of the member states. The third is the CFSP, inter-governmental and probably relying on consensus, with many blanks for a common defence policy. The fourth is the co-operation among ministers of justice and the interior, likewise inter-governmental and no suggestion that it would ever proceed otherwise than by consensus. Despite the involvement of justice departments, no jurisdiction for the Court of Justice.

POST-MAASTRICHT COMPLICATION: RATIFICATION

The conclusion of the agreement at Maastricht in December 1991 was greeted with a good deal of 'Europhoria' across Europe. Ratification was set in hand to meet the target date of 1 January 1993, coinciding with the completion of the Single Market (the 1992 programme). No great problems were foreseen in Britain: in the general election of April all the main parties supported the Maastricht agreement, with the Labour opposition criticizing the opt-outs. Difficulties were foreseen in Dublin, where the progress towards union became adventitiously mixed up with the constitutional ban on abortion, in Denmark with its tradition of minority governments and the strong anti-market movement, and even in Germany, where the government of Chancellor Kohl was accused of selling out the Deutschmark with its guarantee of maintained value for an unknown and possibly politically weakened and vulnerable ecu.

The first jarring note was struck on 2 June 1992, when by the narrow margin of 42,000 votes, less than 1 per cent, the Danish referendum went against ratification. This killed the treaty. Nevertheless, the other member states decided to continue with their own ratification procedures on the basis that the Danes might not have spoken their final word. In June the Irish referendum went 2:1 in favour. In Britain the Bill laid before parliament had commanded a strong majority at second reading, but in the light of the Danish vote, the government withdrew the Bill from the committee stage. At this time the government's message was upbeat. Maastricht had been a triumph for British diplomacy and for the Prime Minister in person – game, set and match.

In France the president announced that there would be a referendum, although this was not required by law. On 22 June the Congress (a joint gathering of the *Assemblée nationale* and the Senate) approved by comfortable majorities both the ratification of the treaty and the constitutional changes represented by the new electoral rights of European citizenship.

But storm clouds began to gather in different weather systems in Britain and in France. In Britain, the pound began to come under intense pressure in August at the hands of foreign currency speculators, who thought that it could be driven down to their advantage. The summer was also marked by mounting disquiet over the damage done by the high base interest rate (10 per cent) which the British government maintained to sustain the exchange value of the pound. The government insisted that it was an essential part of its anti-inflation stategy, which was working, with inflation falling from 11 per cent to less than 4 per cent in two years. But the price was heavy: bankruptcies, job losses, investment starvation, 'negative equity' (houses worth less than their mortgages) and house repossessions. Significant numbers of the government's own supporters began to question the value of the policy and the anti-marketeers among them placed the blame on the needlessly high interest rate dictated by Britain's two-year membership of the ERM.[3] There the DM set the floor and the Bundesbank held to a high interest rate to offset the inflationary effect of huge public sector expenditures on the scale of DM150 billion a year, in the former DGR.

Meanwhile in France, the expectation of a massive Yes vote in the referendum to be held on 20 September began to evaporate. The extremes of Left and Right were opposed. The main opposition parties were pro-Treaty, but did not command the loyalty of all their followers, and leaderships were embarrassed by being obliged to recommend support for the policies of their Socialist opponents. There had already been a good deal of unrest in France, including farm vote protests against changes in the CAP.

On 16 September Britain withdrew from the ERM and allowed the pound to float down. Italy, which had already devalued within the mechanism, also withdrew. On 20 September, the French referendum gave a majority of less than 2 per cent in favour of the ratification of the Treaty on European Union. In two of the three referendum countries roughly half the voters had said that they did not want the treaty.

Meeting in New York on 21 September, the foreign ministers decided that ratification procedures should proceed, but they did not set any timetable for the entry into force of the new treaty. The British government had meanwhile announced that it would defer the ratification process in Britain until the Danish situation was clearer. It also regarded events as a vindication of its own view that the inter-governmental conferences had been too ambitious and had in particular lost touch with public opinion across Europe. It detected 'fault lines' in the ERM, calling in question the plan for EMU (to which it was not committed) and called for full examination of the system, which it had already and unsuccessfully sought to suspend. The message was that governments had to change their style and begin listening to the people. The Prime Minister recalled that he had consistently opposed centralizing tendencies and that it had been a constant aim of British policy throughout its membership of the European Community to restore the authority of the nation-state by diminishing the role of the Commission and the European Court of Justice.

STATE VERSUS COMMUNITY POWER: FEDERALISM, SUBSIDIARITY, SUPRANATIONALISM AND INTER-GOVERNMENTALISM

The view that the treaty served to protect national authority had not been the perception among the negative voters in France and in Denmark, where, as among its British opponents, the excessive and growing power of 'Brussels' was condemned and the Commission was blamed for all ills. The British Prime Minister himself contributed to these criticisms when, at the meeting of the European Council in Lisbon in June 1992, he described the Commission as intrusive.

Much of the anti-Brussels sentiment was ill-informed, and some of it arose from ambiguity in the language used on both sides of the argument. In the penultimate draft of the treaty it was said that the union 'had a federal vocation'. This was opposed by the United Kingdom and was replaced by 'in which decisions are taken as closely as possible to the citizen' (article A, second para.). The meaning is elaborated in article 3b second para.:

> In areas which do not fall within its exclusive competence, the
> Community shall take action, in accordance with the principle of
> subsidiarity, only if and in so far as the objectives of the proposed action
> cannot be sufficiently achieved by the member states and can therefore,
> by reason of the scale or effects of the proposed action, be better achieved
> by the Community.

Subsidiarity is part of the social teaching of the Vatican, set out in the encyclical Quadragesimo Anno of 1931.[4] According to this doctrine, the people should be closely involved in decisions that affect them, and the bodies that take the decisions should be close to them. The encyclical set out to counteract the totalitarianism of fascist Italy and of the Soviet Union. It is not an easy doctrine to apply because there can be endless argument about which level of decision-taking obtains the best results. It can even be argued that in a federal structure, where the federation is constitutionally empowered to act independently of and if necessary despite the authorities which are joined in the federation, subsdiarity, or comparable definitions of states' rights, is what distinguishes federation from unitary state. But in the simplifying presentation, article 3b gives power back to the state, and inhibits the growth of central power. It is worth noting that in the Maastricht version of subsidiarity, decentralization stops at the level of the member state, and does not descend to regional or local authorities, although they might be held to be 'close to the citizen'.

However, the effect of the principle of subsidiarity depends on the nature of the central power. In the Community of the 1957 treaties, this power is in the hands of the member states, and not of an institution independent of them. The word 'supranational' occurs once in EC treaties, in the original 1951 version of the ECSC Treaty. It was deleted when that part of the ECSC Treaty was repealed on the fusion of the institutions (see pp. 32–3 above). The Commission possesses law-making powers, which have been conferred on it by the member states when they have adopted legislation, but they are not comparable with the powers of the Council, which is the Community legislature. If, therefore, 'Brussels' has been overbearing or intrusive and has pushed itself into the nooks and crannies of national life, then either

1. the member states, or a qualified majority of them, have judged, perhaps erroneously at the time, that the intrusions now complained of were needed and were better done by the Community than by the member states; or
2. the Commission has used the powers given to it in Community legislation, perhaps insensitively, but not legally improperly. If it has acted *ultra vires*, the member state which has felt the intrusion can get the Court to stop it.

Since the essence of the Community system is/was the separation of powers, interventions by the Commission, within its responsibilities, are likely to be unwelcome to the member state which receives them and to be rebutted as bureaucratic and the work of busy-bodies.

While British anti-federalists saw the change of wording from 'federal' to 'subsidiarity' as a victory for their opposition to the growth of a central power, exercising sway over the people and over the nation-states and abusing the latter's rights, federalists might say that the words now used are a convenient and informative definition of the nature of federal power. This, according to them, is decentralized and governed by principles which are the essence of subsidiarity, even though federalists had not previously borrowed the term from the social teaching of the Vatican. It was this interpretation of federalism which inspired Vice-President Bangemann (German) to say, on the eve of the crucial House of Commons vote on 4 November 1992, that the Treaty on European Union is federalist.

The government of Mr Major, for its part, thought the deletion of all references to federalism of the first importance, in so far as it re-affirmed the essential role of the government and possibly other institutions of the member states. Whether or not the language of the treaty is justiciable is not material. The importance of the drafting is that it provides a basis for argument at political level that such and such a thing – how to consult local people over the building of a new motorway, whether and how to control the advertising of tobacco, whether there should be the same length of working week everywhere, whether water on bathing beaches should be of a standardized purity, or whether Europe should be a single time-zone – is among those that can be sufficiently achieved at the level of the member states.

Another way of diminishing the real or perceived threat of the growth of central (in the English lexicon, 'federal') power is to demobilize the central institutions. This is inter-governmentalism, of the kind which the Treaty applies to the CFSP, predictably to the eventual Common Defence Policy and to co-operation among ministers of justice and of the interior. It is an example of the 'active and willing co-operation among independent sovereign states' which Baroness Thatcher gave as her definition of European integration in the speech she delivered at the College of Europe in Bruges, Belgium, in September 1988. (In his companion speech, on the same occasion one year later, M. Delors used the word 'subsidiarity' ten times.)[5] In inter-governmentalism there is no separation of powers. The member states act independently of other institutions and consensually or not at all, unless minorities are prepared to yield.

Inter-governmentalism is a mode of action which preserves the authority of the member state, especially by resting on unanimity and by escaping the restriction represented by the institutional powers of the Commission, which is not a government and intending to escape the purview of the Court of Justice. When inter-governmentalism is practised it too must first satisfy the test of subsidiarity – it must be shown or accepted that the European Union should act, but not in the same way as it acts when it is using the classic Community method. Mr Major contends that the validation of this type of action, little known in the EC treaties, marks a stage in the process of decentralization. The inter-governmental titles of the treaty may not be enforceable against a deviating member state, but the political counterweight is that participants are to be deemed to give their full support to whatever is decided; and any one of them can block a decision which it would find adverse. Unanimity is strength.

One of the existing and particular forms of inter-governmentalism is the European Monetary System, which is ultimately based on an agreement among the heads of the central banks, with only ancillary Community legislation. The Commission's role is minor and it has never been envisaged that the European Parliament or the European Court of Justice have anything important to say. This would change radically and towards total centralization under EMU, which is why the United Kingdom reserves its position on the final stage. Interestingly, the British criticism of the ERM during the September 1992 crisis, was that the system was excessively nationalistic, that is serving German economic management purposes, not those of the other participants.

A third way of maintaining national authority, 'sovereignty', is opting out. Community legislation contains countless derogations for individual member states, but they are temporary and transitional. They give time for the member state to apply the obligation which the legislation has created. Permanent derogations, opting out of a decision, are rarer. Examples are article 100a 4 of the Single European Act, which enables a member state not to apply a harmonizing decision (never used), and some R & D programmes in which member states participate or not at their own choice.

VARIABLE GEOMETRY

These tendencies have given rise to the notion of variable geometry – a generic term which also implies that the variability has an objective justification. Near synonyms are 'multi-speed Europe', 'Europe *à la carte*', but they have negative vibrations. 'Graduated integration' tends to imply that the variability is transitional, perhaps over a long period. Variable geometry is not something new, being well established in the (inter-governmental) ERM, in the R & D programmes, which allow for non-participation, and in article 100a 4, which allows for a member state to go beyond what was adopted as a harmonized Single Market measure.

Another example of variable geometry, occurring outside the treaty framework and contracted inter-governmentally, is the Schengen agreement, whose founder members – Germany, Benelux and France – created a single area for the free movement of people without waiting for the known divergent views of the other member states to be reconciled. The Schengen states regard their agreement as a test bed for what the European Union will do.

Extreme variable geometry is represented by the Franco-German brigade, to be expanded to a corps, which is offered as a model for a European army, and which some other member states, but not all, are said to be interested in.

The Maastricht Treaty goes beyond most previous experience:

- There is a two-speed progress towards the Monetary Union, governed by the convergence criteria.
- The United Kingdom is not committed to membership at any speed, and no reason is given.
- Eleven member states accept a programme of social legislation which the United Kingdom excludes itself from.
- If, in the CFSP or in the Justice and Home Affairs co-operation – and eventually in the Common Defence Policy – there is no agreement after due process, each member state can pursue its own line of policy.

Subsidiarity (which can be regarded as federal or anti-federal according to who is using the word) acts against over-centralization and keeps the Community out of matters which the member states can handle better. Inter-governmentalism allows the Union, but not the Community, to act and curbs the possible growth of a central authority independent of and possibly overriding member states, especially on sensitive issues like war and peace. Variable geometry empowers a member state to go its own way without preventing the others from doing whatever it is they want to do. This is the essence of British pragmatism and its aversion to institutionalizing. It also, in the view of the British government, eases the enlargement of the Community and puts a stop to the hanging of a new 'iron curtain' between EC Europe and the rest of Europe. It is, however, by no means certain that all the possible applicants are against centralism, or that in an enlarging union, the central power can continue to be diluted without risking its collapse. In the end the Treaty on European Union establishes a European Union, which is described as a stage on the way to the ever closer union among the peoples, but it is the Europe of the States and it may not be on the way to becoming something else.

The Treaty on European Union could not have been concluded

without opting-out: Britain is not committed to the single currency and will not participate in the Social Chapter adopted by the Eleven. The Danish finance minister said in Washington, on 22 September 1992, that Denmark might need some similar exemptions if the government were to be able to justify holding a second referendum on the treaty, and to have any prospect of success.

RENEGOTIATION?

This raised the problem of renegotiation. Meeting in Washington (fortuitously) on 4 June 1992, Community foreign ministers, including the Danish, ruled out the renegotiation of the Treaty on European Union, which, as President Mitterrand said later, would open Pandora's Box, and release chaos. But sophisticated attempts began to be made to devise some form of 'addition' or 'clarification' which would not compromise the text of the treaty, but could be regarded as interpreting it. If, however, such glosses were to be legally secure, they might need to form part of the treaty. If they were not an integral part, the Court, whose exclusive function it is to interpret treaties, might consider that although they were important politically, they did not qualify, amplify or otherwise affect the meaning of the Treaty, or lack of it.

For its part, the British government was seized by a crisis of confidence in September. Obliged by a sustained run on the pound to leave the ERM after two years' membership, it announced in a special debate in the House of Commons on 24 September 1992:

- that it did not expect sterling to re-enter soon;
- that 'fault lines' in the ERM needed to be examined and rectified, such that the ERM which it would rejoin would not be the same as the one it had left;
- that parliament would not be asked to ratify the treaty until the Danish government had made its position clear;
- that additionally, the ratification Bill would not be brought back for second reading until there was clarity about what powers were for Brussels and what for the states – a valid elaboration of the principle of subsidiarity.[6]

In several of the other member states there was no great sympathy for the remarks about the ERM and irritation that the British government proposed to delay ratification while all the others pressed ahead in time for the end of the year, but other heads of government supported the proposition that 'Brussels' had become too powerful.

For all that the Treaty on European Union does not increase the powers of the Commission but on the contrary reinforces the authority of the member states and for all that it seems to depoliticize inflation-free economic management, to almost half the voters of Denmark and of France, and to significant numbers of Parliamentarians and their constituents in some other countries, Maastricht is a 'treaty too far'. Even if the treaty were ratified:

- the realignment of exchange rates after five years of currency stability among the participants and the entry of all save Greece,
- plus the withdrawal of sterling and the lira from the mechanism,

call into question the possibility of realizing a monetary union and a single currency on anything like the time scale of the treaty.

FROM BIRMINGHAM TO EDINBURGH

On 16 October 1992, the British Presidency convened a special meeting of the European Council in Birmingham. Whatever may have been the game-plan, the proceedings were overshadowed by an unconnected crisis provoked by the announcement of the closure of half of Britain's remaining coalmines, with 30,000 dismissals and by successive retreats by the government from its position.

Despite earlier pronouncements, the Birmingham meeting did not address the difficulties of the ERM, apart from endorsing conclusions which the Finance Ministers had already reached. It:

- reaffirmed that the text of the Maastricht agreement would not be reopened;
- reiterated its commitmnet to the EMS;
- reaffirmed that decisions must be taken as closely as possible to the citizen; and looked forward to receiving at its next meeting reports on adapting the Council's procedures and practices and on guidelines for applying the principle of subsidiarity in practice.

'Making subsidiarity work should be a priority for all the Community institutions, without affecting the balance between them.'

The results were more modest than the presidency had seemed to be seeking, but the coalmine troubles had distracted attention.

Late in October the Danish government, having negotiated with the numerically superior opposition, published its proposals for the reassurances which it thought the population required. They appeared to want legally binding provision for Denmark to opt out of the single currency, of Union citizenship and of an eventual common defence policy.

The Maastricht text already provides for there to be a Danish referendum on the question of joining in on a single currency; and the common defence policy is so skeletal that there is only a principle to opt out of. Union citizenship is also mild and does not jeopardize existing nationality. But the demand for legally binding statements raised precisely the problem of whether Denmark could not be satisfied except by renegotiation. The British government welcomed what it described as the clarification of the Danish position. On that basis, and fortified by the progress which it thought to have been made in Birmingham, it decided to address its domestic problems by conducting a debate in the House of Commons on 4 November 1992 to pave the way for the resumption of the ratification procedure. Despite its majority of 21 it carried the debate by only 3 votes. The main opposition party, Labour, while upholding its pro-European stance, voted against on two grounds: that it would not vote confidence in the government and that ratification should be suspended until the Danish and subsidiarity problems had been dealt with. After the debate it emerged that the timetable for further progress of ratification in the United Kingdom envisaged that the result of the second Danish referendum would be known before the House of Commons completed its examination of the Treaty on European Union, but meanwhile another problem forced itself on the Community agenda and demanded much attention at all levels before the meeting of the European Council in Edinburgh on 11–12 December 1992. In November 1992 in Chicago, the US–EC talks on agriculture within the Uruguay Round of trade negotiations broke down and the United States took the first steps towards imposing punitive tariffs on a range of its imports from the Community.

Further confusion was spread by the revelation by the Commissioner responsible for the talks with the United States that he had been frustrated by the intervention of Commission President, M. Delors. While resolved by the end of the year, this was another distraction and, even more importantly raised questions of good faith and Community allegiance on the part of several actors, as well as overloading the agenda of Community business.

THE EDINBURGH EUROPEAN COUNCIL

At its meeting in Edinburgh on 11–12 December 1992, the European Council must have felt that it was in the Last Chance Saloon. The causes of European unity had not shone under the British presidency – indeed, the President of the European Council had sought to disarm the critics among his own supporters by describing himself as the first of the Euro-sceptics. The Birmingham Council had been a non-event. The London Conference on Yugoslavia held at the beginning of the British presidency had served to demonstrate only the ineffectiveness of the Community and its member states.

To the post-Maastricht problems of Danish dissent and the deferment for domestic political reasons of British ratification[7] were added:

- The split in Community ranks over Delors II on future expenditure, casting its shadow over the 1993 budget.
- The controversy over M. Delors' role in the Uruguay Round bilateral discussions between the Commission and the United States, and the French repudiation of the agreement reached between the two on reducing EC subsidies for agriculture.
- The partial collapse of the ERM and the continuing market pressure on the weaker currencies within it.
- The worsening economic situation in Europe, and especially the forecasts of downturn in Germany.
- Confirmation early in December 1992 that the free movement of people, an element in the Single Market and a requirement of article 8a of the EEC Treaty, would not be realized by the target date of 1 January 1993.

The presidency's own priority at the European Council meeting in

December 1992 was to obtain a new statement about subsidiarity: 'transferring power from Brussels to London' in the words of John Major. At Edinburgh it obtained agreement to a 16-page document, which amplifies the sense of article 3b of the Treaty on European Union, centring on three principles:

1. National powers are the rule and the Community's the exception.
2. Subsidiarity proper, that is, article 3b.
3. The means to be employed by the Community (when it acts within the other two principles) must be proportional to the object to be pursued.

The document also sets out procedures for the application of the principle, including wider pre-proposal consultation by the Commission. It gives examples, provided by the Commission, of pending proposals which will be dropped and existing legislation which will be overhauled in the light of subsidiarity and associated principles.

On the related theme of openness, the European Council decided that the Council's decisions will be more transparent; that the record of formal votes taken in the Council will be published; and that some Council debates will be televised live to the press room in the Council building (to which access is controlled).

The heads of state and government, meeting within the European Council, agreed on a decision concerning the Danish demands for legally binding provisions affecting Denmark in relation to the Treaty on European Union:

1. Citizenship. They declared that citizenship of the Union does not take the place of national citizenship, an individual's nationality being a matter for national law.
2. EMU. The treaty gives Denmark the right to decide on its participation in the third (and final) stage. Denmark has given notice that it will not participate.
3. Defence. Denmark will not participate in decisions and actions of the Union which have defence implications. Accordingly, Denmark will not exercise its presidency when these matters are before the Council.

The Danish government made a companion declaration on citizenship and on co-operation on justice and home affairs. It also announced that the Edinburgh conclusions on Denmark and on subsidiarity gave it satisfaction; only one political party in Denmark maintained its opposition to eventual ratification.

There are two interpretations of the status of the European Council decision, a measure which is not known to Community law. The first is that it is a statement of things already decided by the treaty, made more explicit. The treaty did not impose on Denmark any new obligations regarding citizenship, defence or co-operation on justice and home affairs. It already provided for Denmark to contract out of the final stage of EMU. Thus there was no renegotiation and no amendment of the treaty and the 'decision' changes nothing.

The second interpretation – which shares the view that the decision could not have amended the treaty – is that the decision could function as an inter-governmental agreement, binding in international public law on how the parties will behave with respect to the treaty. It might also have some persuasive value for the purpose of interpreting the new treaty as a superior form of declaration.

It appears that the Council's senior legal adviser, regarded as the author of the decision, assured the European Council that the decision would not require national ratifications; and Denmark for its part accepted that it complied with its demand for a legally binding measure.

Other matters settled at Edinburgh included:

- Future financing of the Community for seven years ahead and new financial perspectives for 1993–9, including a Cohesion Fund worth 16,150 billion ecus at 1992 prices over seven years[8] (Spain nearly brought the entire Council and the Edinburgh package to an end over this issue, and negotiations on it took the Council past its scheduled ending).
- The increase in the number of seats in the European Parliament (see p. 87).
- The negotiations for the accession of Austria, Sweden and Finland should open at the beginning of 1993.
- There will be no change in the location of the insitutions.

Nothing was said or decided about the ERM or about the internal dispute about the GATT Uruguay Round.[9]

These solutions to a string of major problems, however, carefully worked out by the British presidency and patiently negotiated by the Prime Minister, to whom his Community colleagues paid tribute, saved the British presidency from the harsh judgement towards which it had seemed to be heading during most of its term.

THE NEXT ENLARGEMENT OF THE COMMUNITY

The Treaty on European Union corresponds to the 'completing' and 'deepening' components of the celebrated tryptich. On the third, 'widening', it states in article O that any European state may apply to become a member of the Union. The application would not stand a chance if the applicant could not subscribe to the principle of an open market economy with free competition (article 3a 1), the principle of democracy (article F 1) and respect for fundamental rights (article F 2). Eight European states have applied to join the Community. Three more have said that membership is their intention. On ceasing to exist as a separate state in October 1990, what had been East Germany became part of the Community.[10]

Turkey is classified as a European state. The association agreement which it concluded with the Community in 1964 looks forward to membership. There have been difficulties in the functioning of the agreement, notably in connection with the movement of Turkish workers, once eagerly recruited but now not welcomed. Turkey applied for membership on 14 April 1987. In accordance with treaty procedure, the Commission gave a formal opinion on the Turkish application on 18 December 1989. This put off the opening of accession negotiations, partly because of the political and economic situation in Turkey and partly because 'it would be inappropriate for the Community – which is itself undergoing major changes while the whole of Europe is in a state of flux – to become involved in new accession negotiations before 1993 at the earliest, apart from exceptional circumstances.' Alternatively, the Commission proposed that the Community should step up its economic assistance.

Although they moved independently and at different times, the EFTA states are best looked at together.

Austria was the first EFTA state to apply for membership, on 17 July 1989. In an accompanying memorandum, the Austrian government explained that it wished to maintain its policy of military neutrality, but did not consider this an obstacle to membership. The Commission gave a positive opinion on 1 August 1991, leaving open the neutrality issue. This came as the Community was at full stretch in the inter-governmental conferences and its peace-making mission in Yugoslavia. It had meanwhile received, on 1 July 1991, a Swedish application.

This may not have been in accordance with the scenario which the Commission might have been planning for.

When the collapse of communism changed the political constellations in Europe and when the success of the Community's 1992 Single Market programme became evident, speculation grew that Western European countries which had stood aside from the Community might think again. A series of membership applications might have been unmanageable in a Community which was also reflecting, by no means consensually, about its own future. On 17 January 1989, presenting the new Commission's programme to the European Parliament, President Delors launched the idea of a far-reaching discussion with the countries of the European Free Trade Association on the possibility of broader co-operation. The underlying notion was to find a way in which these countries might form part of the Single Market, with freedom of movement of goods (except agricultural) and services. Some observers thought that the proposal might be intended to head off membership applications, by offering an alternative which would be easier for the EFTA countries, as well as for the Community. This was the origin of the negotiations which led, on 21 October 1991, to political agreement on the European Economic Area (EEA). (Formal agreement was reached on 2 May 1992 after the draft text had been changed to respond to an objection from the European Court, which considered that a judicial organ to be set up under the Agreement would be contrary to Community law.) In this agreement the EFTA countries undertook to organize themselves, in relation to the Single Market, in the same way as the Community, to ensure conditions of fair competition both ways. The agreement is subject to ratification by all the parties. It was due to come into force on 1 January 1993, but this was nullified by its rejection on 20 December 1992 in a referendum held in Switzerland. The result of this referendum also placed a question mark beside the Swiss application for membership of the European Community.

Table 12.1 *The European Economic Area (EEA) in figures*

	Area (1,000 sq. km)	Population (million)	Gross domestic product (GDP) in PPS[1]	Per capita GDP in PPS[1]	Level of unemployment as % of active population	Inflation rate (1989/90)
B	30.5	9.9	180.4	19,091	8.1	3.5
DK	43.0	5.1	100.9	19,814	7.9	1.9
D	248.6	79.3	1,276.9[2]	21,131[2]	5.1[2]	2.8[2]
GR	132.0	10.0	94.1	9,850	7.5	22.8
E	504.8	38.9	526.6	14,556	16.1	6.5
F	549.0	56.3	1,114.1	20,207	9.0	3.4
IRL	70.2	3.5	41.1	12,819	15.6	–
I	301.3	57.5	1,086.6	19,187	9.8	6.6
L	2.6	0.4	8.1	24,303	1.6	4.4
NL	41.5	14.9	276.0	19,147	8.1	2.7
P	92.1	10.3	90.2	10,369	4.6	13.7
UK	244.1	57.4	1,092.2	19,726	6.4	9.3
EC	2,259.8	343.5	5,752.1	17,857	8.4	5.7
A[3]	83.9	7.7	142.6	18,615	3.2	3.5
SF	338.1	5.0	100.7	20,140	3.4	4.9
IS	103.0	0.3	5.6	21,828	1.4	–
FL	0.16	0.3	0.9	31,817	–	–
N	323.9	4.2	96.0	22,679	5.2	4.4
S	450.0	8.5	178.5	20,936	1.5	10.9
CH[4]	41.3	6.7	165.2	24,308	2.0	5.3
EFTA	1,340.2	32.3	688.7	21,291	2.7	–

Notes:
1. PPS = Purchasing power standard (a common unit representing an identical volume of goods and services for each country. The PPS enables people's real purchasing power to be measured and countries to be compared).
2. Without the former German Democratic Republic.
3. A = Austria, SF = Finland, IS = Iceland, FL = Liechtenstein, N = Norway, S = Sweden, CH = Switzerland.
4. Switzerland voted 'No' in December 1992.

But if the rationale of the EEA was, in some measure, to avert membership applications, things did not work out that way. Sweden applied on 1 July 1991, Finland on 18 March 1992, the Swiss Confederation on 26 May 1992 and the Norwegian parliament approved an application in November 1992. (The other EFTA members are Iceland and Liechtenstein.) The Commission gave its opinion, as required by procedure, on the Swedish application on 31 July 1992; positive apart from concern that Sweden (and by implication the other EFTA applicants) should accept all the future consequences of the provisions in the Treaty on European Union relating to the common foreign and security policy and the possible defence policy. Commission officials were reported to be talking darkly of 'implicit commitments'.

At Maastricht on 8–9 December 1991 the European Council agreed that negotiations on accession to the Union could start as soon as the Community had terminated its negotiations on its future financing arrangements. It was taken as read that the Union treaty would by then have been ratified. At Lisbon on 26–27 June 1992 the European Council, largely at British urging, considered that the EEA agreement had paved the way for opening the negotiations with EFTA applicants and that preparatory work should be speeded up, with a view to opening negotiations immediately after the Treaty on European Union had been ratified and agreement had been reached on future financing (colloquially, the Delors II package). For their part, all the EFTA applicants said that they could accept the Treaty on European Union, although its terms gave rise to fresh internal debate. As has been seen the Edinburgh package cleared the way for negotiations to begin early in 1993. The Commission was reported to be working on a set of principles of membership which should guide the negotiators on both sides. Thus the EFTA states, regardless of when they applied, are first in line for negotiations to open, and they will be conducted in parallel.

Three other candidacies were discussed at Lisbon. Of Turkey it was said that there was every reason to intensify co-operation and develop relations. This seemed to mark some weakening of Greek opposition to the proposals that the Commission had made when it presented its Opinion in December 1989.

Cyprus applied for membership on 4 July 1990 and Malta on 16 July 1990. The Lisbon European Council put their applications on hold by deciding that relations with them should be developed and strengthened by building on the existing association agreements and by developing the political dialogue.

While communism ruled Eastern Europe, the Warsaw Pact countries refused to recognize the existence of the EEC, dismissing them as the side-kick of NATO. Under perestroika relations were opened with the conclusion on June 1988 of a Declaration of Intent, signed by the EEC and by Comecon, the organization responsible at the time for co-ordinating economic policy in the Warsaw Pact countries (and now no more). This was simply a signal and symbol of change. The Community proceeded between 1988 and 1990 to negotiate trade agreements with Bulgaria, Czechoslovakia, Hungary, Poland and Romania. At its meeting in Strasbourg on 8–9 December 1989 the Community announced that it intended to conclude an association with countries of Eastern and Central Europe, as part of the contribution to their economic and political reform. A year later on 20–22 December 1990 association negotiations opened with Czechoslovakia, Hungary and Poland, which came later to be known as the Visegrad countries from the town in which they agreed on mutual co-operation. The so-called 'European agreements' were signed, after some hiccups, mainly caused by EC import restrictions on sensitive products, in December 1991. (The agreements are still criticized as being too restrictive on the EC side and allowing insufficient trade opportunity to the three countries.) They explicitly aim at the integration of the three countries into the EC. For their part, each of the three has said that it intends to become a member of the EC in the relatively near future.

Similar agreements are on offer to Bulgaria and Romania. The future relationship of the former Yugoslavia and the new independent republics with the EC is in the balance.

13 Conclusion

On 7 February 1992 the Treaty on European Union was signed in Maastricht, but given both the nature of the treaty and the subsequent events in 1992, with the Danish 'no' in June, the close French vote in September, the currency crisis of the same month and the continued British and Danish ratification problems it was still not clear at the end of the year what content is to be given in the rest of the 1990s to the notion of 'European Union'.[1]

The exact constitutional and institutional structures of a European Union are a matter of choice and of negotiation if Europe is going down that road. There is also a choice not to go down such a road, but rather to give priority, over a lengthy period, to completing and cementing the Community, and to inter-governmental co-operation of the Twelve, that is, the road chosen at Maastricht. Both could arguably be called further European integration.

A European Union which was a new state would, it is to be supposed, do what a twentieth-century state does, which means that whatever its structure – and 'federal', 'confederal' and subsidiarity are words which unfortunately are not rigorously defined either – there would be a unitary principle somewhere in it. It is perhaps useful to reflect on the boundary conditions which might distinguish a future European Union from the 1993 model.

The first consideration has to be constitutional, although constitutions are not ends in themselves: under what structure of government does the citizen participate in the decisions which are taken in his or her name? Most of the discussion turns on the future relationship between different political forces, those mediated by:

- The unanimous or majority tendencies and actions of the governments of the member states of the Union, represented by and accountable to their national electorates.
- The majority view of the European Parliament, whose members are also accountable to their voters at five-year intervals.
- The collegial advocacy and the authority of the Commission, however appointed, and to whomever it is answerable.

The member states are not at all responsible to the directly elected European Parliament; and the Council has not gone very far down the road of submitting itself to European parliamentary control. Another way of saying the same thing is that the Council, holding the Community's legislative power, has not wanted to share much of that power with the Parliament.

In a more fully developed structure it is empirically unusual and perhaps organically unnatural for the lower house (for example, a future European Parliament) to be the revising chamber which pronounces on Bills normally originating in a higher chamber (for example, a Council of the European Union). The House of the People (that is, the European Parliament) would want a larger share of the power than this kind of projection would allow. In order to exercise it, it would need a continuity of purpose which cannot easily be secured by the fluctuating alliances within the present European parliamentary parties as at present constituted. Since a plurality seems unlikely, and proportional representation is not conducive to it, a reasonably stable coalition with an ideological base would be needed. The House of the People, and the whole system, may also need an executive to propose the programme and see it through. This gives colour to the idea that at least the chief executive's should be an elective post.[2]

The second minimal distinguishing attribute of European union is that it should practise economic management in regard to the level of employment, prices and growth. Although central, the management need not be centralized – there could be a lot of devolution. But a central, unitary management of the economy, and one in which the factors of production can circulate freely, gives rise or emphasis to the problem of regional disparity. Conditions are not everywhere equal: there are areas of prosperity and areas of deprivation. Unless some steps are taken to provide for redistribution of wealth, the use of resources will be allocative – drawn towards the geographical areas which offer the best prospects. This allocative principle, unless tempered, will incite opposition to integration from those who are not favoured by it. While some movement has been made in the direction of meeting this problem, the scale of resources agreed for that effort at Edinburgh in December 1992 appears woefully inadequate for the task. The MacDougall Report of 1977, 'The Report of the Study Group on the Role of Public Finance in European Integration', had argued that in a small public sector federation central expenditure would need to be about 5–7 per cent of GNP, plus 2.5–3 per cent of GNP if defence expenditure became a federal responsibility.[3] This compares with less than 1.5 per cent of Community GNP being spent on the Community budget in the early 1990s.

A third distinguishing feature or boundary condition of European union is an economic and monetary policy, even an economic and monetary union. The functions of an economic and monetary union would include:

- Decisions on public spending priorities. This implies a large consensus on objectives, or the acceptance of leadership in the selection. The union need not be responsible for anything like all public expenditure but it needs to be able to influence a large part of it in order to avoid regional disparities.
- The creation or reduction of credit; the maintenance of inflation, including its regional variation; the maintenance, or otherwise, of planned exchange rates between the currency unit which the union uses in its national accounting and (if they continue to exist) national currencies.[4] Even in a deregulated economy all these decisions will influence the volume and location of investment, the condition of the labour market, economic growth and the end-division of added value.

The division of added value again implies a consensus or an acceptance of leadership in social policy, in fields usually thought to be of the closest interest to voters. This puts the union, as the EEC's first Commission president Walter Hallstein, said of it, squarely in the business of politics.

Progress in these areas, however, similarly appears to be very much in the lap of the gods, given the 1992 misgivings and hesitations abroad in a number of states about moving to the third stage of economic and monetary union.

A fourth minimum attribute of a European Union would be a common foreign and defence policy.[5] The Union would need it practically and psychologically, to feel itself as a single whole in its dealings with the world outside. In its fully developed form, the foreign and defence policy of the Union would be unitary and, as in existing models, centralized: there cannot be separate foreign policies for different parts of the territory of the Union, and in order to be valid international interlocutors the Union's representatives and negotiators must be able to commit the Union, subject always to whatever are the Union's internal rules of ratification of international agreements – which could involve a parliamentary stage.

There is still no 'kind of United States of Europe'.[6]

A QUESTION OF PERSPECTIVE

That, however, raises the question of the importance of perspective in any attempt to assess the significance of the European Community and European Union in their current form and stage of development, and in assessing whether that form and stage are merely a phase in *Europe: Journey to an Unknown Destination*, or whether that journey has already come to an end.[7] Perspective is also crucial in any assessment of what has already been achieved on that journey.

There have always been sceptics as to the practicality of attempting or making the journey, and those sceptics have not been confined to the United Kingdom. In the late 1940s, for example, Sean Lemass, who was later responsible for the Irish application in 1961, still had 'doubts as to the practicability of maintaining a permanent organization for European co-operation'.[8] Even in the late 1950s British sceptics still believed that the new European Economic Community, which came to life in 1958, was a mere flash in the pan, it being perceived that it would not last long, especially, but not only, because of the lack of British participation. If it were to survive, it was felt that it would probably be in a watered-down form, reverting to a general free trade agreement arrangement, as had been and was being discussed in the OEEC, and with central institutions being bereft of real power and authority, rather like the Council of Europe by that time. In 1958 no one knew quite what to expect and, as seen earlier, some expected Euratom to be significant. The negotiations leading to the two Treaties of Rome had been difficult, with success being by no means guaranteed. At several points during the negotiations, and indeed during the preceding decade since the halcyon days at The Hague in 1948, the entire journey could have been derailed, the entire enterprise scuttled. There was no inevitability about the destination or the smoothness of the journey, then, later, now, or in the future.

It is thus important to record the fact that over thirty years later the enterprise still exists and from some perspectives flourishes. The company making the journey has expanded, from the original six to nine in 1973, to ten in 1981, and to twelve in 1986. The company now encompasses some 345 million people, a greater population than that of either the United States (237 million) or the former Soviet Union (275 million). It comprises the world's largest trading unit, having some 18 per cent of world trade compared to the 17 per cent of the United States and the 9 per cent of Japan. Indeed, if intra-Community trade is included, the share of world trade involving the Twelve approaches some 40 per cent. More than 130 states have diplomatic relations with the Community as such, while some 120 or so agreements relating to trade, aid and economic co-operation have been signed between the Community and other states. In addition, the Community participates in over thirty multilateral agreements.[9]

The Community has clearly become a pole of attraction to others, a phenomenon that has become more pronounced with the onset of the single internal market in 1992. The prospect and arrival of 1992 stirred several European non-members into re-evaluating their position. In January 1993 four states began to negotiate for membership of the revamped Community and the new Union. Moreover, events in 1989 completely opened up the question of the nature of relations with the Community for Eastern and Central European states, and, indeed, the future institutional relationships which might exist in Europe as a whole. Some of the Eastern and Central European states are committed to seeking membership of the European Community/Union as soon as is practicable.

One hundred, even fifty years ago, it would have been inconceivable that twelve European and sixty-six African, Caribbean and

Pacific (ACP) states would freely and voluntarily sign trade and aid agreements such as Lomé. It would have been impossible to conceive of twelve fractious, blooded European states, including France, Germany and Britain, taking a common position in harmony at a multilateral Conference on Co-operation and Security in Europe (CSCE); these same states now, on a range of issues, voting in common at international forums like the United Nations, with one of their number regularly speaking on behalf of all and negotiating for all; moreover, these same states allowing a Commission to take their place and speak on their behalf in the General Agreement on Tariffs and Trade (GATT) and elsewhere, the group speaking with one voice in many trade and commodity negotiations. Although many have been disappointed that there has not been greater cohesiveness among the company on the journey, more evidence of common, united action and purpose, that Europe's potential to play a world role has been hindered by its fissile tendencies and lack of agreement on the formation of a common foreign and security policy, such considerations ought not to obscure what progress has been made in travelling forward, not only in terms of a voice in the world but in a range of other matters as well.

It may be that it is difficult to find examples of federations of states which had existed for any length of time or in any real sense as independent, sovereign states, but the Community exists and is, perhaps, a greater advance towards international co-operation and integration on a voluntary basis by states than has ever been seen before. The Community is different from the purely inter-governmental institutions of the late nineteenth and early twentieth centuries in which member states refused 'to accept any formal limitation on their sovereignty, insisting on the maintenance of a national veto'.[10] In those first practical steps towards the creation of permanently existing international organizations, co-operation was limited to collaboration among independent, sovereign states and the powers of institutions were heavily circumscribed. The states remained as distinct entities, and indeed were intended to remain as such, the objective of organisations being to help those states perform their roles better, not to portend or imply the withering away of the state. The states were subject to no superior authority or law, and domestic law was solely the preserve of the organs of the state, especially the government. While the new organizations had 'secretariats', they were literally that: a group for taking notes, preparing meetings in a formal sense and recording the decisions of others. Those secretariats did not take decisions.

In late twentieth-century Europe the situation is very different. The philosophical ideas of Sully, Penn, Simon and Cattaneo, discussed in Chapter One have been transformed into living institutions and systems. The role of at least one secretariat has been transformed. Now the European Commission's permission is required before a state can derogate from its obligations under Community law. States are no longer free to decide for themselves whether special problems or circumstances entitle them to suspend or deviate from their obligations to others. States too increasingly have allowed themselves to be outvoted on a number of issues. In the Community system, all the member states have found themselves, at one time or another, circumscribed in their behaviour. This is a revolutionary change in the conduct of international politics in international institutions. States have always had their freedom of decision and action constrained by the limitations on their own power set by the power of others, but the institutionalized and legitimized way in which this occurs in the Community system is rather different and new.

Whatever their intentions and behaviour, in the Single European Act and in the Community parts of the Treaty on European Union, the member states have committed themselves to an expansion of qualified majority voting, and the areas where a *de jure* veto power remains have been narrowed, now involving fundamental, constitutional-type questions within the Community, such as enlargement, any redistribution of power among the institutions and any move into new, unchartered areas of policy. Furthermore, although states can still in practice stop decisions, policies and agreements being reached, they have found it all but impossible to go back on decisions and policies previously introduced. In other words, governments are now constrained in their decision-making and, apart from retaining the unilateral right to abrogate their commitments and membership, states are no longer sovereign in the traditional sense. J. D. B. Mitchell observed that 'already by 1973, the Treaty of Rome had become a constitution having its effects within the internal law of the whole Community and having consequentially effects . . . on the constitutional situation and internal law of each' of the member states.[11] As noted in Chapter Five, certain decisions are 'directly applicable', as is made clear in article 189 of the EEC Treaty.

Moreover, in addition to the ENEL case referred to earlier, other cases such as the seminal Van Gend en Loos and Simmenthal have clearly established that Community law does enjoy primacy over national law.[12] Community law now pervades much of the legal systems of the twelve member states and is, therefore, part of the environment of every court. Furthermore, given the treaty – the legal position regarding qualified majority voting – some Community institutions can enjoy primacy, in some cases, over national governments. This position was hardly imaginable to many a generation ago. Although there remains the practical legacy of the 1965 crisis, any comparison with the extent of collaboration and co-operation in the period before the formation of the Communities is striking and significant. To some extent, albeit on a minor scale, the Community can now make the 'authoritative allocation of values', in Easton's memorable phrase, within the various national societies which go to make up the Community.[13]

Also striking is the creation, existence and evolution of the European Parliament. Whatever the debate about its precise powers and functions (Chapter Five), it is a novel feature of the international environment that millions of citizens from twelve states should vote for their directly elected representatives to a European Parliament. While the turnouts of 61–2 per cent may have disappointed those with lingering 1940s aspirations, that should not divert attention from the significance of such elections being held for such a body in the first place. That turn-out, incidentally, was higher than the turn-out in recent US presidential elections. Without becoming whimsical, the symbolic coming together of 518 MEPs from twelve states ought not to be underestimated, especially given their ability to question the actions (and inaction) of governments, to thwart the will of governments over some aspects of the budget and to be awkward about the passage of Community legislation. Too often the focus is on the constraints the Parliament faces, its limitations, at the expense of any appreciation of what an innovative, far-reaching experiment it has proved to be, and how unique it remains.

As well as these institutional changes, the Community has transformed relationships between its member states, and it has transmogrified the environment in which those relationships occur. Leading up to the Franco-Prussian War of 1870 there was no international organization in existence for promoting a peaceful settlement of international disputes or for providing a mechanism for such settlement between these or any states. Similarly, there was no organization or mechanism capable of stopping the second and third conflicts in 1914 and 1939. Between 1870 and 1945 millions had died because of conflict between the French and their neighbours to the east, yet on 9 May 1950 Robert Schuman, the French Foreign Minister, could talk of the contribution that an organised and living Europe could bring to civilization by maintaining peace. He and Monnet, who submitted the plan to him, tackled that central problem of Franco-German relations, specifically advocating the rassemblement of the nations of Europe and, crucially, 'the elimination of the age-old opposition of France and Germany. Any action taken must in the first place concern these two countries.' Of course, Schuman also went on to say that by establishing solidarity of production of coal and steel it is plain that 'any war between France and Germany becomes not merely unthinkable, but materially impossible'.[14] That central aim has now been achieved.

While critics might argue that the Community has done little to contribute to the avoidance of a 'European' war, and the situation in 1993 in Yugoslavia stands as a challenge to all European states, its contribution in the Franco-German area should not be gainsaid. Similarly, although it has not solved all the problems existing between Dublin, Belfast and London, common membership of the Community does provide potentially a mechanism whereby old sores can be circumvented, with old bilateral battles being subsumed by the Community process. The impact of the Community may make the border less of an issue in the future. In other words, several parts of the Community which have been violently opposed to each other for decades have been brought into a new pattern and environment of relationships.

In considering the question of perspective, it is perhaps worth recalling the motivations underlying the moves for European unity after the war, in addition to the central Franco-German issue. Those promoting a vision of a united Europe were concerned first about the repair of material destruction, economic recovery and growth. The advocates of a fundamental change were preoccupied with both immediate and long-term concerns. The latter focused on war prevention, on how to bring traditionally warring powers actively together in a new relationship. The former focused on the immediate necessity for action given that continental Europe was a 'charnel-house' – that is, a vault of dead bones.[15]

Beyond doubt the Communities have contributed significantly to the socio-economic transformation of Europe, so that today the 345 million citizens of the Twelve enjoy a very high standard of living relative to the rest of the world, with a GDP per capita that is some 270 per cent of the world average, and with high levels of personal utility consumption and acquisition, levels which trail only North America, Japan and Scandinavia. The Community is an economic giant, and its citizens (in general) are the inheritors of and the participants in 'the affluent society'. This has brought other benefits too, such as a transformation in life-expectancy levels.

The second concern of those promoting a united Europe was for military defence against the Soviet Union and protection from American economic strength. On the first the record was rather mixed since for a generation after the Western Europeans turned quaking to the United States for support in the late 1940s, over 300,000 US military personnel were in Europe to provide for the protection of those Europeans. There remained little doubt that most people in Western Europe felt that the Community states, individually or even collectively, could do little to resist a Soviet attack. The coupling of the United States with West European security was and is still widely perceived as necessary, as evidenced by the 1990–1 debates on CFSP, despite all the changes since 1989.

In this sense the European states still perceive themselves to be unable unilaterally to provide for a basic prerequisite of their citizens' needs – security. On the other hand, as against the expectations of many a generation ago, Western Europe was neither swamped nor intimidated by the Soviet Union, and indeed has outlived it. Moreover, not only has there been the development of the British and French nuclear systems, but with economic recovery Europeans generally have also begun to make a greater contribution to their own defence. In the late 1980s, 90 per cent of the manpower, 95 per cent of the divisions, 85 per cent of the tanks, 95 per cent of the artillery and 80 per cent of the combat aircraft stationed in Europe were provided by the Europeans, as were 70 per cent of the ships in European waters and the Atlantic.[16] Chapter Ten indicated signs of an evolving European identity on security and defence issues, partly because of disenchantment with the quality of American leadership and partly because of an awareness of particular European interests and perspectives on major issues, although Chapter Ten also showed that security has remained a difficult issue for the Twelve.

If not swamped by the Soviets, then neither have the Europeans been suffocated by the economic embrace of the Americans, despite occasional alarms that they might. As late as 1967 J. J. Servan-Schreiber in *Le Défi Americain*[17] expressed concern at the danger of American technological and economic penetration, concerns that returned in the 1980s, for example, in connection with the British debate over American or European solutions to the Westland helicopter problem, and in fears over the technological leap the United States might make as a result of its investment in the Strategic Defence Initiative programme.

There have, of course, been problems in the relationship with the United States, such problems surfacing periodically in 'chicken wars', disputes over the European contribution to a gas pipeline for the Soviets and hormone-injected meat. The main problem has been American concern at the perceived protectionist nature of much Community activity, especially with regard to the CAP, coupled with divergences over security questions. More than a decade ago, President Nixon drew attention to the potential for serious dispute: 'can the principle of Atlantic unity in defence and security be reconciled with the European Community's increasingly regional economic policies?'[18] The question remains whether the crises in the transatlantic relationship are transient as they have been in the past, or whether a structural change is beginning to take place as the United States becomes more concerned about its other, Pacific, shore, and more assertive in its stand against what it still perceives as European protectionism, as evidenced by the problems of the Uruguay Round of the GATT talks in 1992–3.

The problem for the Europeans is how far they can assert their cohesion, their identity, without damaging their relations with third parties, and without, in particular, weakening the American commitment to protect them. It may, however, be counted as a success that West Europeans still face that dilemma some forty years after the signing of the North Atlantic Treaty. Europeans have not succumbed to the alternatives of either total estrangement from the United States or subservience to it.

The vision of a united Europe was, thirdly, inspired by concern for a role in the world. The problem of relations with the United States will remain of vital importance to Europeans and the objective clearly is not to become divorced from the Atlantic partnership since that would be counterproductive in terms of security and anathema to the majority of European opinion. The objective is rather to evolve a European identity, through CFSP, so as to become more equal partners with the United States – as both Kennedy and Monnet envisaged in 1962, Monnet calling for a 'relationship of two separate but equally powerful entities, each bearing its share of common responsibilities in the world'.[19] Again, perspective is important since, while that symmetry in position has not been achieved, it is clear that the asymmetry has been reduced.

Europe was once the cauldron of international relations but it has had to adjust to the loss of empires and the movement of truly global power to two extra-European superpowers. Stutteringly, Europeans have tried to adapt to the new realities and to begin to establish a new role for themselves, albeit on a smaller scale than before. EPC has been a significant element in this development and even more important has been the Community's impact through its external relations activities, as shown in Chapter Seven. Again, despite all the tensions, it is increasingly possible to identify the emergence of a particular European view and contribution. While the citizens of Europe focus on centrifugal predispositions of the Twelve, states outside the Community are struck by its strength, its relative cohesion and its centripetal tendencies. While it still has far to go to become a 'superpower in the making', it is becoming increasingly less accurate to regard the Community as an economic giant but a political dwarf.[20]

A fourth ingredient was a belief in Europe and the European ideal. This clearly relates to much of the foregoing, but in general terms it might be regarded as the one area where the ratchet effect has failed to work – instead of there being evidence of general advance, despite occasional slippage, with respect to the European ideal, the process seems to have been one of gradual, if not steady, decline. In terms of the hearts and minds of many of its citizens, the imperatives, the faith, the *cri de coeur* underlying the European ideal have been somewhat dimmed. The belief in the construction of a new Europe involving a new pattern of political relationships, as an experiment, has been distorted as the economic instruments identified to achieve political change and objectives have gradually become regarded as more important than the objectives themselves. The means are in danger of consuming the ends. The fact that the true nature of the European Community cannot be understood simply by focusing on the provisions of the founding treaties has been obscured. As the cohort who lived through the ravages of war, despair and destruction died, it was replaced by a new generation of citizens and adults which was brought up to focus on the economic dimension of the Community. In the 1970s, however, the sheen went off the economic miracle as progress ran into the wall of OPEC price increases and world recession. Given this, the shortcomings of the Community appear only too apparent to the new generations of Europeans, especially to those facing personally the consequences of economic recession in the 1990s; ironically facing these problems just as they were expected to endorse the Treaty on European Union.

Indeed, when considering perspective, the shortcomings are also apparent if the current situation is compared to the aspirations of the founding fathers. Their motivation was not the price of eggs, bacon or steel but rather a revolution in international behaviour. When some resistance groups met in Geneva in 1944 they talked of the need 'to go beyond the dogma of absolute sovereignty of the state and unite in a single federal organization',[21] while at the Congress of Europe at The Hague in 1948 resolutions referred to 'the urgent duty of the nations of Europe to create an economic and political union in order to assure security and social progress'.[22] Schuman in May 1950 saw his proposals on coal and steel as 'a first step in the federation of Europe'.[23] As against such passionate appeals, it can be argued that states have been reluctant to 'transfer and merge some portion of their sovereign rights' as demanded at The Hague,[24] and sceptics can also argue that there has been little real movement towards European union or federation. It can further be argued that in parts of the Treaty on European Union and in the debates of 1992 the member states have reverted back to inter-governmentalism to some extent and have shied away from any transfer of power with regard to crucial decisions. But again perspective is important, for as has been shown 'some portion' of sovereignty and 'some portion' of the freedom to take decisions have been transferred, and whatever the limitations unique direct elections have been held.

It may be that to some extent the Community has become a victim of its own success, that as it has partially, or in some cases fully, achieved some of its basic objectives, particularly in the economic sphere, many have begun to feel that the need for radical solutions has passed, that a somewhat patched-up system of states could suffice, that the Community has achieved enough to satisfy its members – that is, they know that the current stage of development is not the optimal solution to Europe's problems and needs, but to many it is reasonably satisfactory and 'good enough'. The economic rejuvenation of post-war Europe has lessened the perceived need to continue with political rejuvenation, with some such as the British perceiving no linkage between the two at all. With economic recovery since 1945 and a return to political stability and peace have come the renewed arrogance of national political systems and some desire to restore as much autarky as is possible in an interdependent world.

One is reminded of the distinction between a pessimist and an optimist: the pessimist sees a glass as half empty, but the optimist sees it as half full. That may be a somewhat trite analogy but it is important not to become too preoccupied with the declining glamour, euphoria and bezazz of the Community idea. It can be demonstrated that compared to the 1880s and 1890s, to the 1920s and 1930s, or even to the 1940s much progress has been achieved, that the glass is becoming full. The Community states have achieved a degree of interdependence that would be difficult and economically costly to unravel. The notion of a 'European reflex' has not only applied to EPC as whole sectors of national governmental activity have acquired a European dimension and different domestic departments are forced to ensure that their initiatives and decisions are compatible with Community policy. Individual societies and states have discovered that there is no going back, that while not necessarily enamoured of the Community the alternatives are much less attractive, a fact accepted reluctantly by the British and by the Danes.

Schuman and Monnet who launched the Communities were aware, as Schuman put it in his seminal speech of May 1950, that 'Europe will not be made all at once, or according to a single plan. It will be built through concrete achievements which first create a *de facto* solidarity', that his own proposal was 'the first concrete foundation of a European federation indispensable to the preservation of peace'.[25] It is possible to be too impatient with respect to the progress of the foundations of the new Europe, but it has clearly been demonstrated in the preceding chapters that a number of foundation stones have been laid, that a *de facto* solidarity is being created. Further such steps are being laid daily as the Community conducts its business in a routine fashion. Other steps are more than routine, of course, such as the creation of a genuinely single 'common' market, an objective dating back to the 1950s, reaffirmed in 1985, and largely brought to fruition by December 1992. This created, as it was put in the SEA, 'an area without internal frontiers in which the free movement of goods, persons, services and capital is ensured'.

One final point on perspective is that it must always be borne in mind that the Community experiment does involve that element of 'journey to an unknown destination', and does encompass more than a common market, a mere economic arrangement. The very words 'community' and 'union' are symbolic of the nature of the endeavour. European construction is not solely or primarily about economic transactions or a single integrated market but about the future nature of the political relations between states, nations and peoples.

Where the Community stands today, then, depends very much on the perspective used. If one compares the situation as the Community enters the 1990s with the aspirations of the founding fathers much remains to be done, but let it not be forgotten that there is another perspective, namely that of 1870, 1914 and 1939. The fundamental rationale remains: 'They shall beat their swords into plowshares, and their spears into pruning hooks: nation shall not lift up sword against nation, neither shall they learn war any more.'

Part Four: Further Reading

Belmont European Policy Centre, *The New Treaty on European Union, Volume 2: legal and political analyses*, Brussels, Belmont European Policy Centre, 1992.

Bulmer, S., George, S. and Scott, A., eds., *The United Kingdom and EC Membership Evaluated*, London, Pinter, 1992.

Francioni, F., ed., *Italy and EC Membership Evaluated*, London, Pinter, 1992.

George, S., *An Awkward Partner, Britain in the European Community*, Oxford, Oxford University Press, 1990.

Ginsberg, R., *Foreign Policy Actions of the European Community*, London, Adamantine, 1989.

Harrison, R., *Europe in Question – Theories of Regional Integration*, London, Allen and Unwin, 1974.

Holland, M., ed., *The Future of European political cooperation: essays on theory and practice*, London, Macmillan, 1991.

Keatinge, P., ed., *Ireland and EC Membership Evaluated*, London, Pinter, 1991.

Keohane, R. O. and Hoffman, S., eds., *The New European Community: decisionmaking and institutional change*, Boulder, Col., Westview, 1991.

Laursen, F. and Vanhoonacker, S., eds., *The Intergovernmental Conference on Political Union: institutional reforms, new policies and international identity of the European Community*, Dordrecht, Martinus Nijhoff, 1992.

Lodge, J., ed., *The European Community and the Challenge of the Future*, 2nd edn., London, Pinter, 1993.

Lyck, L., ed., *Denmark and EC Membership Evaluated*, London, Pinter, 1992.

Martin, D., ed., *Europe: an ever closer union*, Nottingham, Spokesman Books, 1991.

Nuttall, S., *European Political Cooperation*, Oxford, Clarendon Press, 1992.

Schweitzer, C. C. and Karsten, D., eds., *Federal Republic of Germany and EC Membership Evaluated,* London, Pinter, 1990.

Swann, D., ed., *The Single European Market and Beyond*, London, Routledge, 1992.

Taylor, P., *The Limits of European Integration*, London, Croom Helm, 1983.

Van Meerhaeghe, M. A. G., ed., *Belgium and EC Membership Evaluated*, London, Pinter, 1992.

Wallace, H., ed., *The Wider Western Europe: reshaping the EC/EFTA relationship*, London, Pinter, 1992.

Wallace, H., Wallace, W. and Webb, C., eds., *Policy-making in the European Communities*, Chichester, John Wiley, 1977 (1st edn.), 1983 (2nd edn.).

Wallace, W., ed., *The Dynamics of European Integration*, London, Pinter, 1990.

Wilke, M. and Wallace, H., *Subsidiarity: approaches to power-sharing in the European Community*, London, Royal Institute of International Affairs Discussion Papers 27, 1990.

Notes

CHAPTER I

1. Richard Hoggart and Douglas Johnson, *An Idea of Europe* (London, Chatto and Windus, 1987).
2. Paul Kennedy, *The Rise and Fall of the Great Powers* (London, Unwin Hyman, 1988).
3. H. A. L. Fisher, *A History of Europe* (London, Edward Arnold, 1938).
4. Training manuals for British conscripts in 1939 talked of the nation going from peace to total war overnight. It was expected that from the first hours of hostilities there would be air attacks on civilian populations (as at Guernica during the Spanish Civil War), using poison gas (as in the Italian conquest of Abyssinia).
5. Brian Bond, *War and Society in Europe 1870–1970* (London, Fontana, 1984).
6. Claude Delmas, 'Corée 1950', *Editions Complex* (Paris), pp. 111–31.
7. The Edict of Nantes, by which King Henry gave the Huguenots religious freedom, was 'the first public recognition of the fact that more than one religious communion can be maintained in the same polity', Fisher, op. cit., p. 579.
8. W. Nicoll, 'Pour la constitution en 1963 d'un Parliament européen composé de délégations nationales siégeant en hemicycle avec pondération de vote', *Revue du Marché Commun*, Paris, No. 302, December 1986, p. 592.
9. 'Law is to do what blood and iron have for centuries failed to do. For only unity based on a freely-taken decision can be expected to last; unity founded on the fundamental values such as freedom and equality, and protected and translated into reality by law', Commission of the European Communities, *The ABC of Community Law* (OOP, 1986), p. 28. This is the milk of Kant's doctrine.
10. The vision was common to Burns in 'A man's a man for a' that', and Schiller in 'An die Freude', which to Beethoven's setting became the 'European Hymn'.
11. Coudenhove-Kalergi appears at vital points over the years. In 1943, in

exile in New York, he proposed a 'European Federation' which the Roosevelt administration disfavoured, anxious to avoid trouble with the Soviet Union. See Boyd France, *US–European Community Relations*, (Washington, European Community Information Service, 1973), p. 6. In 1965, Coudenhove-Kalergi supported General de Gaulle's perception of European unity. His movement had already been written off in 1952 by out-and-out federalists like Spinelli.

12. James Joll (ed.), *Britain and Europe: Pitt to Churchill 1793–1940* (London, Adam and Charles Black, 1961), p. 15, footnote. In his semi-fictional biography of Briand, *Moi Aristide Briand* (Paris, Plon, 1981), Vercors has him 'proposing as a first step the creation of a Common Market, which by facilitating the movement of goods, capital and people would show that something coherent and complete was happening. . . . The governing idea would be union, not unity, with no danger of the stronger nations dominating the weaker. . . . The replies showed the fierce tenacity of national egoisms' (pp. 307–8).

13. Quoted by Harold Macmillan, *Tides of Fortune 1945–1955* (London, Macmillan 1969), p. 151.

14. 'Patriotism is not enough, I must learn to love all peoples and hate none' were the last recorded words of Edith Cavell, killed by firing squad in Brussels on 12 October 1915 for aiding escaped British prisoners of war.

15. Passive resistance, *ahimsa*, was the Gandhian response to British police power.

16. W. Shirer, *The Rise and Fall of the Third Reich* (London, Secker and Warburg, 1974), pp. 25–62.

17. Christopher Saunders, *From Free Trade to Integration in Western Europe?* (London, Chatham House/PEP, 1975), p. 10; Sidney Pollard, *European Economic Integration 1815–1970* (London, Thames and Hudson, 1974), Chapter 6.

18. 'A continental-European economy under German leadership must comprise all the peoples of the continent . . . it appears necessary to designate this not as a German extended-area economy, but fundamentally always to speak of a European economic community' Third Reich Association for Economic Planning, May 1940, quoted in *The Times* letter column, 12 January 1993, in the context of a revisionist view of Winston Churchill. See also *Fatherland*, a novel by Robert Harris, a modern historian, about a post-war victorious Germany. (London, Hutchinson, 1992)

19. Nigel Nicolson (ed.), *Harold Nicolson: The war years 1939–45: diaries and letters*, Vol. II (London, William Collins, 1967), pp. 101–2, 139.

20 Macmillan, op. cit., Appendix 1.

21 Boyd France, op. cit., p. 6.

22. *The North Atlantic Treaty Organisation Facts and Figures* (NATO, 1989), pp. 7–8.

23. For the scale of the US contribution to the European Economic Recovery Programme, 1947–53, see Paul A. Samuelson, *Economics* (New York, McGraw-Hill, 1955), p. 672. Although it was not US policy to push the OEEC countries towards economic or political organization which they might not want, the first administrator of the Economic Co-operation Administration, Paul G. Hoffman, did not take long to become forthright. In late 1949 he looked forward to 'a single large market within which quantitative restrictions on the movement of goods, monetary barriers to the flow of payments and eventually all tariffs are permanently swept away'.

24. The first French economic plan envisaged that France would continue to manage a section of German heavy industry. It was when the British and Americans said that they could not support such an arrangement that the French Foreign Minister looked for other ways of resolving the problem.

25. The Schuman plan launched the first of the European Communities, for Coal and Steel. The others are the Economic Community and Euratom. Together they are described as the European Communities, despite the expressed wish of the European Parliament that the official name should be 'The European Community'. The 'Common Market' is a colloquial name for the European Economic Community. European Political Co-operation is not a Community, or regarded as belonging to the European Communities as defined above. In the Treaty on European Union, 1992, discussed in Chapter Twelve, the European Economic Community is formally replaced by the European Community. The other Communities remain, but it seems to be the intention that the generic name for the Communities should be the Community, in line with established usage. This is reflected in the title of this work.

26. British ministers were not told of the announcement of 9 May 1950 in advance and were irritated when they learned that others, including the US Secretary of State, Dean Acheson, had had advance notice. On 19 May President Truman said, 'Mr Schuman's proposal is an act of constructive statesmanship. We welcome it.' Britain declined to attend the conference which Schuman called on 20 June 1950 to discuss details of the plan.

27. The North Atlantic Treaty was signed on 4 April 1949 by the United States and Canada; by the five countries which had signed the Brussels Treaty on 17 March 1948 (France, the United Kingdom, Belgium, the Netherlands and Luxembourg); and by Italy, Portugal, Denmark, Norway and Iceland.

28. Consultative Assembly, Council of Europe, 11 August 1950: *Proceedings*, pp. 222–8.

29. Fondation Paul-Henri Spaak, *Pour une Communauté Politique Européenne* (Brussels, Bruylat, 1984), Chapter 3.

30. European Parliament (Text of the Statute of the European Community), pp. 57ff.

31. Ibid., pp. 95–9.

32. William Slany (ed.), *Foreign Relations of the United States 1955–57. Vol. IV: Western European Security and Integration* (Washington DC, US Government Printing Office, 1986), p. 323.

33. Ibid., p. 421.

34. Pollard, op. cit., pp. 112–16.

35. François Clerc, *Le Marché Commun Agricole* (Paris, Presse Universitaire de France (Que sais-je?), 1970), p. 20.

36. Britain abandoned free trade when it passed the Import Duties Act in 1932. The Act imposed a 10 per cent tariff. Imports from the colonies were exempt. Imports from India and the Dominions were also provisionally exempt, as an autonomous measure. This exemption became contractual in the Ottawa Agreements concluded in 1932. Under these agreements Britain secured 'preferences' in India and the Dominions. The creation of these preferences had been pioneered from 1904 to 1906 by Joseph Chamberlain. See R. Grinter, *Joseph Chamberlain* (London, Edward Arnold, 1971), pp. 33–8, 46–61. The 1932 Act was promoted by his son, Neville Chamberlain, better known as British Prime Minister at the time of the 1938 negotiations with Hitler.

37. D. Jay, *After the Common Market* (London, Penguin, 1968).

38. This nomenclature recurs throughout. France is the one EC country whose head of state (president) has executive responsibilities and attends summit meetings.

CHAPTER 2

1. Articles 39 and 40 of the EEC Treaty, which provide that the common organization of agricultural markets *may* include any measures required to attain the objectives set out in article 39, in particular regulation of prices.

2. W. Nicoll, 'Historique de la composition de la majorité qualifiée en vertu des traités', *Revue du Marché Commun*, Paris, No. 295, March 1980, p. 135.

3. 'Determined to lay the foundations of an ever closer union among the peoples of Europe. . . . Resolved thus by pooling their resources to strengthen peace and liberty. . .'

4. In the Note which it handed to the Six, the Soviet Union said that, since they all belonged to NATO, 'it is obvious that the entire activity of the Common Market and of Euratom will be subordinate to the objectives of NATO, whose aggressive character is well known.' France, Belgium, Germany and Italy replied in identical terms that their aims were

peaceful and that the Soviet proposals could be discussed at the May meeting of the Economic Commission for Europe, a UN body in which East and West participated.

5. Pierre Gerbet, *La Construction de l'Europe* (Paris, Imprimerie Nationale, 1983), p. 237.

6. Cf. n.1 above.

7. The Yaoundé countries were: Burundi, Cameroon, Central African Republic, Chad, Congo, Dahomey, Gabon, Ivory Coast, Madagascar, Mali, Mauretania, Niger, Rwanda, Senegal, Somalia, Togo, Upper Volta and Zaire. Mauritius (a Commonwealth country) became a member of the Yaoundé Convention in 1973.

8. European Parliament (Text of the Statute of the European Community), p. 106.

9. Ibid., pp. 107–8.

10. On the silver jubilee of the Franco-German Treaty the two countries concluded a new agreement, which provides for the setting-up of a Finance Council and a Defence Council. It also set up a Franco-German infantry brigade, which has been formed.

11. Harold Wilson, *The Labour Government 1964–1970* (London, Weidenfeld and Nicolson, and Michael Joseph, 1971), pp. 184–5.

12. France exploded its first atomic bomb (under the Euratom dispensation) in the Sahara on 13 February 1960. The first French nuclear submarine was launched on 29 March 1967.

13. The boycott was not total. French delegates came to meetings in Brussels of CAP Management Committees.

14. W. Nicoll, 'The Luxembourg Compromise', *Journal of Common Market Studies*, Vol. 23, No. 1, September 1984, pp. 35–43.

15. Uwe Kitzinger, *Diplomacy and Persuasion* (London, Thames and Hudson, 1973), pp. 45ff.

16. This statement by the Six was reinterpreted in London as 'a firm assurance of a secure and continuing market in the enlarged Community on fair terms for the quantities of sugar covered by the 'Commonwealth Sugar Agreement'. In the event the assurance was respected in the Lomé Convention (*Hansard*, 9 June 1971, col. 1062).

17. Norwegian representatives immediately stopped attending the EC meetings to which they had been invited and returned all the documents they had received since January 1972.

18. In February 1982, following home rule for Greenland and a referendum there, it withdrew from membership of the European Communities, although there is no provision or procedure for withdrawal in the treaties.

CHAPTER 3

1. See J. Lodge and V. Hermann, *Direct Elections to the European Parliament: A Community Perspective* (London, Macmillan, 1982); and J. Lodge (ed.), *Direct Elections to the European Parliament, 1984* (London, Macmillan, 1986).
2. See Roy Pryce (ed.), *The Dynamics of European Union* (London, Croom Helm, 1987), passim.
3. *The Falklands War* (*Sunday Times* Insight) (London, Sphere Books, 1982), pp. 116–18. Max Hastings and Simon Jenkins, *The Battle for the Falklands* (London, Pan, 1983), p. 124.
4. See Patrick Keatinge and Anna Murphy 'The European Council's Ad Hoc Committee of Institutional Affairs (1984–1985)'. In Pryce, op cit., pp. 217–37.
5. Richard Corbett, 'The 1985 Intergovernmental Conference and the Single European Act'. In ibid., pp 238–72.
6. Single European Act, *Bulletin of the European Communities Supplement 2/86*; and P. Ludlow, *The Making of the European Monetary System* (London, Butterworth, 1982), p. 22.
7. For a fuller discussion, see Trevor C. Salmon, *Unneutral Ireland* (Oxford, Clarendon Press, 1989), Conclusion.
8. 'Completing the internal market', White Paper from the Commission to the European Council (Milan, 28–29 June 1985), the EC Commission, Brussels, COM Documents 1985/310 final.
9. Only two association agreements – those of Greece and Turkey – provide for membership of the Communities to be examined when association has sufficiently prepared for it.
10. Commission of the EC, 'Le Défi' (Introduction to the Cecchini Report) (Paris, Flammarion, 1988).
11. See Christian Franck, 'New Ambitions: from The Hague to Paris Summits (1969–1972)'. In Pryce, op. cit., pp. 130–48.
12. Report on European Union by Leo Tindemans, December 1985, *Bulletin Supplement* 1/76.
13. Otto Schmuck, 'The European Parliament's Draft Treaty Establishing The European Union'. In Pryce, op. cit., pp. 188–216.

CHAPTER 4

1. This 'flagrant violation' of the treaty was attacked by an MEP in the debates on 16 November 1988.
2. Article 10 of the treaty establishing a single Council and a single Commission of the European Communities.
3. All of the original Six have seen one of their nationals appointed as president. The Dutch president – Mr Mansholt – held office for only a

brief period when Mr Malfatti of Italy resigned in 1972. Of the new six only the United Kingdom has provided a president in Roy (later Lord) Jenkins, 1977–81.

4. For an inside account of the Commission, and its president, at work, see Roy Jenkins, *European Diary 1977–81* (London, Collins, 1989).

5. Article 179 (EEC).

6. Article 13 of the Protocol on the Privileges and Immunities of the European Communities.

7. The work of some councils is shared between the top-level official committees. COREPER I (Deputies) is generally responsible for the internal market and consequently prepares work for ECOFIN on financial services and for the Agricultural Council on veterinary directives.

8. A frequently used gloss is a statement in the Council minutes. In these statements the persons making them say how they interpret a Community decision and what they intend to do about it. The statements may be made by the Council and/or the Commission or by one or more member states. Such statements are not published.
   Statements in the Council minutes almost certainly do not have legal force.

9. The two Committees of Permanent Representatives are staffed by Brussels residents. The Special Committee for Agriculture is partly resident and partly non-resident. The high-level article 113 Committee (trade policy) is entirely non-resident.

10. Confessionals are a form of bilateral negotiation in which the Council President suspends the plenary meeting and invites his colleagues to meet him individually to explain to him what they want or why they cannot accept his compromises.

11. Capital-to-capital contacts are bilateral, except in the tripartite gatherings of the members of Benelux and business meetings in the Troika of the last, current and next presidency. Gatherings of three or more would normally be frowned on, as threatening to create an inner circle.

12. The absence of officials from meetings of the European Council is a matter of convention, and was confirmed as the European Council's desired method of work. Officials from member states and from the Commission attend all other Council meetings. In a 'restricted' meeting the number of officials present is reduced to one or two. Very occasionally, there are meetings of 'ministers only'. Work usually continues at ministerial lunches, with two officials present: the chair of COREPER and the senior member of the Council Secretariat.

13. The ministerial discussion may establish what is agreed textually or in substance with instructions for a final text to be prepared. The draft on which delegations finally agree is further examined by the Council's 'jurist-linguists' (legal revisers) to ensure that it says the same thing in all languages, and otherwise contains no legal drafting blemishes.

14. P. Soldatos, *Le Système institutionnel et politique des Communautés Européennes dans un Monde en Mutation* (Brussels, Bruylant, 1989), pp. 168–71.

CHAPTER 5

1. Cases 138 and 139/79.
2. Case 13/83, judgment given on 22 May 1985.
3. In practice, the Parliamentary opinion usually takes the form of a series of proposed amendments. To ensure coherence between its first and second readings, Parliament adopts such amendments by absolute majorities of its members: in first reading, it uses second reading rules. It urges the Commission to amend its proposals in the light of these amendments, and if the Commission is unwilling or hesitant, Parliament often defers its first reading vote – on which there is no time limit – and uses the interval to negotiate with the Commission. At its first reading, the Council is often faced with a proposal which the Commission has amended and which replaces the original.
4. The Committees of Enquiry proceed on the distant model of a US Congressional or Senate Committee, but have no powers to compel witnesses to testify. They hold 'hearings' to which they invite interested parties. In at least one of them (on the carriage of toxic materials) ministers from some member states spoke. The Committees of Enquiry produce reports, which are their property and cannot be amended in debate on the floor of the House. The Committee of Enquiry usually also produces a draft resolution, which sets out what should be done to remedy a particular evil and on which the House votes. An essentially similar task to that of a Committee of Enquiry can be taken up by a *rapporteur* within a Standing Committee – for example, the Report on Religious Cults.
5. See W. Nicoll, 'Le dialogue législatif entre le Parlement et la Commission: la procédure de renvoi en commission du parlement européen', *Revue du Marché Commun*, Paris, No. 316, April 1988, pp. 240–2.
6. Case 314/85, judgment given on 22 October 1987.
7. *ABC of Community Law* (OOP, 1986), p. 29.
8. The abortive Draft Treaty of the European (Political) Community took into its third article Part I of the Convention for the Protection of Human Rights and Fundamental Freedoms concluded in Rome on 4 November 1950 and the Protocol signed in Paris on 20 November 1952.
9. Taken from a lecture given by (later Sir) Jean Pierre Warner, then Advocate-General, in Luxembourg, summer 1977: 'Community law from the point of view of the national judge'.

CHAPTER 6

1. From January 1989 common positions adopted by the Council are published in the *Official Journal*. The Explanatory Memorandum on the draft budget and the motivation of common positions in the co-operation procedure are not published in the *Official Journal*. They are distributed to Members of the European Parliament as sessional papers, which do not have a security classification.
2. A convenient list of Euro-Trade Associations is published by Editions Delta, Brussels. See also W. Rogers (ed.), *Government and Industry* (Amsterdam, Kluwer, 1986), Chapter 6, Part D.

CHAPTER 7

1. The exclusive competence of the Commission to speak for the Community is not contested, but de Clercq, External Relations Commissoner and a former minister of the Belgian government, remarked in 1988 that when there is a GATT ministerial meeting it would be too much to expect the trade ministers of EC member states (which formally remain GATT contracting parties) to be silent.
2. For the other side of the coin – the prospective effect on UK wage costs of CAP price levels – see D. Jay, *After the Common Market* (London, Penguin, 1968).
3. By the autumn of 1988, following the rise in world prices and shortages after a protracted North American drought, Community stocks had been heavily drawn down, at relatively low cost.
4. The CFP negotiations of 1977 gave rise to the only occasion on which the United Kingdom practised the 'empty chair' by declining to attend a Council meeting held in Berlin, on the grounds that the United Kingdom was being unfairly treated in contemporaneous agricultural negotiations.
5. The European Community's *Transport Policy Periodical*, 3/84, OOP, p. 21.

CHAPTER 8

1. 'Powers of investigation in the enforcement of competition law', *OOP Periodical*, 1985, p. 33.
2. Giving rise to the first Monetary Compensation Amounts.
3. Communiqué of the Conference of the Heads of State and Government of the European Community's Member States, 2 December 1969, The Hague, *Bulletin of the European Communities*, 1–1970, pp. 11–18.

4. The worked out example given on p. 50 of *The Economy of the European Community* (OOP, 1984) is: The divergence threshold for a currency with a weighting in the ecu of 20% is reached when it deviates from the ecu central rate by

$$\frac{2.25 \times (100-20) \times 0.75}{100} = 1.35\%$$

5. According to Lord Owen, who was Foreign Secretary at the time, the author of the idea that the United Kingdom could belong to the EMS but not the ERM was Michael Butler, later British ambassador to the EC and later still advocate of the 'hard ecu', which the British government ran as preferred alternative to the proposed single currency. David Owen, *Personally Speaking* (London, Pan Books, 1987), p. 117.
6. Nigel Lawson, *The View from No. 11* (London, Bantam Press, 1992), p. 930.
7. Sir Alan Waters, economic adviser to the Prime Minister at the time, has said that he drafted these conditions, but had no expectation that they would stick. Public Lecture at Georgetown University, Washington DC, April 1992.
8. See *Leading Europe into the 1990's*, (London, Conservative Central Office, May 1989), pp. 34–5.

CHAPTER 9

1. One reason for British opposition to increased Community spending was the logical Treasury rule that whatever was spent by the Community scored against the budget of the government department concerned.
2. *Thirty-Third Review of the Council's Work* (OOP, 1985), p. 71.
3. The Vredeling proposal is memorable for the vast amount of counter-lobbying it provoked when the European Parliament came to deliver an opinion on it.
4. See 'Structural Funds in an Objective 1 Region', *European Business Journal*, Vol. 14, Issue 3, 1992, pp. 33–42.
5. Especially by the shock-wave sent out by the publication in the United States in 1962 of Rachel Carson's book, *The Silent Spring (London, Hamish Hamilton, 1963)*.
6. *Official Journal references*: C112, 20 December 1973; C139, 13 June 1977; C46, 17 February 1983; C328, 7 December 1987.
7. Lawnmower noise is a sensitive subject. In many Belgian communes it is an offence to use garden power-tools on a Sunday or public holiday.

CHAPTER 10

1. See EEC Treaty of 25 March 1957 and Treaty on European Union of 7 February 1992.
2. Declaration of Political Principles of European Union, approved by the International Council of the European Movement at Brussels, 28 February 1949. Reproduced in Richard Vaughan, *Postwar Integration in Europe* (London, Edward Arnold, 1976), pp. 37-9.
3. The Messina Resolution is reproduced in Miriam Camps, *Britain and the European Community* (London, Oxford University Press, 1964), pp. 520-2.
4. *Bulletin of the European Communities*, 12–1973, pp. 118–22.
5. A. Silj, *Europe's Political Puzzle: A Study of the Fouchet Negotiations and the 1963 Veto*, Occasional Papers in International Affairs No. 17 (Harvard, Mass., Harvard Center for International Affairs, 1967).
6. Communiqué of the Conference of the Heads of State and Government of the European Community's Member States, 2 December 1968, The Hague, *Bulletin of the European Communities*,1–1970, pp. 11–18.
7. Report by the Foreign Ministers of the Member States on the Problems of Political Unification, *Bulletin of the European Communities*, 11–1970 pp. 9–14.
8. Ibid.
9. See Ralf Dahrendorf, 'A new goal for Europe', in M. Hodges (ed.), *European Integration* (Harmondsworth, Penguin, 1972), pp. 74–87.
10. Phillippe de Schoutheete, *La Co-opération politique européenne* (Paris, Fernand Nathan, 1980), p. 118.
11. Second Report of the Ministers for Foreign Affairs, Copenhagen, September 1973, *Bulletin of the European Communities*, pp. 12–21.
12. See Simon Bulmer and Wolfgang Wessels, *The European Council* (London, Macmillan, 1987); Annette Morgan, 'From Summit to Council: evolution in the EEC' (Chatham House Papers No. 27, London, RIIA and PEP, June 1976); and Emil Kirchner, *Decision-making in the European Community: the Council Presidency and European Integration* (Manchester, Manchester University Press, 1992).
13. The European Identity, issued during Conference of Heads of State or Government, 14 December 1973, *Bulletin of the European Communities*, 12–1973, pp. 118–22.
14. Report on European Union by Leo Tindemans, December 1975, *Bulletin Supplement*, 1/76.
15. Report of European Institutions presented by the Committee of Three to the European Council ('Report of the Three Wise Men'), Luxembourg, 1980.
16. Phillippe de Schouteete, 'European political co-operation: achievements

and prospects', *European Documents*, No. 1061, Agence Europe, Brussels, 3 July 1979.

17. Report on European Political Co-operation, London, 13 October 1981, *Bulletin Supplement*, 3/81, pp. 14–17.

18. The plan set out to create an 'Act' and evolved as a Solemn Declaration. See Gianni Bonvicini, 'The Genscher–Colombo plan' and the 'Solemn Declaration on European Union' (1981–1983) in R. Pryce (ed.), *The Dynamics of European Union* (London, Croom Helm, 1987), pp. 174–87.

19. Single European Act, *Bulletin Supplement*, 2/86.

20. Judgment of the Irish Supreme Court, 9 April 1987. The Irish people voted in a referendum on 26 May 1987: 69.9 per cent of those voting were in favour of the proposed amendment and 30.1 per cent were against, with a turnout of 44 per cent. For a fuller account, see Trevor C. Salmon, *Unneutral Ireland: An Ambivalent and Unique Security Policy* (Oxford, Clarendon Press, 1989) Conclusion passim.

21. London Report, see n.17 above.

22. Christopher Hill, 'National interests: the insuperable obstacles'. In C. Hill (ed.), *National Foreign Policies and European Political Cooperation* (London, Allan and Unwin, 1983), p. 189.

23. Camps, op. cit., pp. 520–2.

24. Roger Morgan, *High Politics, Low Politics: Towards a foreign policy for Western Europe* (The Washington Papers No. 11, Center for Strategic and International Studies, Georgetown University; London, Sage Publications, 1973, pp. 21–25.

25. William Wallace, 'Cooperation and convergence in European foreign policy' in Hill, op. cit., p. 10.

26. European Parliament, *The Week*, Strasbourg, 9–13 September 1991, PE 152.616/rev. pp. 17–18.

27. Address to the International Institute for Strategic Studies, 7 March 1991, see *Survival*, Vol. 33, No. 2 (March/April 1991).

28. Alfred Cahen, 'The emergence and role of the Western European Union'. In M. Clarke and R. Hague (eds.), *European Defence Co-operation* (Manchester, Manchester University Press, 1990), pp. 62–3.

29. See, for example, interview with Willem van Eekelen, Secretary-General of the WEU, *International Herald Tribune*, 20 August 1990, and Willem van Eekelen,' The WEU and the Gulf crisis', *Survival*, Vol. 32, No. 6 (November/December 1990).

30. See *NATO Review*, Vol. 39, No. 6 (December 1991).

31. Idem.

32. See n. 27 above.

33. *Financial Times*, 6 September 1990.

34. Conclusions of the Presidency: European Council, Rome, 27–28 October 1990 (SN 304/90 rev. 2).

35. *International Herald Tribune*, 6 November 1990.

36. Trevor C. Salmon, 'Testing times for European political cooperation: the Gulf and Yugoslavia, 1990–1992', *International Affairs*, Vol. 68, No. 2 (April 1992), pp. 233–53.

37. Treaty on European Union, Luxembourg, Office for Official Publications of the European Communities, 1992.

38. Ibid., Declaration on Western European Union: Declaration on the Western European Union and its relations with the European Union and the Atlantic Alliance, pp. 242–6.

39. Genscher, Foreign Minister, Federal Republic of Germany, 11 April 1991, *International Herald Tribune*.

CHAPTER 11

1. See Finn Laursen and Sophie Vanhoonacker (eds.), *The Intergovernmental Conference on Political Union: institutional reforms, new policies and international identity of the European Community* (Dordrecht, Martinus Nijhoff, 1992).

2. See Adrian Poole, 'Belgium and Luxembourg', who cites *La Belgique et la Communauté Européenne, Textes et documents*, No. 317 (Brussels, Ministère des Affaires Etrangères du Commerce Exterieur et de la coopération au Développement, 1979) p. 7, in Carol and Kenneth Twitchett (eds.), *Building Europe* (London, Europe Publications, 1981), p. 145; and M. A. G. Van Meerhaeghe (ed.), *Belgium and EC Membership Evaluated* (London, Frances Pinter, 1992).

3. On the Netherlands, see Philip Everts and Guido Walraven, *The Politics of Persuasion, Implementation of Foreign Policy by the Netherlands* (Aldershot, Avebury, 1989).

4. Since 1991 Belgium has been converting itself into a federal state consisting of the two self-governing regions – Dutch-speaking Flanders and French-speaking Wallonia – the Brussels region and the small German-speaking area.

5. Belgian Memorandum 19 March 1990, see Laursen and Vanhoonacker op. cit., p. 270.

6. But see letter to Prime Minister Andreotti of Italy 12 December 1990. In Laursen and Vanhoonacker, op. cit., pp. 315–17.

7. Aidan Cawley, *de Gaulle* (London, Collins, 1969), p. 443.

8. *Agence Europe*, 26 June 1990.

9. See *Agence Europe*, 10–11 December 1990.

10. Bonn had obtained a special Protocol in the Treaty of Rome by which trade between the two Germanies was regarded by the whole Community not as external trade but as intra-Community trade, not subject to the Common Customs Tariff.

11. See Simon Bulmer and William Paterson, *The Federal Government of Germany and the European Community* (London, Allen and Unwin, 1987); and C. C. Schweiizer and D. Karsten (eds.), *Federal Republic of Germany and EC Membership Evaluated* (London, Pinter, 1990).

12. Jean Monnet, *Memoirs*, translated by Richard Mayne (London, Collins, 1978), pp. 288–92.

13. *Agence Europe*, 20 April, 1990.

14. See Geoffrey Pridham, 'Italy'. In Carol and Kenneth Twitchett (eds.), *Building Europe* (London, Europa, 1981), p. 14 and pp. 80–118 for an excellent short background on Italy's attitude to European integration. See also Francesco Francioni (ed.), *Italy and EC Membership Evaluated* (London, Pinter, 1992).

15. Pridham, op. cit., p. 84.

16. *Fifth Report on the Implementation of the White Paper* (Brussels, Commission of the EC, 1990).

17. Guido Carli, President of the Confindustria, quoted in *Europaische Zeitung*, January 1979, cited in Pridham, op. cit., p. 103.

18. *Agence Europe*, 26 June 1990.

19. Italian proposals on CFSP, 18 September 1990; reproduced in Laursen and Vanhoonacker, op. cit., p. 292.

20. Sean Lemass, Prime Minister, speaking to the Daíl, *Dail Debates*, Vol. 191, Col. 205ff and 266, see Trevor C. Salmon, *Unneutral Ireland: an ambivalent and unique security policy* (Oxford, Clarendon Press, 1989) p. 211 and passim; and Trevor C. Salmon, 'Ireland', in Twitchett and Twitchett, op. cit., pp. 191–216.

21. Speech to Royal Irish Academy, 10 November 1975, see Salmon, 'Ireland', op. cit., p. 203.

22. Calleary, Minister of State, Department of Foreign Affairs, *Dail Debates*, Vol. 371, Col. 2297 (1987). For fuller discussion, see Patrick Keatinge (ed.), *Ireland and EC Membership Evaluated* (London, Pinter, 1991).

23. *Ireland Today*, 1037 (May–June 1987), 1039 (August 1987); and Salmon, *Unneutral Ireland*, op. cit., pp. 286–311.

24. *Irish Times*, 2 November 1990.

25. The Protocol was designed to prevent legal abortion being introduced into Ireland under EC rules, but had the unintended effect of disallowing Irish women to appeal to the European Court of Justice if prevented from travelling abroad for abortions.

26. Carsten Holbrad, *Danish Neutrality: a study in the foreign policy of a small state* (Oxford, Clarendon Press, 1991), pp. v and 57.

27. See Clive Archer, 'Denmark', in Twitchett and Twitchett, op. cit., 168–90, especially p. 171.

28. In February 1982, following home rule for Greenland and a referendum there, it withdrew from membership of the Communities.

29. G. Nielsson, *Denmark and European Integration* (PhD, University of California). Quoted in Archer, op. cit., p. 179.
30. Mr Möller, footnote, in 'Report of the ad hoc Committee on Institutional Questions to the European Council', *Agence Europe*, Documents Nos. 1349/1350, 21 March 1985, p. 2.
31. For the background on Denmark, see Lise Lyck (ed.), *Denmark and EC Membership Evaluated* (London, Pinter, 1992).
32. This and following quotations taken from Memorandum from the Danish Government, 4 October 1990. Reproduced in Laursen and Vanhoonacker, op. cit., pp. 293–303.
33. Emphasis added.
34. See Carsten, op. cit., pp. 108ff.
35. Treaty on European Union Protocol 12.
36. See Stephen George, *An Awkward Partner: Britain in the European Community* (Oxford, Oxford University Press, 1989); and Simon Bulmer, Stephen George and Andrew Scott (eds.), *The United Kingdom and EC Membership Evaluated* (London, Pinter, 1992).
37. Paul Kennedy, *The Realities Behind Dilpomacy: Background influences on British External Policy 1865–1980* (London, Fontana, 1981).
38. F. S. Northedge, *Descent From Power: British foreign policy 1945–1973* (London, Allen and Unwin, 1974).
39. Clement Attlee, Labour Prime Minister, *House of Commons Debates*, 5th Series, Vol. 450, cols. 1314–19, 5 May 1948.
40. Speech quoted in Randolph Churchill (ed.), *Sinews of Peace* (London, Cassell, 1948), p. 202.
41. Winston Churchill, as Prime Minister, *House of Commons Debates*, 5th Series, Vol. 515, Cols. 889ff, 11 May 1953.
42. Sir Anthony Eden, British Foreign Secretary, University of Columbia, 11 January 1952, in Nicholas Mansergh, *Documents and Speeches on British Commonwealth Affairs 1931–1952*, Vol. I (London, Oxford University Press for the Royal Institute of International Affairs, 1953), pp. 1156–7.
43. Miriam Camps, *Britain and the European Community 1955–1963* (London, Oxford University Press, 1964), p. 4.
44. Attlee, Prime Minister, *House of Commons Debates*, 5th Series, Vol. 477, Col. 472, 5 July, 1950, speaking on the Schuman proposal. Harold Macmillan, a future Conservative Prime Minister, agreed.
45. Camps, op. cit., p. 339.
46. Cf. ibid., p. 274 who sees it as a 'radical change in British policy'.
47. Harold Macmillan, Prime Minister, *House of Commons Debates*, 5th Series, Vol. 645, Cols. 928ff, 31 July, 1961.
48. Harold Wilson, Prime Minister, *House of Commons Debates*, 5th Series, Vol. 735, Col. 1540, 10 November 1966.
49. Harold Wilson, Prime Minister, *House of Commons Debates*, 5th Series, Vol. 795, Cols. 1080–97, 10 February 1970.

50. 'The United Kingdom and the European Communities', London, HMSO, Cmnd. 4715, 1971.

51. It is said that the Conservative government took over virtually word for word the opening statement drafted by George Thomson.

52. F. S. Northedge, 'Britain and the EEC: past and present', in Roy Jenkins (ed.), *Britain and the EEC* (London, Macmillan, 1983), p. 26.

53. Harold Wilson, Prime Minister, *House of Commons Debates*, 5th Series, Vol. 888, Cols. 1456ff, 18 March 1975.

54. For major debate, see ibid., Vol. 889, Cols. 821–1370, 7 April, 1975.

55. Harold Wilson, Prime Minister, ibid, Vol. 893, Cols. 29–30, 9 June, 1975.

56. Conservative and Unionist Party General Election Manifesto, May 1979.

57. Labour Party, General Election Manifesto, June 1983.

58. Margaret Thatcher, Prime Minister, 'Europe: the future', paper produced for the Fontainebleau European Council, 25–26 June 1984. Reproduced in *Journal of Common Market Studies*, Vol. 23, No. 1 (September 1984), pp. 73–81.

59. J. Pinder, 'Positive integration and negative integration: some problems of economic union in the EEC', *World Today*, Vol. 24 (1968), pp. 88–110.

60. Speech given by the Rt Hon. Mrs Thatcher at the opening ceremony of the 39th Academic Year of the College of Europe, Bruges, 20 September 1988 (British Embassy Press Service).

61. John Major, House of Commons, 20 November 1991.

62. *European Parliament News*, 6–10 July, 1992.

63. Treaty On European Union, pp. 191–3.

64. House of Commons, 20 November 1991.

65. In 1977 Greece's GDP per capita was 46.4 per cent of the Community average, Portugal's 27.4 per cent and Spain's 51.6 per cent, see Loukas Tsoukalis, *The European Community and its Mediterranean Enlargement* (London, George Allen and Unwin, 1981), p. 19 and passim for the background and membership debates.

66. See 'Statement on Greek Presidency of the Council', *EC Bulletin*, 7/8-1983, pp. 111–18; and 'Statement on the work programme of the Greek Presidency', *EC Bulletin*, 7/8-1988, p. 170.

67. See Greek Memorandum, 'Contribution to the Discussions on Progress Towards Political Union', 15 May 1990, in Laursen and Vanhoonacker (eds.), op. cit., pp. 277–81.

68. See WEU states declaration attached to the Treaty on European Union.

69. Conclusions of the Presidency, European Council in Edinburgh, 11–12 December 1992.

70. See Tsoukalis, op. cit., p. 53.

71. Ministry of Foreign Affairs: Memorandum of the Portuguese Dele-

gation: Political Union with a view to the Intergovernmental Conference, Lisbon, 30 November 1991, in Laursen and Vanhoonacker, op. cit., p. 304 and pp. 304–12.
72. 'The Road to European Citizenship', 24 September 1990. Reproduced in ibid., pp. 328–32 and, for the 21 February memorandum, pp. 325–8.
73. Spanish Foreign Minister Ordonez, *Agence Europe*, 6 September 1991.
74. See Laursen and Vanhoonacker, op. cit., pp. 336–44.

CHAPTER 12

1. See Kohl–Mitterrand letter to the Irish Presidency 19 April 1990, reproduced in Finn Laursen and Sophie Vanhoonacker (eds.), *The Intergovernmental Conference on Political Union: institutional reforms, new policies and international identity of the European Community* (Dordrecht, Martinus Nijhoff, 1992), p. 276.
2. Treaty on European Union (Luxembourg, Office for Official Publications of the European Communities, 1992).
3. For the case made by Conservative MPs against Maastricht, see William Cash, *Against a Federal Europe* (London, Duckworth, 1991); and Michael Spicer, *A Treaty Too Far* (London, Fourth Estate, 1992).
4. Mark Wilke and Helen Wallace, *Subsidiarity: approaches to power-sharing in the European Community* (London, Royal Institute for International Affairs, 1990).
5. *Bulletin of the European Communities*, 10/1989 (OOP), pp. 110ff.
6. For a commentary on what the British Prime Minister described as the Rubik cube', see *Sunday Times*, 6 December 1992, p. 41. See also William Nicoll, 'Maastricht revisited', in G. Rosendahl (ed.), *The State of the European Community* (USA, Lynne Riener, 1993).
7. With the exceptions of Denmark and the United Kingdom, the other ratifications were proceeding according to timetable and were expected to be completed by the end of the year.
8. After the 16 September devaluation of sterling, British GNP was below 90 per cent of the Community average. Britain announced that it would not seek to benefit from the Cohesion Fund.
9. *Text Conclusions of the Presidency*, European Council, Edinburgh, 11–12 December 1992, Sn 456/92.
10. 'The European Community and German Unification', *Bulletin of the European Communities*, Supplement 4/90.

CHAPTER 13

1. The European Court of Justice in 1975 had observed that 'it is not yet

clear what the expression [European Union] imports'. That remains true in 1993. Suggestion of the Court of Justice on European Union, *Bulletin Supplement*, 9/75, p.17. See also Report on European Union by Leo Tindemans, December 1975, *Bulletin Supplement*, 1/76; A New Phase in European Union (European Parliament, May 1985); Attainment of the Economic and Monetary Union, *Bulletin Supplement*, 5/73; Commission, Report on European Union, *Bulletin Supplement*, 5/75.

2. For a discussion of possible institutional structures, see Commission, Report on European Union, op. cit., p. 30, paras 95–111. More recently there have been proposals that a 'President of Europe' should be elected.

3. Report of the Study Group on the Role of Public Finance in European Integration (MacDougall Report) (Brussels, OOP, 1977), p. 20.

4. In its 1973 paper, already quoted, the Commission said, 'the ultimate objective should be for monetary resources to be an exclusive field of competence of the Union, just as the common customs tariff is already' (p. 17, para. 36). According to the Padoa Schioppa Report, commissioned by President Delors in 1987: 'In the monetary area it is necessary to move towards a European central banking system with considerably enhanced policy coordination and executive responsibilities' (p. 13). Padoa Schioppa *et al.*, *Effiency, Stability, and Equity*, (Oxford, Oxford University Press, 1987).

5. Tindemans, op. cit.

6. The famous call for one was made by Winston Churchill in Zurich in September 1946. For the text, see Randolph S. Churchill (ed.), *The Sinews of Peace* (London, Cassell, 1948), p 202.

7. Andrew Shonfield, *Europe: journey to an unknown destination* (Harmondsworth, Penguin, 1973).

8. Sean Lemass, *Dáil Eireann Debates*, Vol. CXI, Cols. 2003ff (1948).

9. See *The European Community in the World*, European File 16/88 (October 1988).

10. Carole Webb, 'Theoretical perspectives and problems', in H. Wallace, W. Wallace and C. Webb (eds.), *Policy-Making in the European Community* (Chichester, John Wiley, 1983), 2nd edn., p. 22.

11. J. D. B. Mitchell, 'The sovereignty of Parliament and community law: the stumbling-block that isn't there', *International Affairs*, Vol. 55, No. 1 (January 1979), pp. 34–5.

12. Ibid., pp. 33–46.

13. David Easton, *A Framework of Political Analysis* (Chicago, University Press, 1965), Chapter 4.

14. Robert Schuman, 9 May 1950, *Keesing's Contemporary Archives*, Vol. 7 (1948–50) (Keynsham, Keesing's, 1950), pp. 10701–2.

15. Roger Morgan, *West European Politics since 1945* (London, Batsford, 1972), p. 1. For a graphic account of the situation, see Richard Mayne,

The Recovery of Europe (London, Weidenfeld and Nicolson, 1970), pp. 29–30.

16. Eurogroup, *Western Defense: The Eurogroup Role in NATO* (Brussels, Eurogroup, May 1988), p. 10.
17. J.-J. Servan-Schreiber, *Le Défi Americain*; published as *The American Challenge* (Harmondsworth, Penguin, 1969).
18. Speech in Chicago, 15 March 1973.
19. Action Committee for the United States of Europe, 26 June 1962, Michael Palmer *et al.*, *European Unity* (London, Allen and Unwin for PEP, 1968), p. 142.
20. Johan Galtung, *The European Community: a superpower in the making* (London, Allen and Unwin, 1973).
21. Uwe Kitzinger, *The European Common Market and Community*, (London, Routledge and Kegan Paul, 1967), pp. 29–33.
22. Richard Vaughan, *Post-War Integration in Europe* (London, Edward Arnold, 1976), pp. 35–7.
23. Schuman, op. cit.
24. Vaughan, op. cit., pp. 35–7.
25. Schuman, op. cit.

Index

Spain (*continued*)
  attitudes to Treaty on European
    Union, 213, 214, 230, 236, 269,
    271–5, 285, 300
  early attitudes, 42, 43–4, 52–3, 271–3
  EMU, 145, 154
  EPC/CFSP, 197, 200, 202
Special Agricultural Committee, 67
Spinelli, A., 9, 54–5, 231
Stabex, 125
Standing Committee on Employment,
  171
state aids, 20, 148
Steichen, R., 64
Stresa, 26, 128
Stresmann, G., 6
structural funds, 51, 101, 150, 172–3, 268
subsidiarity, 5, 65, 228, 232, 236, 245,
  260, 261–2, 263, 267, 270, 275,
  290–4, 296–7, 299–300, 306
Sully, 4, 312
supranational, 12, 15, 41, 91
Sutherland, P., 148
Sweden, 25, 31, 38, 212, 234, 300, 301,
  304
Switzerland, 25, 31, 38, 212, 232, 234,
  302–3, 304
Syria, 126
Sysmin, 125

terrorism, 51, 285, 286
Thatcher, M., 44, 105–8, 171, 246, 254,
  256, 257–8, 292
Thierry, A., 5
Thomson, G., 252
Thorn, G., 45
three wise men, 54, 190
Tindemans, L., 54, 190
transport, 16, 81, 108, 138–42
Treaty on European Union, 105, 119,
  179, 185, 213–63, 280–305, 312, 318
  appointment of Commission, 62, 93
  CFSP, 201, 207–12, 218, 222, 227, 231,
    237–8, 243, 244, 260, 267, 271, 275,
    281, 285–6, 287, 292, 294, 297, 299,
    309, 315, 317
  cohesion, 105
  Committee of the Regions, 109, 242,
    263
  'democratic deficit', 81–6, 111, 218,
    224, 226, 228, 270–1, 280, 282
  EMU, 159–60, 282–4, 296–300
  European Council, 75, 76

European Parliament, 92, 166, 178,
  218, 223, 231–2, 237, 242, 245, 262,
  266, 270, 275, 280, 281, 282, 300
  home affairs/justice, 218, 245, 260,
    281, 285, 286–7, 300
  immigration, 178
  institutional balance, 218–19, 222–3,
    224, 226, 228, 231–2, 236–7, 242,
    245, 260, 262, 266, 270–1, 275, 280,
    282
  law, 95, 97
  legislative procedures, 81–6, 166
  Ombudsman, 92, 242, 262, 274
  pillars, 176, 281, 285–7
  ratification, 215, 223–4, 227–9, 237–8,
    273, 287–9
  research and development, 166
  single currency, 214, 217, 232, 234,
    242, 244, 261, 263, 267, 281, 283–4,
    297
  social charter/chapter, 170, 171, 214,
    261–3, 284–5, 294–5, 297
  subsidiarity, 242, 245
  variable geometry, 294–5
Trevi Group, 179, 286
Truman, H., 10, 12
trusts, 20, 148
Tunisia, 126
Turkey, 52, 120, 126, 210, 264–5, 267,
  301, 304

UNCTAD, 123
UNICE, 112
United Nations, 4, 124, 194, 203, 245,
  271, 311
United States of America, 28, 163, 168,
  190, 194, 212, 217, 220, 237, 271,
  310, 315–17
  Britain, 11, 31–2, 246, 247, 249, 260
  defence, 10, 11, 13, 14–15, 31–2,
    202, 260
  early attitudes to Europe, 17–18
  integration, 31
  trade, 31, 120–4, 133–4, 149, 297–8
  US–EC Declaration, 123–4

Val Duchesse dialogue, 171
Van Gend en Loos, 99, 313
Van den Broek, H., 64
Van Miert, K., 64
Veil, S., 43
Ventotene manifesto, 9
Visegrad, 305